W9-BIQ-167

What People Are Saying About
Auschwitz #34207 ...

"Nancy did a beautiful job of telling my story and all I went through. It's unbelievable that I'm still here. Unbelievable."

—Joe Rubinstein
Holocaust Survivor

"Nancy Sprowell Geise has done a remarkable job telling the story of Joe Rubinstein in *Auschwitz #34207*, and what a story it is. Taken from his home in Radom, Poland, Joe's experiences in Auschwitz were delivered with unrelenting honesty. A powerful story, worth being told and retold, one of authenticity and integrity, written so very skillfully"

—Michael Berenbaum. Director
*Sigi Ziering Institute
and Professor of Jewish Studies
American Jewish University*

"Author Nancy Geise presents this compelling story of the strength of the human spirit with extraordinary style and simplicity. Joe's life will help us all keep the promise to 'never forget,' as this treasured generation of firsthand witnesses are becoming fewer in number. May this work serve to empower and inspire for generations to come."

—Katharine Teicher
*Senior Adult Program Director
Aaron Family Jewish Community Center Dallas*

"A fantastic book! Heartbreakingly descriptive and full of suspense, love, suffering, and victories large and small. It's an incredible story about a man full of love for life and others. I've never read about the Holocaust experiences before from INSIDE the suffocating boxcar rides, fatal separation lines, and frozen barracks like Nancy Sprowell Geise has described. It feels so painfully real, so tragic, and so inspirational all at the same time! It's a book I'll read over and over again. It is a gift to treasure!"

—Sally Robinson
Worksmart USA, LLC CEO

"Joe's story demonstrates the resilience of the human spirit to not only survive but also heal from such great atrocities. This well-written book opens a window to the trauma and suffering experienced by one man that is representative of what so many individuals suffer when hate and evil rule the day. That Joe was able to live a happy and full life after what he suffered points us to the hope we can all have no matter how dire our circumstances."

—Reverend Cindy Frost
First Presbyterian Church
Fort Collins, Colorado

"*We're free. We're free …* The phrase Joseph and Irene Rubinstein whispered when their harrowing nightmare ended in New York. *We're free. We're free …* A phrase that few Americans today can truly grasp as well as the torment that seeded it.

Gripping, riveting, appalling, biographer Geise mirrors the voice of Rubinstein as he survives the unspeakable torture and cruelty of the Holocaust … later to become one of New York's premier shoe designers. After reading *Auschwitz #34207*, you are linked with Joseph Rubinstein through a number never to be forgotten."

—Dr. Judith Briles
The Book Shepherd Author and Publishing Expert

"Words do not come easily to describe the strong emotions felt during the reading of Joe Rubinstein's story of his surviving the Holocaust. My whole sense of being is somewhat more sensitive and more grateful for our blessings in simple, everyday living actions:

    ... a good hot cup of coffee in the mornings

    ... good nutritious food each day

    ... hot water and soap for daily shower

    ... a warm comfortable bed

    ... the love and support of family and friends

    ... the freedom of speech and choices.

And, with each one, I think of what Joe Rubinstein was able to endure. *Auschwitz #34207* is a marvelous story."

—Ethlyn Irwin
Retired Occupational Therapist

"Debut biographer Geise (*The Eighth Sea*, 2012) tells the remarkable story of Joe Rubinstein, a survivor of the Holocaust... With its thorough chapter endnotes, helpful timeline, extensive research citations and suggested discussion questions, this biography may serve as an ideal teaching tool for students of the Holocaust.

"A riveting, well-documented account of survival that's harrowing, inspiring and unforgettable."

—*Kirkus Reviews*

(The complete Kirkus Review can be found at the back of this book.)

AUSCHWITZ
#34207

The Joe Rubinstein Story

AUSCHWITZ
#34207

The Joe Rubinstein Story

A Remarkable Journey of Triumph and Survival

Nancy Sprowell Geise

MERRY DISSONANCE PRESS   CASTLE ROCK, COLORADO

Auschwitz #34207: The Joe Rubinstein Story
A Remarkable Journey of Triumph and Survival

Published by Merry Dissonance Press, LLC
Castle Rock, CO

Library of Congress Control Number: 2014921314
Geise, Nancy Sprowell, Author
Auschwitz #34207: The Joe Rubinstein Story
A Remarkable Journey of Triumph and Survival
Nancy Sprowell Geise

FIRST EDITION
2015

ISBN 978-1-939919-12-0
1. Biography
2. Historical
3. World War II/Holocaust

Cover and book design by NZ Graphics, NZGraphics.com
Front cover photo: Courtesy of Nicholas DeSciose,
copyright © 2014 DeSciose Productions, www.desciose.com
Back cover photo of Joe with tattoo and Author photo:
Courtesy of Crystal Geise, copyright © 2014 Crystalis Photo,
www.crystalisphoto.com

This book is dedicated to the millions of Holocaust victims who did not live to share their stories.

Contents

Foreword

Auschwitz #34207: The Joe Rubinstein Story lives because Nancy Sprowell Geise has taken Joe's memories of his concentration camp experiences and climbed into Joe's skin with her remarkable story-telling skills to tell his story—a redemptive story for the heart and soul of the world that needs to be told and shared. In this narrative, Nancy becomes Joe. She lives his dreams and his nightmares. What a monumental gift she has given to Joe personally, to his family, both living and dead, and to the conscience of every generation.

There are simply some stories where you are never the same after you have read them, especially the stories that describe people and events that try to kill hope in others. Joe's story is one of those stories. They can break your heart. But Joe Rubinstein was a survivor and has gone on to thrive joyfully in life. He is now ninety-three years old and is one of the most gentle, loving, and kind human beings you will ever meet. How did what was unbearable become bearable for Joe? How did his years in the concentration camps not take away completely his will to live, his will to endure, his will to hope, even his will to thrive? How did Joe become a renowned shoe designer, a husband, a father, and a grandfather after he was liberated?

From time to time as you read Joe's story, your anguished souls may have to pause and take time to rest. Honor that, but then return to read more—all the way to the end. For somehow, through the many camp horrors Joe experienced, there remained an inextinguishable "warm light" in Joe, a flicker of light in the "quiet space" (as author Nancy Sprowell Geise described) of his ravaged soul. It is a remarkable testimony to the human spirit.

From this sacred flicker of light, I want to light candles of reverence to Joe. I want to embrace him and let him rest for a few minutes in my peaceful arms. I want to tell him that he has given something too precious for words to the human race with the triumph of his amazing spirit, something enduring to humanity, something transcendent in the human condition: HOPE WHEN THE SITUATION SEEMED HOPELESS. Every reader who reads Joe's story will want to join me in that procession, winding our way to him in a reverential procession of lighted candles, to embrace him and his imperishable spirit.

For me, Joe's unfathomable story is an affirmation of mystery as truth. This truth is memorably and penetratingly expressed by Peter J. Gomes (1942-2011), appointed in 1974 as Plummer Professor of Christian Morals at Harvard College, when he wrote: "Hope is not stoical endurance, although it does help us endure, but whereas endurance has a certain almost fatalistic quality to it, hope itself goes beyond that which must be endured." That must be hope's greatest power and truth and mystery, that it is unconquerable, because that is the heart and mind and soul of Joe Rubinstein.

John T. Forssman
February 11, 2014

About The Foreword

When considering whom to ask to write this Foreword, my thoughts kept returning to my high school English teacher of many years ago, a man for whom I have the greatest respect and admiration. Mr. Forssman taught extensively on the Holocaust. His insights and reflections touched me so deeply that they have remained with me for decades. I continue to marvel at his mastery of recognizing and developing narrative themes, so central for both writers and readers.

For over forty-three years, Mr. John Forssman taught English and Literature. Many of those years were at Ames High School, Ames, Iowa. He was one-half of the dynamic duo in the English department. The other half was the late and very great, Mrs. Grace Bauske.

I am, and will forever be, eternally grateful to have had the opportunity to sit in their classrooms and those of so many other gifted teachers.

Nancy Sprowell Geise
Ames High School,
Class of 1979

Note from the Author

When Joe Rubinstein first asked me to write his story nearly two years ago, he was ninety-two and sharing many of these stories for the first time. The sequence of events and some of the facts about places and names are understandably forgotten. He kept no diary, but his memory for detail is remarkable.

In order to be fully present to his life, I wrote as if I were Joe. For instance, when Joe made statements such as, "It was frigid" or "I was very scared," I used such feelings to describe the scenes in expanded detail. The same was true for some of the physical attributes of those he encountered but can no longer recall.

In the Chapter Endnotes I have referenced the places where the events and/or the individuals portrayed were either a compilation of the people he encountered or representative of his broader experiences.

Joe shared that he prayed every day during his time in captivity. Thus, many of his thoughts and prayers in these chapters were expressed by Joe during our many interviews but were sentiments that he shared with me in fragments—rarely in the totality of the way I have written them. At the end of this book, I have included a collection of Joe's thoughts, in his own words.

One note of caution: this book includes a few heartbreaking and graphic photos. Each of these photos tells its own story, far beyond what I have the ability to put into words. Each is a small glimpse into the atrocities Joe witnessed.

Nancy Sprowell Geise—August 5, 2014

Map of Germany, Poland, and the Czech Republic
(Showing some of the cities and Nazi concentration, labor, and death camps)*

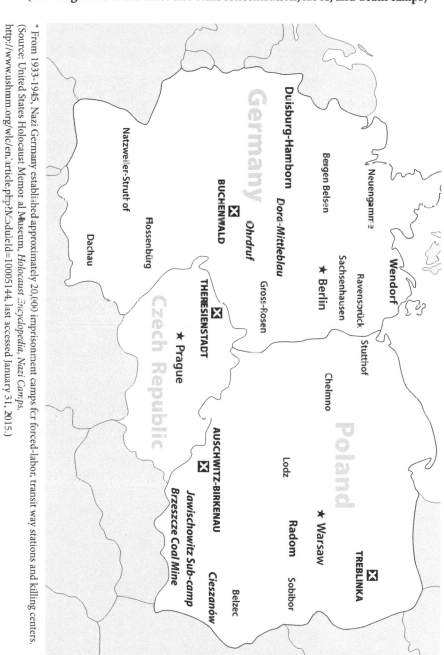

* From 1933-1945, Nazi Germany established approximately 20,000 imprisonment camps for forced-labor, transit way stations and killing centers. (Source: United States Holocaust Memorial Museum, *Holocaust Encyclopedia, Nazi Camps.* http://www.ushmm.org/wlc/en/article.php?ModuleId=10005144, last accessed January 31, 2015.)

PART ONE

Poland will be depopulated and settled with Germans.
~Adolf Hitler, August 22, 1939[1]

Prelude

I saw it with 'mine' own eyes.
~Joe Rubinstein

Cieszanów, Poland
September 1940

"It's the Swinehund. Someone's gonna get hurt." The voice behind me was whispered and strained. We had no words bad enough to describe our labor camp commander, Hermann Dolp—Swinehund was as close as we could get.

I let out a long, slow, nervous sigh, relieved that Abram was with another crew and nowhere in sight. The sun was hot overhead. I hoped it was too early in the day for Dolp to be drunk. His wrath was bad enough even when he wasn't.

Dolp's horse whinnied, shrill and piercing; the kind that would shake even its rider—the kind my father's horses used to make when they wanted to return to the barn and he wouldn't let them. I wiped my filthy, sweat-soaked sleeve across my brow, struggling to see through the sun's blinding glare. Horse and rider had stopped at the edge of the trench where a group of thirty or so of us were digging below. Thick froth dripped from the horse's mouth, its nostrils flaring wildly against the heat. I didn't need to see the condition of the horse to know its rider was a brute. We all knew it. My hands tightened around the rough handle of my shovel. Even the rider's black and tailored uniform assailed its insult against our torn and filthy garments. Our ragtag crew had been digging trenches every day for over a month—trenches for the German army that had invaded our country.

We were mostly Jewish, and since the invasion it was the only work we could find. We weren't paid in money, but rather in food. I was nineteen. Most of the men were in their early twenties, and some, like my brother Abram, were several years younger.

I wiped again at the sweat running into my eyes.

Without a word, Dolp shifted in his saddle, then pulled a gun out of the holster at his waist. I saw the glint of steel flash in the sun. I heard the distinctive clicking of his trigger.

Several men around me fell to the ground. I couldn't move. I couldn't breathe. Someone screamed, "No!" The gun clicked again. Then silence. I heard nothing. No cries, no screams—nothing. I braced for Dolp to turn toward me. Instead, he shoved the pistol into his holster. With a flick of his wrist and a press of his spurs against his horse's flank he rode away, his horse's tail snapping hard as if in protest.

I just stood there, the shovel frozen in my hand. [2, 3, 4]

The Taking

They told me I had everything I needed.
Then they took me.
~Joe Rubinstein

Radom, Poland 1942

In the quiet space between night and the first light of dawn, the stillness of my world was shattered by a pounding on the door. Moments before, I was sleeping hard, curled beneath a mound of blankets against the unforgiving cold. Sometime earlier in the night I woke, my heart racing, my body trembling. The nightmare had come again—the nightmare of Dolp killing those around me with no more thought than his horse's tail swishing away a biting fly. Just as I had for nearly a year-and-a-half since it happened, I couldn't stop the click, click, click of his gun from echoing in my head. I heard it when I was awake and I heard it in my nightmares.

As always, I spent the long night convincing myself that I would feel better in the morning and that I was safe, Abram was safe, and what we had suffered was behind us. Still, I could not shake it, that sense that it was beginning again—a reality worse than any nightmare. I had finally fallen back to sleep when the pounding began.

I sat up, searching the darkness. The shadow of my brother in his bed across the room was still. I heard nothing from the room my mother shared with my younger sister. I was grateful. Mother had looked exhausted the night before. I wanted to get to the door before the knocking could awaken her.

The cottage was dark. Our windows were covered each night for the blackout—required now by the Germans to keep the Allied planes from finding and bombing our city. I had no idea what time it was but sensed it was very early.

The knock came again, more urgent than before. It scared me. Someone at the door at that hour could only mean trouble. I didn't want trouble. I wanted to ignore them, to go back to sleep, to hide beneath the covers and pretend none of it was happening ... the war, the invasion, the fear, the brutality.

As the oldest male in the house, it was up to me to handle whatever was on the other side of that door. I pushed off the straw mattress and moved across the floor. Wanting to protect my younger brother Abe from whatever was out there, I shut the bedroom door behind me. It didn't seem like enough.

I moved quickly, my hand trembling as I reached for the front door handle. My palm touched cold metal and with it, a flash of hope—*maybe it's Chaim and Anszel bringing Marsha and the baby. Oh, God, let it be them!*

I turned the lever and cracked open the door, the early light of dawn filtering in. My gaze dropped to the floor. It seemed safer some-how not to see all of what was there. A heavy black boot in the shadows greeted my bare toes. I pushed against the door, but a black-gloved hand shoved it open. The slap of frigid air hit my skin so hard I thought I had been struck. I shrank from it. Two German soldiers, shoulder to shoulder, stood before me with machine guns in hand.

Everything tilted. I reached for the door, trying to stop the spinning. I felt small. I had no choice but to look at them. In the soldiers' faces I could see my future—a future only of darkness.

The pressure in my head was pushing hard against my ears. One of the men was talking. It took me a moment to understand. He was speaking German. I understood enough of the language to know that he was asking about my father.

I couldn't breathe. *How could I speak?* When my voice came, it was thin and weak. I stuttered, trying to remember enough German words to make him understand. I said my father was dead. He asked if I had other older brothers living at home. I said no. It was the truth. Anszel was married and had an infant son, and Chaim had not lived with us for months. We hadn't seen any of them since the ghetto was closed. Mother worried constantly about them but decided that they must be in the second ghetto in Radom.

The other soldier, with his helmet tilted far back on his head, motioned for me to come out the door. I tried to think. *The rumors were true then … rumors of the Nazis rounding up men again and taking them away from the ghetto!*

"No, please," I begged, "I can't! My mother … she's a widow. She needs me!"

The man jerked his head toward the outside. My mind raced. *This can't be happening! What do they want from me? I've already dug trenches for them! Surely I'm not being taken! What's my crime? I haven't done anything wrong!*

I wanted to argue with them. I needed to talk to Mother, to tell her not to worry, to tell my sister Laja to be brave and not to cry, to ask Abram to look after them until I could come home. I wanted to shout for them to get word to Chaim and Anszel. *Anszel would know what to do. He always did!* So many things I wanted to say to my family. I pulled against my undershirt and told them I needed to change my clothes and put on shoes. *I need time to speak to my mother!* I turned, but strong fingers digging into my shoulders stopped me.

"Nein!" the man barked harshly. "You have everything you need."

I looked at my thin undershirt, pajama bottoms, and bare feet. *All I need? How is that possible?* [5, 6, 7]

Eye of the Storm

We worked hard and loved one another.
~Joe Rubinstein

I was born in the calm, in the quiet and good times of the 1920s, when the world paused from its madness—between the great and terrible war and the one yet to come.

The Great War and its 37 million casualties had solved nothing. The old ways, the old alliances, and old enmities had only dug deeper into the souls of men. A new order in Europe was held together by the thinnest parchment and fed the cold rage that was building.

If they hadn't been so weary from the first war, maybe my parents, or grandparents, or somebody would have noticed. They might have felt the pressure of something menacing out there slowly churning and gaining momentum in the misty distance. But in the eye of a storm it is calm—no hint that the worst is yet to come; no hint that the world will once again turn against itself.

When my mother went into labor on that sixteenth day of September, 1920, my parents were overjoyed and relieved that the terrible previous decade was behind them. They didn't know what the future held, but they were certain that nothing could be worse than what they had come through in the past few years; nothing could be worse than war and losing a child.

One hour after my brother Chaim was born, my cry filled the tiny apartment at #5 Lubelska Street* in Radom, Poland. I was born Icek Jakub Rubinsztejn. My arrival in the world had been a surprise to everyone except my mother and the midwife, who kept their suspicions of twins to themselves, fearing disappointment if they were wrong.

Disappointment was the last thing my parents needed after the recent death of their eldest son, eleven-year-old Solomon.**

Mother cried tears of joy for hours after our birth. Over and over she whispered prayers of thanks and prayed that we would have long and healthy lives. She was overcome with gratitude that Anszel would again have a brother.

Word of our births spread quickly. My mother's family, the Kirshenblatts and Wiesmanns, along with my father's family, had all lived for many years near Radom. Everyone rejoiced in the birth of twins to the grief-stricken Rachel and Ruwin Rubinsztejn. News that we were identical brought even more excitement. If it had not been for a small mole on the tip of my right ear, no one, not even our parents, could have told us apart.

*****

My mother's name was Reszka, but she was called "Rachel." She was eighteen when she met and married my father. At over six feet, three inches tall, he was a young man not easily missed. My grandfather Mendel Wiesmann told me he and my grandmother Ruchla feared that my mother was too young to be getting married. Once they realized how much in love their daughter was with the young Ruwin, they did not interfere. They liked my jovial father, who made his living as a baker, and so they had consented to the marriage.

One year later, Mother gave birth to Solomon. Dawid was born the next year. They called him by his middle name "Anszel." My twin, Chaim, became "Chi." Our friends and neighbors insisted on calling me "Uzick." Mother would correct them, but it didn't stop them. I was nearly three when Abram, "Abe," was born and six when my sister, Laja, completed our family.

Our family lived in a tiny first floor apartment in a complex that housed ten other families. My parents were both raised in devout Jewish homes where prayer and fellowship with other Jewish families was everything. In our home we spoke Yiddish, a language combining elements of both Hebrew and German, and we were each fluent in Polish as well. Radom was a busy industrial city of nearly 75,000 people, with the Jewish population making up about a third. I grew up thinking of our home as being in the heart of Radom and Radom in the heart of Poland and Poland in the heart of Europe.

All of us children slept in one room on bunk beds with mattresses stuffed with straw. In the next room my parents also used a bed made of straw, one that was so uncomfortable for Father's large frame that he frequently took to sleeping on the floor. Even once they saved enough money to purchase a regular mattress, Father had become so accustomed to sleeping on the floor that in the morning Mother would often find him there.

With no running water or toilets, all the families in our building used an outhouse. The apartment was in wretched condition. The owner was a kind man, and we grew up playing soccer with his sons, but he said the five zloty a month we paid in rent was not enough to cover the expense of repairing the building. Our apartment was damp and cold in the winter and miserably hot and humid in the summer. When it rained, water leaked through holes in the roof, and when it was windy, even when the windows were closed, the candle flickered on our kitchen table. During blizzards, Mother stuffed the window sills with rags to keep the snow from drifting inside. Our building had no electricity, so candles and kerosene lamps lit our nights. Outside our apartment was a water pump. Because the well there was said to be unsafe, we took turns hauling buckets of water from a pump in the next block. We did not have an oven in our kitchen, so Mother did all her cooking on a metal stovetop.

Shortly after my parents were married, Father (whom I called Tatte) grew weary of breathing the dust from grinding the flour. He said flour was everywhere and he couldn't stand it. He was determined to make a change and saw a need for more transportation in the country. My grandparents were unhappy about Tatte's decision to change careers, fearing their daughter would be left alone too often. Grandfather spoke to Tatte about it, but his concerns fell on deaf ears.

Grandfather's fears were confirmed when my father's new job kept him away for much of the time. Tatte traversed Poland in every kind of weather, driving his wagon teams hundreds of miles every week, even making several trips a month to Warsaw, seventy miles away. His business grew steadily. Eventually he secured enough money to purchase eight draft horses, several heavy wagons, three buggies, and hire multiple drivers. They were all used for delivering people and goods as he carved out a good living for our family. It was not without consequences for my mother, who often bore the burden of caring for our growing family alone, but if she was unhappy, I never heard her complain.

Tatte's barn, where he housed his horses, wagons, and kept the family chickens, was the hub of his business and a short walk from our apartment. Whether it was to collect fresh eggs or just because I had nothing better to do, I loved making the trek to the stable to watch Tatte load the wagons and harness, brush, and feed his horses. Even though I was young, my father's strength awed me. He could single-handedly move a massive wagon and pivot it into place; it was work usually reserved for several men. The first time Mother saw him move a cart by himself she cried out, "You're gonna kill yourself!" Father just smiled and flexed his strong arms, teasing her.

Overwork was not the only vice for which Father frequently endured an earful from Mother. I remember she used to admonish him when he came home smelling of alcohol and cigarettes. Mother was afraid for him and for us. He smoked and drank a lot. Yet her arguments were lost on him. I can still hear Tatte's howls of laughter as he exclaimed that he needed to drink to keep warm on the cold night routes.

Those early years were good years for our family. Father came home from a long trip once while we were having dinner. He was wearing a heavy fur coat and hat. His face was red and he was louder than usual. When he leaned downed to kiss Mother on her cheek, I caught of strong whiff of beer. He scooped a handful of coins from his trousers and tossed them to each of us around the table, exclaiming with glee, "It's been a good month. Do what you want!"

Mother was very protective of her children. I think it was partly because she had already buried one son. I wish I could have known my brother Solomon, or at least a little more about him. Mother and Tatte rarely spoke of him. I think it was because it hurt too much. All I really knew was that he had been gravely ill for a long time and that my parents had loaded him into their wagon and taken him to doctors throughout Poland to search for a cure for his ailing lungs, a cure that would not come.

I remember Mother telling Tatte that he was never to discipline us; that was her job. I think she was worried that because of his strength and size, combined with his spirits, he might hurt us. He must have had the same concern because he never laid a hand on any of us, not even for a spanking.[8]

* Lubelska Street was later changed to Zeromskiego. At some point Joe believes they also lived at #9 Lubelska Street.

** The exact age of Solomon at the time of his death is unknown.

The White Shroud

I will never forget that white sheet covering my father.
~Joe Rubinstein

Tatte's skin was blue, and he kept making a strange noise that scared me when he breathed; it sounded like my baby sister's rattle when I shook it. Blood welled up to the corners of his mouth when he coughed. We were all there—my mother, Anszel, Abram, and seven-year-old Chaim and I—gathered around our father on a thin straw pallet on the floor of our tiny apartment. In the corner Grandmother quietly rocked my sister, Laja, and Grandfather sat next to her not saying anything. I didn't understand what was happening. I only knew something was wrong with Tatte and that Mother was very sad. Her body shook and her eyes were red and swollen, the way mine looked after I had been crying hard. I wiggled my hand in hers, trying to make her feel better, but it didn't seem to help.

Mother said cancer in his lungs caused him to be so sick. I was scared. Father had been ill for months, but I had never seen him like this, not even when he came home from Warsaw after an operation. Mother had told me then that the operation was going to make him get better. *Why wasn't he better?*

Mother kept urging Father to get into the bed, but he would not move. Mother's voice sounded strange as she cried out, "Why? Why are you leaving me now? Five children need you here! I don't want to do this alone! I can't ... I can't do this alone!" He opened his eyes, and I thought they looked very sad too. His voice came in jerks as he whispered "Rachel." His tongue ran across his swollen, purple lips. "You're not alone. God is with you, you're in His hands now." I didn't know what he meant. It didn't seem to make Mother feel any better; she was crying harder than before.

Mother squeezed my hand and then let it go. Her fingers were trembling when she lifted Father's hand and held it gently against her wet cheek. She was speaking to him in a soft voice and it didn't sound like all of her words were coming out. She kept asking him not to leave, telling him that she didn't want him to go, that he needed to stay and watch all of us grow, to help her with the baby, that his drivers needed him. She told him that it wasn't time yet. Father didn't answer. Mother's voice grew louder when she cried out, "Where are you going?" I didn't think Father heard her. Then his eyes parted open, and his hand moved ever so slightly, his index finger pointing upward. I stared hard at that finger and watched it slowly drifting down. His eyes closed. I couldn't hear the rattle anymore. Mother's shoulders were shaking as she cried out, "No, no, no, no!" She grabbed both his hands in hers, squeezing them. His hands had always been so strong, able to do anything, fix anything, and now they were completely still. Mother looked around at the four of us boys and shook her head, as if she'd just realized we were there. An odd look came over her, like she had just made a decision. She wiped the tears from her face, took a deep breath, and looked at my father for a long time. Then she pulled Father's white sheet over his face.

I hated that white sheet. *Why is she covering Tatte?* I wanted him to yank it off and laugh, then give me a big bear hug and start to wrestle. Instead, Tatte didn't move and the sheet that lay over him remained still.

* * * * *

Poland was frigid in December. Tatte always hated the cold. He covered himself in heavy fur blankets and drank to stay warm when he drove his wagons, and now it just wasn't right that he was lying there in the cold ground, wearing only a white sheet that Grandfather called Tachrichim and his white prayer shawl, called a tallit. Grandfather told us on the way to the burial that when we die we must come before God wearing only the white shrouds. Grandfather read to us the Torah's commandment, "Unto dust shall you return," (Genesis 3:19) and told us that according to Jewish tradition our father's body would be placed directly in the ground, unlike our Catholic neighbors who buried their loved ones in caskets. It didn't seem fair that, even in the winter, Tatte had to be buried covered only by two boards. I couldn't stop crying at the thought of Tatte in that cold grave.

A solemn rabbi with a long salt-and-pepper beard cut a black ribbon and said a few prayers from the prayer book. As the rabbi talked, Grandmother's eyes kept finding mine and I saw that hers were red like Mother's. Grandmother nodded to me and mouthed something; I think she was trying to tell me to be strong. I didn't feel strong. I felt the cold clump of earth in my fingers as my brothers and I followed our mother's instructions and each threw a handful of dirt into Tatte's grave. I didn't want to do it, but Mother said we had to, to show God we had accepted that our father was gone. I flinched as my dirt made a dull thud when it hit the boards. I didn't know what Mother meant by "accepting that he was gone." I wanted Tatte back. I wanted to throw in my coat instead of dirt, but I knew Mother wouldn't let me. I wanted him to be warm; I didn't know how he ever would be. When it was Grandfather and Grandmother's turn, they tossed in their handfuls of dirt. Grandfather paused for a long time, staring into the grave before shaking his head and turning away.

A month later, with our neighbor at the reins of his one horse-drawn wagon, Mother and I rode back to the graveyard on the outskirts of Radom. Mother asked me to stay in the buggy and out of the wind. I was huddled beneath the blankets but peeked out to watch her as she moved between the distant grave markers. When she finally stopped and knelt down, her back was toward me. Her shoulders were stooped and shook. I wondered if her eyes were red again. A soft glow appeared at her hands.

On the ride back, I asked Mother what she had been doing. She said that she was lighting lanterns of love on the graves of my father and brother. I smiled as I buried my face in the blanket. I knew that she was lighting those lanterns to keep them warm. [9]

Strength Through Family and Faith

I don't know how our mother did it.
~Joe Rubinstein

After Father died, life quickly became increasingly difficult for Mother. With little money and five children to raise she devoted a good portion of her time to keeping us fed. A local store that sold bulk and canned food had no available space for selling fresh produce. Mother had a knack for gardening, so on a nearby plot she started planting fruits and vegetables. Her space was limited, however. So, from late spring through the fall, my siblings and I would accompany Mother every Thursday to an outside market where the locals peddled their fruits and vegetables. We all took turns following Mother, loading the cart until it brimmed with strawberries, cucumbers, potatoes, cabbages, carrots, and onions. The next day we would rise at dawn and push the cart several blocks to a shop where Mother would set up a small stand outside to sell our own produce as well as the fruits and vegetables from the market.

The shopkeeper was grateful he was able to make his customers happy and to be of some help to our struggling family. The income from that stand was meager but served as our primary source of income for many years until my brothers and I were old enough to secure work of our own. Mother spent hours and hours at that stand selling produce. If there was enough food remaining at the end of the day, she would return to the shop the next day and stay until the cart was empty. We spent much of our time helping her.

In the winter we ate what Mother had canned during the summer and fall. She stretched every meal to make it go further than I believed possible. Soup was usually our main dish. If it had not been for Mother's cousin and her husband who owned a restaurant and kosher butcher shop, I don't know how we would have survived. Every week they asked me to come by, and they would give me leftover veal or beef salami and bread. As I walked down the busiest street in town, the delicious aroma from their shop filled the air and my mouth watered in eager anticipation. They made wonderful meals and the restaurant was crowded. They had older children so when I returned home, my arms often overflowed with not just food, but with hand-me-down clothes for Abram and Laja.

Every week they saved the discarded bones their customers didn't want for Mother to use in her special soup. As we eagerly slurped the delicious broth, Mother would exclaim, "People don't know what they are throwing away!"

*****

Sometimes before Chaim and I went to bed, we watched Mother free her shiny black hair from the bun she always wore at the nape of her neck and brush it. With her hair down, she looked so young and beautiful. I knew she missed our father; I could see it in her eyes. When she caught us looking at her she would smile, trying to mask her sorrow. I wanted to ask her why life was so unfair. She did not deserve to lose both a son and her husband and to raise five children on her own. She hadn't done anything wrong. Instead, I remained quiet, feeling weighted down with a new and disheartening understanding: people don't always get what they deserve.

I wanted to do something to make her life easier. I promised myself that for as long as I could, I would try to help her. I knew it was what my father would have wanted.

The week Tatte died, Anszel had told Mother not to worry because he would make sure we all helped her. We looked up to our oldest brother who was wise beyond his years, and we listened to him as if he were our father. We would soon discover that he was tougher on us than Tatte had ever been. Anszel would not allow any of his brothers to be idle. He lectured to us that we owed it to Mother to help. On the days he didn't think I was working hard enough, he forced me to look at Mother's hands, which were red and chafed from scrubbing our clothes on the washboard. If we dared to argue, he threatened us with his belt strap. Anszel had no sympathy for my pleas when I told him that I was too tired to work, or for the times I made excuses for why I forgot to do a promised chore. On more than one occasion, he would look at me disapprovingly and told me I was the laziest one in the family. I hated being the cause of such disappointment. Next to Mother, there was no one I looked up to more than Anszel. I wanted to be like him. I couldn't stand the thought of letting him down. But as much as I wanted it to be otherwise, I couldn't deny that there was something to his claim that I was lazy. It was true. I much preferred to sleep or play soccer than do my chores, but Anszel would hear none of it. He demanded that we rise early to do our chores before school. After school, there was even more work. Only after Anszel was convinced we had completed all our chores did he permit us free time.

Chaim, Abram, and I created most of our fun by playing games with other boys in the neighborhood. We were all competitive and loved playing even after dark. Trumping all sports was soccer, which we played at every opportunity in the street in front of our apartment. The times when Anszel joined us were the ones I liked most, for he was so much bigger, taller, and faster than everyone else.

As neighbors, we played together, giving little thought to our family backgrounds. I don't think any of us cared who was Jewish and who wasn't. Instead, we laughed, fought, teased, and celebrated together and were the closest of friends. Many of my Catholic and Protestant friends would invite me to celebrate Christmas and Easter at their homes. Mother was not happy about it, worrying it would somehow weaken my faith. I tried to reassure her, but she remained unconvinced.

Mother was grateful her children were all healthy and never had a serious illness or injury among us. There was only one time when I woke to find a doctor tending me because I had knocked myself out cold. That happens when one horses around on a roof and slips off. Aside from the roof accident, I think our family's vitality had a lot to do with Mother's wholesome cooking of food from her garden and fresh chicken and eggs from our brood.

* * * * *

My favorite time of the week was *Shabbat*. We ushered it in every Friday night when my mother lit two candles just before sunset and recited a blessing. On the nights Grandfather was not with us, Anszel, as the family's eldest male, would remove the cover from the two challah loaves. Following a blessing, he tore the bread into pieces and passed it around the table. Once we each had a piece, we would gleefully devour our mother's savory meal, which was never complete without her special borscht soup made of beets, garlic, and onions; often she strained the soup and we enjoyed it as a beverage. After we ate, we gathered to sing songs called zemirot.

The next day always brought an equally wonderful meal. I don't know how she did it when she had so little to work with yet, somehow she always managed. To me, she was the best mother ever.

Our grandparents helped us as much as they could. On holidays, we feasted together with as many family and friends as we could fit into one home. My mother's two brothers emigrated to America as soon as they were old enough to leave home. We had never met them, but Mother's sister and her two kids lived with Grandfather and Grandmother, and we saw them several times a week. My father's parents passed away before I was born, but Father's sister Geitel and her husband, Bernard Ackerman, used to join us for holidays before they moved away when I was a teenager.

At Passover each year, Mother gave us new clothes that she had lovingly wrapped in newspaper. Anticipation was bright on our faces as we opened the packages, each of us knowing the hours Mother had worked to afford such gifts. If the clothes were inexpensive and poor quality, we didn't notice. Of all the gifts, it was the shoes that I was most eager to unwrap. With money tight and the speed at which we outgrew our old shoes, we often went barefoot. Though our new shoes were cheaply made with rubber soles and canvas tops, I didn't care. I was just thrilled to have a new pair and fascinated by how they were designed.

Each month Mother made the journey out to visit the graves of Solomon and Tatte to light lanterns over their graves. Once I heard her whisper to Tatte's grave that she was sorry she hadn't saved enough money to buy them proper headstones. I hated how it weighed so heavily on her and tried to tell her that I thought Tatte would care more that we had enough to eat, or that she had a new dress, rather than a stone at his grave. Mother would hear none of it and every week after selling produce at the market she would slip a few extra coins in a small tin box. It was several years before those coins added up to the price of the headstones. The day we walked away from the cemetery, after having seen and touched two new stone markers neatly engraved with the names of my father and Solomon, I thought Mother looked taller. It reminded me of how I felt after I emptied the buckets of water that I had carried in a yoke over my shoulders the several blocks to my grandmother's house.

On the anniversaries of the deaths of Solomon and Tatte, everyone in the family gathered to light candles and say blessings for them.

During every commemoration, I tried to remember the fun times with my father, his laughter, his strength, and how much he loved my mother. [10]

From Generation
to Generation

I'm glad they died before they knew what
would happen to us.
~Joe Rubinstein

M other told me that Father attended the synagogue every day. After his death my mother's father, Mendel Wiesmann, who was equally devout, assumed the role of teaching us about our Jewish faith. Each morning Grandfather donned his yarmulke and his white tallit prayer shawl with blue embroidery, saying, "Blessed are You Lord, our God, King of the Universe, whose mitzrot add holiness to our lives and who gave us the mitzrah to wrap ourselves in the tallit."

Carrying the lunch Grandmother had made, Grandfather left his apartment each morning and walked to the synagogue to pray wearing his tallit katan, or smaller tallit, between his outer shirt and his undershirt.

At the synagogue Grandfather would don his tefillin, a box tied to his upper arm that held scrolls of parchments with verses from the Torah on them, its leather straps running down his arm to his hand. Another box was tied to his forehead with the straps hanging down over his shoulders. All the while, Grandfather was praying, grateful for the reminder that God brought the children of Israel out of Egypt. Some days I accompanied Grandfather and watched the rituals with wide-eyed fascination, wondering if I would be able to remember all the words and steps that would one day be required of me.

After we left the morning service, Grandfather and I made the daily trek of nearly two miles to his work at a factory that produced laundry detergent and other cleaning products. Standing outside the plant door, I gagged after just one whiff of foul-smelling agents used in the plant. I asked Grandfather repeatedly how he could stand working there. His simple reply was always the same, "Somebody has to do it." I felt sorry for my grandfather having to do such work, but I was amazed by his attitude. Like my mother, Grandfather never once complained. Instead, he reminded me how grateful he was that God gave him work and hands to do it. Grandmother, however, took issue with one aspect of factory work: the smell. When he returned each night, she would not allow him inside without first having shed his clothes and sponging off in a metal basin she left outside their apartment door.

One year Mother spent months saving her money to buy Chaim and me new suits and black leather shoes for our Bar Mitzvah ceremony. We were very proud of our new clothes and matching yarmulkes as we were each called up to recite blessings. Afterwards our family and friends came together to celebrate. With everyone's contributions of a vast array of food, we feasted. My aunt's potato dumplings were my favorite.

In the days that followed, Grandfather insisted that Chaim and I, as was required of all males over the age of thirteen, begin wearing the tefillin when we went to the synagogue to pray. We reluctantly agreed, but after Grandfather passed away, and despite my mother's strong protestations, we eventually stopped doing so.

Grandfather died when he was nearly ninety years old, and Grandmother followed him not long afterwards. They were buried in the same graveyard as my father and brother. They lived healthy and happy lives, and neither was very ill until shortly before their deaths. They had become second parents to us after the death of our father, and I loved them dearly.

Grandfather and Grandmother left this earth believing their legacy of family and faith would live for generations in the lives of their children and many grandchildren. They died knowing nothing of what was to come to their beloved family. I am glad they died before the war, before they could know. [11]

Promises Kept

I just wanted to help my family.
~Joe Rubinstein

As soon as he was able, Anszel secured a job at a local shoe factory. I occasionally accompanied him to work. Despite my growing fascination with shoes, I felt a great aversion to that factory, in part because it reminded me of the smelly factory where Grandfather had worked. Chaim did not share my disdain and when he was old enough, he joined Anszel in working there. When I was twelve I was hired by a local lumberyard. The owner was a Jewish man named Kiekleski. He had a long, flowing white beard and was rumored to be the wealthiest man in Radom. The man below him in rank was the yard foreman, my supervisor. Like the owner, the foreman was a kind man and was married to a highly regarded English teacher.

I had little interest in school, but Mother insisted I go. I would stay each afternoon until about two o'clock and then hurry to the lumberyard. I worked side by side with the owner's sons. I was paid well—three zloty a week for moving heavy timber that would eventually be used for making wagon wheel spokes. Though the work was hard, I enjoyed it, and liked how strong I was becoming.

One day, after hearing that my father had passed away, Mr. Kiekleski asked me if I would like to come to his home for dinner. Mr. Kiekleski was the only person I knew to own a car. As we pulled away from the lumberyard in his gleaming black-and-chrome Opel I felt the air leave my lungs. I could not stop smiling as we gained speed and wished that my father had lived long enough to have such an experience. He would never have believed how much distance we could cover in so short a time. When we reached their grand home, I was unable to hide my dismay at its size and beauty. I had never seen anything like it. Mrs. Kiekleski treated me like one of the family, even making sure that I left with a basket brimming with food to take home for my family. To my astonishment, that one dinner invitation became a frequent event. Not long after, the couple invited me to accompany their daughter on a shopping trip, encouraging me to pick out anything I wanted. Mother, too, was overwhelmed and profoundly grateful for their generosity.

Before long, I was earning more than five zloty a week. I was so relieved to be able to help lighten Mother's burden. Each week, I couldn't wait to press my earnings into her hand and receive the warm embrace that always followed. Often, as I pulled away, I saw her eyes brimming with tears of gratitude.

We had recently moved into a tiny, two-bedroom cottage. Mother loved that little house with a garden that was bigger than the home, and it wasn't long before she had transformed the yard into a thriving garden. We helped her build a coop for our chickens and we were soon enjoying fresh eggs every day. Mother was so happy to be out of the apartment, to have a garden that she could see from her kitchen, to have enough land to grow food for her family. I would catch her sometimes, gazing out that window, willing her plants to grow. Some mornings she would come in from the garden covered with dirt and sweat, and beaming her wide, beautiful smile. I hadn't seen Mother so happy since before Tatte died. Life was good—very good.

When Abram was old enough he began working for a local tailor, and Laja helped with babysitting our neighbor's children. With Anszel's assistance and all of us pitching in, we were able to help our family make enough to live on. Those who knew Mother were not surprised by her hardworking children. We were simply emulating her. All my siblings were tenderhearted, and if someone needed help, they were there. Next to Anszel, I was the one most comfortable talking to strangers. I couldn't help it; I loved people and loved hearing about their lives.

All my brothers were good looking, sharing our father's blue eyes and our mother's dark hair. Because we looked so much alike, Chaim and I attracted a lot of notice, especially as we grew into our teenage years, but it was Anszel who turned heads. He was tall like Father, towering over me, and he lived up to the meaning of his given name, Dawid, or "shining." Stunningly handsome, he was sought after by many adoring young women. Their mothers, too, had long ago determined that the young man who had looked after his family since he was a boy himself would make an excellent suitor for their daughters. Much to their great disappointment, Anszel had his sights on only one girl, the pretty, blond-haired sister of one of our friends. Soon, Marsha and Anszel were inseparable, and when they were old enough, they wed.

When Anszel and Marsha moved across town into an apartment of their own, Anszel promised our mother that he would continue sending home a portion of his earnings to help the rest of us. It was a promise he diligently kept.

As our teenaged years ebbed, Chaim was eager to be out on his own, and when an opportunity came for him to rent an apartment that he could afford, he moved out. I was sad, knowing life would never be the same without my brother—my best friend. Since the day we were born, we had slept every night in the same room. He asked if I wanted to move with him, but every time I considered doing so, I remembered the promise I had made to myself about helping my mother for as long as I could. Knowing that she still needed help with Abram and Laja, I could not bring myself to leave them. Eventually, I came to realize how grateful I was for that decision, for it was during those years that Abe and I grew very close, playing cards at night and soccer on the weekends.

Occasionally I went to local dances that were crowded with young people of all ages and faiths. It was at one of these events that Veronica, a brunette with pretty green eyes, captured my attention. I was soon smitten with her. She was Catholic and one Sunday I went to Mass with her family. When I told Mother where I had been, her feelings were clear—her lips and eyes narrowed with anger. I felt my stomach twist. Mother was the last person I ever wanted to disappoint and I knew that my actions hurt her. The burden she had carried in raising five children on her own had gone far beyond keeping us fed. Our religious upbringing was personal to her; she viewed any deviation as her failure. As badly as I felt for Mother, I felt no remorse for what I had done. I wanted her to understand that neither celebrating Christian holidays with our neighbors in their homes or going to church with Veronica posed a threat to my own beliefs.

Later that night, as the evening sun was shedding the last of its light, I watched Mother sweeping our wood floor. The stroke of her brush was soft and rhythmic—comforting. When she paused to look at me, I said with more enthusiasm than I felt, "I really enjoyed it, seeing how Veronica's family worships." Mother's expression became tight and forced. Before she had time to reply, I quickly added, "Learning about someone else's religion is not going to change what I believe. I am what I am. I'm Jewish, and nothing will ever change that." Mother eyed me skeptically. While not happy, I could see that my words had brought her some measure of relief and, for that, I too was relieved.

She must have decided it was a battle she could not win. Eventually she resigned herself to accepting that my first girlfriend was not Jewish and accepted that I was not about to be bound by the same restrictions that had dominated her own upbringing. Veronica and I had a lot of fun dancing in our spare time, often with Abe in tow. Our courtship lasted a couple of years before we slowly drifted apart.

Mother was determined I would benefit from learning to make clothes so, in addition to working at the lumberyard, I took a job working a few hours a week for a one-man tailor shop. I found little reward in the work but enjoyed getting to know the owner who made me a finely tailored suit for which I was very grateful. The tailor taught me how to work with a needle, thread, and fabric and told me on more than one occasion that he was surprised at how easily I absorbed the skills of his trade and how quickly I was able to stitch. He thought I had a future in making clothes, but I had my sights set on something different. [12]

The Girl in the Corner

How could anyone live that way?
~Joe Rubinstein

The first time I saw her, I wasn't sure what she was. We had come to the large, drab apartment at the invitation of friends to celebrate Passover. The owner of the apartment, a middle-aged widow whose expression was perpetually so strained and tense it looked as if it had been painted on, rented the extra rooms in her apartment for special occasions. The first thing I noticed about the apartment was that it was cold. The heat from the stove was woefully inadequate. To feel any of its warmth, I had to stand inches from it. Next to the temperature, what caught my attention were the occasional noises, guttural and unnatural, coming from behind a closed door adjacent to our room. We looked at one another and shrugged uneasily. I had no idea what the noises could be. If they were coming from an animal, it was no animal I had ever heard before.

Throughout the day, the widow came and went quickly through the wooden door, glancing over her shoulder as if she hoped no one would find her comings and goings odd. At the end of the second day of Passover, just as everyone else was leaving, I stopped to tie my shoe. The widow appeared from the room, startled to see me. She had left the door ajar and I couldn't help myself from peering through the opening. I heard her gasp, waiting for my reaction. I wanted to hide my shock and revulsion but knew it was too late. The woman saw my face.

"It wasn't a problem," she said flatly, "until she grew too heavy for us to move."

"My God!" I whispered. It was all I could say, unable to comprehend the sight before me. In the farthest corner of the room, on a mat of blackened straw, was a large mass, a heap of a person. I had no idea how old she was. Long, dark hair hung in straggled disarray over her face. The mass was rolled sideways, with twisted legs and arms jutting out at awkward angles.

"How long has she been like this?" I pulled my gaze away long enough to see shame tinged with resignation settling into the widow's eyes.

"Since she was born."

"How old is she?" I asked breathlessly, looking again into the room.

"Twenty-six. My husband could carry her until she was about ten." She shrugged helplessly. "But he passed away many years ago. She's been here ever since."

I blinked hard, trying to believe what I was witnessing. "Isn't there anyone to help you?"

I don't know why I bothered to ask. The answer was only too clear. I felt my chest tighten and my stomach churn. The girl had no life, no ability to move, and seemingly no mind. She had no way to even crawl. She depended on her mother to bring her food, to feed her, to clear away the straw when she soiled herself. The longer I stood there, the more I noticed the terrible smell emanating from the room.

"A wheelchair?" I asked desperately.

"Even if I had the money, I could not lift her in and out of it."

I knew it was true. The girl was enormous. She didn't look like she had the strength or ability to even sit up. I rubbed my hands across my arms wanting to get away as quickly as I could. "Is it always this cold in here?"

"I have little coal to spare."

That night, in the warmth of my own room, I could not stop thinking of the widow and her poor daughter. The next day I told the lumberyard foreman what I had seen at the woman's home. As I was preparing to leave later that day, he appeared, pushing a wheelbarrow. He motioned to the scrap pile of lumber. "I spoke with Mr. Kiekleski. We'd like you to take a load of that wood to her home. It's hard and burns better than coal. If she agrees, tell her you will bring her some more later. And tomorrow, take some to your mother also."

I could not stop the smile spreading across my face.

It was nearly dark when I knocked on the woman's apartment door. Her eyebrows were furrowed as she peered through the crack in her front door. I told her that the lumberyard owner had sent me with firewood. When she saw the heap in the cart behind me her dark eyes grew wide, her hands covered her mouth as she cried out in gratitude. After I had carried in the wood and stacked it on the floor next to the stove, she kissed me on each cheek and told me she had never known such kindness. I felt my ears warm with embarrassment. I tried to explain that it was the lumberyard foreman and the owners who were more deserving of such praise, but she wouldn't hear of it. She kept repeating, "Thank you, thank you, sweet boy, for your kindness." She flicked her coarse hands over her cheeks, wiping away the steady stream of tears. "Most people, they ...," she paused, her voice fighting to remain steady. "... they don't know what to do. They're repulsed by this." She swept her hand toward the bedroom. "They don't know what to do, so they do nothing."

A lump had formed in the back of my throat and I swallowed hard. My gesture of firewood seemed like something so small and inadequate for the help she really needed, and yet, to her it seemed to mean so much.

"I'll come back when you need more. The foreman said it was okay."

Again the woman cried.

I didn't know what else to say so I pulled my cap over my head, smiled meekly, then nodded my head in retreat.

The next evening I brought her more wood. And so began my odyssey of delivering firewood nearly every day after work, not only to the widow and to my mother, but to many other elderly neighbors who, after seeing my load, asked if I had any extra pieces to spare. I was grateful that the wheelbarrow was strong and its wheels turned with ease, except on rainy or snowy days. I hated those days, but the ardor of it was made easier by one thought. I couldn't help but grin every time I thought of Anszel calling me lazy. Laziness might have been my tendency but at least I had found a way around it. In this case I was motivated by doing something to help others stay a little warmer.

And every time I started to feel a bit lofty about my good deeds, the image of that wretched girl in the corner would cause me to shudder. A little wood didn't seem like very much—not much at all. [13]

Finding a Path

He taught me more than I ever dreamed possible.
~Joe Rubinstein

There were warnings all around. As I moved into my teenage years hateful anti-Jewish posters began appearing around town and, for the first time, I started to notice the unkind expressions on the faces of strangers and even on the faces of some of our neighbors occasionally. At first I thought I was imagining their scowls as we walked out of our Jewish school. Looking closer, I saw contempt on their faces. I was confused by what was happening. It made no sense. We hadn't done anything wrong.

Slurs against Jews, blaming us for every sort of trouble in the world, began appearing in newspapers and even on the lips of the children who had played soccer with us all our lives. One of the boys we played with got angry after another boy made a goal against him, screaming, "That was lucky, you ugly Jew!"

Reports began circulating of a rising radical group in Germany that was rapidly gaining popularity. This group hated Jews and anyone else who was different from them.

A one-day campaign to boycott Jewish businesses turned into a regular occurrence throughout Radom. For many Jewish businesses already struggling to survive, this was a fatal blow. Mr. Kiekleski decided to close the lumberyard and move his family out of Poland. I was shocked. *Have things really gotten that bad?**

I had no idea what I was going to do. Jobs for Jews were becoming increasingly difficult to find, and our family needed my income. When the lumberyard was in its final days, our yard foreman came to work sporting a new pair of tall leather riding boots, the finest I had ever seen. I could not stop looking at them and admiring their superior workmanship. The foreman saw my interest and asked if I would like to meet the boots' maker. I could hardly contain my excitement. The next day, the foreman introduced me to Mr. Nagel, a Jewish Englishman with a strong British accent. The foreman told him that I was one of the best workers in the lumberyard. It was flattering to hear his words and even more astonishing when Mr. Nagel asked if I would like to work for him.

Mr. Nagel designed and crafted shoes from his small apartment shop. While he did not make a lot of them, his custom-made shoes and boots were of the highest quality I had ever seen. The shoemaker had four daughters who also assisted him. Every day I watched and learned from him as he shared with me his lifelong knowledge of shoe design and craftsmanship. It was fascinating to see the dexterity and speed of his fingers; I am certain he had done the work for so long that he could have made the shoes with his eyes closed. He showed me how to hold and stretch the leather and how to make the stitches as small as possible. I loved the feel of the leather in my hands, the smell of it, and the way it conformed to my grasp. I marveled at how something so strong could be so flexible.

I learned the art of shoe design, slowly gaining the confidence to build on his sketches and develop ideas and styles of my own. Mr. Nagel smiled and nodded his head each time he saw a new design, telling me why he thought it was good and suggesting ways it could be improved. He allowed me the freedom to draw as many new shoes as I wanted.

As I worked, his youngest daughter kept watching me. She had a round, pretty face with eyes that were so dark brown they were nearly black. I was unnerved by her constant attention and spoke to Chaim about it. He told me it sounded like the girl was crazy about me. At first I thought he was wrong, but it soon became apparent that he was not. I began to notice how closely she leaned toward me when we worked, saying she wanted to get a better look at my sketches even though she could see them just fine from her chair next to mine. She laughed when I talked to her, even when what I said was not funny. Mr. Nagel seemed happy about the way his daughter was acting. Over tea and small sandwiches, he asked me all about my family and my dreams. I told him the truth: I wanted to be like him, to design beautiful shoes.

Mr. Nagel, like the lumberyard owner, could not have been kinder to me if I had been his own son. He had his tailor make me the most beautiful winter coat I had ever seen and gave me a matching hat. I had never felt as grand as when I wore them. He paid me two zloty a week, gave me lots of food to take home to my family, and was teaching me more than I had ever dreamed possible about making shoes. I had never been happier. [14]

---

* Mr. Kiekleski may have moved his family to England prior to the invasion, although that is not confirmed.

Neighbor Turns on Neighbor

They asked them, "Who are the Jews?"
And our neighbors told them.
~Joe Rubinstein

In the eye of a storm, it is calm. That is what I was: calm, blissful, and innocent. I knew little of what was happening outside my small world of Radom. I was a teenager who cared mostly about having fun and working hard to ease the burden on my widowed mother.

While we sat side by side making shoes, Mr. Nagel began sharing his political views with me. It was the first time anyone had done so in such depth. He was a highly educated and thoughtful man. He told me with certainty of his fear that the world was turning a blind eye to the growing strength of the Nazi party and to its promise to restore Germany to its previous greatness.

Mr. Nagel was also convinced the radical Nazis had first gained control of the schools to indoctrinate children and now were controlling the German press and the military. He could not understand the ridicule that he, and others like him, endured when he warned of the German military buildup. He repeatedly asked me, "Did the world learn nothing from the past war? How can we be so foolish?" Despite being accused of being extreme and overreacting, he did not back down.

While he spoke to me about his fears of the Nazis, I never heard him speak of a man named Hitler. If he mentioned him, I must have been too focused on learning how to make shoes to absorb his political opinions. I had no interest in politics. I respected Mr. Nagel, but I didn't want to adopt his fears. If I had read the newspapers more fully, or taken my school studies more seriously, maybe then I would have listened carefully when the shoemaker told me that he was convinced the world was in grave danger and that Poland would be a target for the Nazis.

As the months passed, I noticed dark circles under his eyes. Every day, he looked more and more tired. He told me he was unable to sleep at night thinking about the Nazis. One morning, instead of working, he stood at his apartment window, his eyes scanning the street below. When I asked him what was wrong, he told me that he had heard alarming reports coming out of Germany about what was happening to the Jews there and he feared it would soon spread across Europe.

I came into work one morning and found Mr. Nagel and his wife packing boxes. His face was tight and pale. Her eyes were red and puffy and their daughters were nowhere to be seen. They were moving back to England. I was shaken and it must have shown. He covered my shoulders with his arm and asked if my mother had talked about leaving Poland. *Leave Poland? Where would we go?*

Later that night, Mother told me she had thought about moving, but with barely enough to live on, we certainly had no money for travel. And unlike Mr. Kiekleski and Mr. Nagel, we had no place to go. At least in Radom, we had a home and the ability to grow what we needed to eat. Anszel and Marsha had no means of leaving either. And Solomon, Father, and our grandparents were all buried here. City officials had reassured us that England and France had both pledged to protect their ally, Poland. With their might and our military, we were reassured that Poland was safe.

The next week we were shocked when my mother's cousin appeared at our door with a scarf over her head, her eyes red. She was carrying several baskets heaping with food. She told us that they had been granted approval to go to the British-mandated Palestine. They were closing the butcher shop and restaurant and leaving immediately. She explained that they wanted to take us with them, but because there were so many of us, it was impossible. She pressed a pouch of money into my mother's hand, hugged us all, said a blessing for our safety, and then she and my mother wrapped their arms around each other and wept.

Unable to find work, life at home was becoming increasingly dire. I was relieved one day when a military truck appeared, the men looking for volunteers to help dig trenches around the city for fortification. The urgency in the faces of those asking for recruits startled me and filled me with more fear than anything I had yet heard. *Is it really so serious that Radom is in danger*? I could not imagine the Germans invading Radom.

Abram and I rose before daylight each morning and boarded a truck loaded with many other local men and began digging trenches. We spent the day working and were given sandwiches during our noon break. We weren't earning any money, but even working for a few bits of food was a relief. Each day as I dug, I prayed that the trenches would never be needed.

Until the day Poland was invaded, I had never heard of Adolf Hitler's dream—of a glorious world of *Lebensraum*, of more "living space" for the "racially superior" German people. I had no idea his dream was Poland. [15]

Nowhere to Hide

We hid under our small table.
~Joe Rubinstein

On August 23, 1939, longtime enemies Germany and the Soviet Union signed a non-aggression pact permitting Germany to invade Poland without the intervention of the Soviets. Their pact contained a deadly secret clause—an agreement that would mean the end of Poland and the life my family knew and loved.

Before dawn on the morning of September 1, 1939, I was jarred awake by the sound of distant explosions and knew immediately that the worst had happened: Poland was being attacked. We had nowhere to hide, no safe place to retreat. Instead, Mother, Abram, Laja, and I huddled together under our hand-hewn kitchen table, praying for the fighting to stop. Laja started to cry. As I listened to her sobs, I pictured the trenches we had dug, wondering if they were enough to keep the Germans out. I never wanted them tested. Later that day as I joined a handful of our neighbors timidly emerging from our hiding places, we could see no evidence of the bombings, but later, rumors began to spread that several industrial plants and our airport had been hit, killing a few of our citizens.

The world had been torn open. Eventually it would be learned that nearly a half million German troops had stormed into Poland using a military strategy known as the *blitzkrieg*, or "lightning war." The 1,700-mile border between Poland and Germany swarmed with German soldiers and tanks; U-boats attacked Polish naval forces in the Baltic Sea; and more than a thousand German airplanes took flight, bombing Polish airfields and cities. The pounding assaults across Poland came from the north, south, and west. Polish troops were overwhelmingly outmatched. Even within Poland, the minority ethnic German Volksdeutscher Selbstschutz groups fought a brutal campaign against the Polish people and military. Three days after the invasion, Britain declared war on Germany, followed quickly by declarations from Australia, New Zealand, India, and France. World War II had begun. [16]

The Dark Surge

They were everywhere. How could this happen?
What happened to our soldiers?
~Joe Rubinstein

I looked wide-eyed through the window of our small cottage to the eerily vacant street beyond. I could not see the Nazis but I knew they were out there. The roar of their tanks and motorcycles on a distant street reverberated in my chest. The terrible truth dawned on me. The Germans had come—come to Poland, come to Radom, come into my life. The photos, the ones Mr. Nagel had shown me weeks ago with articles written about the German army on the march, flashed as clearly into my thoughts as if I were holding the pictures in my hands. I had not wanted to look too closely then.

Only blocks away, boots drummed against the cobbled pavement with deafening precision—boom, boom, boom. Wave after wave of German *Wehrmacht* kept coming. I imagined them passing near the corner where I had sold vegetables with my mother every summer since I was a young boy. Column after column they came, marching to the same even beat.

I could not stop thinking about Mr. Nagel's photo of the German army. I was struck by a jarring realization and wondered why I hadn't noticed it before—it wasn't people I had seen in those pictures, rather it was a Nazi machine—a heartless, soulless machine of death that was rolling over my town.

I shrank away from the window—knowing with terrifying certainty that Mr. Nagel had been right. While the world slept, this machine had been built. The fear I felt at that moment seeped into the very marrow of my bones. Like a wave crashing ashore, I knew this could not be stopped. This machine could do anything it wanted.

I looked around the room at the faces of my mother, brother, and sister. Each held the same look of disbelief and shock that I felt.

What has happened to our soldiers? Where have they gone? No one had seen them in Radom for at least two days. For the past week, everyone had been whispering the same questions: *What happened to Poland's army and our air defenses? What about our trenches? Did they do no good? How could this have happened so quickly? Where are England and France, who pledged to defend us? Where is our government? How could we have lost so quickly? What can we do? What madness is this? What is going to happen to us?*

Later, stories of what had happened began to circulate. The Germans had come with massive forces of tanks, troops, and an extensive bombing campaign. Our army was overwhelmed. The attacks were leveled in all directions, often from behind the trenches, catching our troops off guard. Those who fought were slaughtered and many others retreated with barely a fight. Many soldiers never made it to the front.

At the time I knew nothing of the details of the invasion. I only knew that within hours of marching into our city, the Nazis consumed and overran Radom like a vicious plague.

The grainy, distant images of the German army in Mr. Nagel's photos were replaced by openly hostile soldiers walking our streets. The Nazi red-and-black flag was hung from nearly every public building and private residences alike. *Where have they all come from?* I grew increasingly certain of another heartbreaking reality, that some of our friends and neighbors may have been secret Nazi supporters for a long time. It was the only explanation for how widespread the Nazi support was. Everywhere I turned I heard people shouting *Heil Hitler*; I heard it from even those I knew to be Poles. The Nazis were everywhere, like ants covering a loaf of discarded bread, and with them came the brutality, slowly at first, then swift and deadly. I couldn't believe how quickly it had all happened and how completely our lives changed.

When I crawled into bed the night they invaded Radom, all I could think of was Grandfather telling me to pray. I knew then that was our only hope. I closed my eyes and prayed more fervently than ever before.

Although I knew nothing of it at the time, two weeks later, on September 17, 1939, the Soviet Red Army invaded eastern Poland with over 800,000 troops. The "deadly secret clause" of the non-aggression treaty called for Poland to be divided between Germany and the Soviet Union. Our country had no way to defend against both Germany and the Soviet Union, no way to retake cities like Radom that had fallen under German control.

Rather than surrender or negotiate peace with Germany, the Polish government ordered all its units to evacuate and reorganize in France. Less than a month from the start of the invasion, a line was drawn across Poland. The Soviet Union would control the east, and Nazi Germany, with its avowed hatred of Poland and Jews, took control of the west—including the cities of Warsaw, Krakow, Lublin, and Radom. And with it, the fate of our lives was horribly sealed.

Life as we knew it ceased. Strict regulations were enacted and the consequences of not complying were brutal. On threats of death, we were forced to wear armbands with the "Star of David" insignia. Jews caught walking on the sidewalks were often beaten, Jewish schools were closed, and Jewish bank accounts were frozen. We were prohibited from keeping more than a small amount of cash in our homes. Our allotted food rationing was meager compared to other Polish citizens. We were desperate for jobs. Abram and I became forced laborers—digging trenches again, only this time for the Nazis.

*****

September 1940, Cieszanów, Poland

It was the kind of day that I had always loved—blue sky, warm air, and the sun shining hot overhead. If I were back in Radom I would have savored that moment. I yearned to be home, playing soccer with my brothers, enjoying the sunshine. I wanted to be anywhere but where I was, shoveling dirt all day.

We had no choice but to sign up. Not long after they occupied Poland, the Germans required able-bodied Jews to dig trenches along the line now dividing Poland between Germany and the Soviet Union. Two fewer mouths at home would be a relief to our mother. So, eleven months after Poland was invaded, Abe and I boarded a train with a crowd of other young Jewish men and boys and left Radom. I was just shy of my twentieth birthday, and Abe was only days away from his seventeenth. We dreaded going to where we would be living and working so closely with the Nazis who hated us. We had seen far too often how brutal they could be. But after a year of not having much to do, nor having enough to eat, we were eager and relieved for any kind of work. However, after a month of the exhausting back-breaking digging, I could think of little else besides going home.

I had just been thinking about Chaim, wondering where he was, when someone whispered from behind me, "It's the Swinehund. Someone's gonna get hurt."

* * * * *

A few weeks after witnessing Dolp's murderous shooting spree, I grew violently ill and began vomiting blood. It was no surprise given the quality of the food and water of our rations. I was examined by a camp doctor who ordered me back to Radom. I was relieved but didn't want to leave Abram under the control of the mad commandant. I had no choice. I was put aboard a truck with other ailing workers and sent back to Radom. Through my fevered illness I fretted about not wanting

Mother to see me so sick. I knew it would only make her more anxious about Abram. Instead of going home I went to see Anszel. He took one look at me and ordered me into his bed. When he learned that Abram wasn't with me, Anszel wanted to leave and find Abram. I told him about Dolp and how if he went anywhere near that camp, he would be shot. Since his wife Marsha was pregnant with their first child, he eventually agreed that he couldn't risk it.

Anszel was furious about what we had endured and shared my same sense of helplessness. Although he was not able to help Abram, Anszel put all his effort into helping me. Their neighbor was a Jewish doctor who examined me and then gave Anszel and Marsha instructions on what to do. Over the next couple of weeks, no hospital could have treated me any better, but even Anszel was at a loss for how to help stop my torturous nightmares—the ones of Dolp and his clicking gun.

When I recovered from whatever it was that had made me so sick, I returned home. To our great relief Abram came home a few weeks later. He was thin and exhausted, but otherwise in good health. His homecoming was a tear-filled and emotional reunion. Neither Abe nor I spoke to Mother of what we had experienced while we were gone. There was no point in upsetting her. It was over, and we were safe—or so we thought.

Six months later the Nazis forced all area Jews, some 30,000 of us, into two small sections of Radom that they called ghettos; one of them encompassed our small cottage. Unlike nearly everyone else, we had no need to move, but our quiet street quickly became crowded, loud, and filthy. There were not enough outdoor toilets to accommodate the number of people, nor enough of anything else—water, food, or freedom. Most of the families were crowded into small apartments. Our home was already so tiny that no others moved in with us. [17]

**Soviet foreign minister Viacheslav Molotov signs the Nazi-Soviet
Non-Aggression Pact. Moscow, Soviet Union, August 23, 1939.**
*Soviet leader Joseph Stalin (white uniform) and German foreign minister Joachim von
Ribbentrop stand behind Molotov. Photo provided to the museum courtesy of National
Archives and Records Administration, College Park, Md. Caption and photo courtesy
of The United States Memorial Holocaust Museum (Photo Archives).*

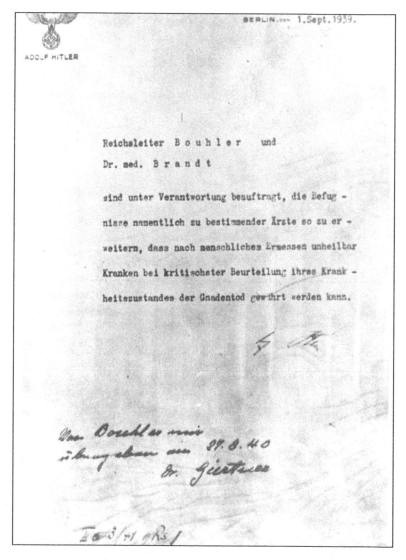

BERLIN. 1.Sept.1939.

ADOLF HITLER

Reichsleiter B o u h l e r und

Dr. med. B r a n d t

sind unter Verantwortung beauftragt, die Befug -

nisse namentlich zu bestimmender Ärzte so zu er -

weitern, dass nach menschlichem Ermessen unheilbar

Kranken bei kritischster Beurteilung ihres Krank -

heitszustandes der Gnadentod gewährt werden kann.

Adolf Hitler's authorization for the Euthanasia Program (Operation T4), signed in October 1939 but dated September 1, 1939. Berlin, Germany.
(Operation T4 was the Nazis' first organized system of mass murder, authorizing the killing of the physically and mentally ill in Germany and German-annexed territories.)
Photo provided to the museum courtesy of National Archives and Records Administration, College Park, Md. Photo courtesy of The United States Memorial Holocaust Museum (Photo Archives).

View of the main square in Radom, Poland. 1939-1940.
Photo provided to the museum courtesy of Archiwum Dokumentacji Mechanicznej Instytut Pamieci Narodowej, courtesy of Krakauer Zeitung. Caption and photo courtesy of The United States Holocaust Memorial Museum (Photo Archives).

Polish farmers sell their produce in an outdoor market in Radom.
November 1, 1940. Radom [Kielce] Poland. Photo provided to the museum courtesy of Heide Brandes. Caption and photo courtesy of The United States Memorial Holocaust Museum (Photo Archives).

Polish infantry.
Photographer and photo date are unknown (Public Domain).
http://commons.wikimedia.org/wiki/File:Polish_infantry_marching

German soldiers parade through Warsaw to celebrate the conquest of Poland.
Warsaw, Poland. Thursday Oct. 5, 1939. Photo provided to the museum courtesy of National Archives and Records Administration, College Park United States Holocaust Memorial Museum, courtesy of Richard A. Ruppert. Caption and photo courtesy of The United States Memorial Holocaust Museum (Photo Archives).

Radom ghetto market.
Photograph from the private archive of Chris Webb.

German troops in the Radom ghetto.
Photograph from the private archive of Chris Webb.
(Background apartment building is similar but smaller than the building where
Joe spent his early years.)

Forced labor in the Radom ghetto.
Photograph from the private archive of Chris Webb.

Radom ghetto.
Photograph from the private archive of Chris Webb.

Jews captured by SS and SD troops during the suppression of the Warsaw ghetto uprising are forced to leave their shelter and march to the Umschlagplatz for deportation.

Monday, April 19, 1943 – Sunday, May 16, 1943. Warsaw, Poland. Photo provided to the museum courtesy of National Archives and Records Administration, College Park Instytut Pamieci Narodowej Panstwowe Muzeum Auschwitz-Birkenau w Oswiecimiu. Caption and photo courtesy of The United States Memorial Holocaust Museum (Photo Archives).

Two young brothers, seated for a family photograph in the Kovno ghetto. One month later, they were deported to the Majdanck camp. Kovno, Lithuania, February 1944. They did not survive. Tuesday, February 1, 1944.
Photo provided to the museum courtesy of Shraga Wainer. Caption and photo courtesy of The United States Holocaust Memorial Museum (Photo Archives).

**Studio portrait of four Jewish siblings all of whom
perished in the Holocaust.**
*1919. Radom, [Kielce] Poland. Photo provided to the museum courtesy of Lewis Shabasson.
Caption and photo courtesy of The United States Holocaust Memorial Museum
(Photo Archives).*

PART TWO

*It had nothing to do with humanity, it couldn't have;
it was a mass — a mass of rotting flesh.*
~Franz Paul Stangl,
Commandant of the Treblinka Extermination Camp.[18]

*The things I saw beggar description. The visual evidence
and the verbal testimony of starvation, cruelty and bestiality
were so overpowering as to leave me a bit sick. In one room,
where they were piled up twenty or thirty naked men,
killed by starvation, George Patton would not even enter.
He said that he would get sick if he did so. I made the visit
deliberately, in order to be in a position to give first-hand
evidence of these things if ever, in the future, there develops
a tendency to charge these allegations merely to "propaganda."*
~General Dwight D. Eisenhower,
Supreme Commander of the Allied Forces, after visiting
the Ohrdruf Concentration Camp.[19]

The Truck

The teenager next to me said he was going to get off the truck. I told him then he needed to be ready to die today because they would kill him.
~Joe Rubinstein

My bare feet stung as I stepped outside onto the cold ground. My undershirt and pajama bottoms were ridiculously inadequate against the frigid early morning air. Behind me I could hear the heavy footsteps of the soldiers taking me from my family. The same soldiers had knocked on our door just before dawn, demanded that I come with them, and told me I had everything I needed. Despite the cold, I felt my face grow hot with rage. I fought the urge to turn and spit on the soldier walking so closely behind me that the end of his gun pressed against my back.

A large flatbed truck filled with the dark shadows of others sat idling noisily on the street in front of our cottage. Its exhaust filled the cold air. That truck waited for me like a caged animal eager for its next meal. I forced my gaze down the street, fighting the urge to run. I knew if I did, the guards would shoot me. I couldn't bear the thought of my mother hearing the shot, looking out the window, and seeing me face down on the street. *If they're going to kill me, it won't be where my mother will see it.* I sucked in my breath at a terrible thought: *Maybe that's what they want, to take me away to kill me where no one will know. But why? I've done nothing wrong. It makes no sense!* A horrid notion hit me then. My chest tightened in panic. *Am I being taken to the same place Abe and I worked digging trenches for the Nazis—that terrible place where a madman was in command? A madman whose gun I still hear echoing in my nightmares?*

The soldier with the helmet tilted far back on his head motioned for me to get into the truck. I yelped as the rough metal touched my foot. For a moment I feared my skin had already adhered to the cold metal. All thought of my feet disappeared when I saw the men in the truck. Several were huddled together with no protection from the cold. Even though the sun had not broken over the horizon there was enough light for me to see their faces, at least the faces of those who hadn't pulled their shirts over their heads to fend off the biting wind. A couple of them looked vaguely familiar, although I didn't know any of them by name. Some wore nightgowns and slippers. Two or three had slacks, long sleeves, and shoes. Most were like me, barefoot and in little more than undershirts. Three or four of the men had coats and had draped them around the shoulders of those next to them.

A handful of the men looked at me as I climbed in. Most just hung their heads. It was clear they were all frightened, all angry, and all very cold.

Surely they don't intend to keep us in here with no blankets, no cover of any sort? We can't survive! I calmed myself, thinking it made sense that they had taken the oldest male in each home because they needed us to work. They would need us alive. They would not have gone to all this trouble to simply allow us to freeze to death now. *When we dug trenches, they needed us alive then too, but that didn't stop the madman. He killed his workers anyway!* I forced the thought aside and moved forward into a corner of the truck bed. I turned to look at our cottage and began furiously shaking my legs to keep the blood flowing. I was relieved our front door was still closed. I wanted the soldiers and this truck far away from my family. I wanted them to be safe. *Please, Mother! Don't come out after me. Wait until we are out of here. Please wait!*

Two of the guards climbed onto the back steps of the truck; more were in the cab. The truck lurched and I grabbed the side to keep from falling. As the truck drove away, I could not bear to look back. Instead,

I tucked my head close to my chest, inside my undershirt. It didn't help much. My feet were almost numb, and I rubbed my hands and legs continuously, wondering how long it would take a person to freeze to death.

"Where are they taking us?" I asked no one in particular, raising my head from my undershirt. I knew before asking that no one on this truck could answer my question. Shrugs and silence were the only responses.

The truck turned a sharp corner and then stopped. Another young man was forced into the truck. He looked a few years older than I. His eyes were wide, tearful. I looked more closely at the faces of those surrounding me. Each person's skin was an odd mix of red and blue with blotches of white. Every ear and nose was bright red, every lip slightly blue. Each face held the same stricken expression, and everyone was trembling uncontrollably, moving in as close to each other as possible. There were more in the truck than I had first realized. The Nazis had had a busy night.

As the truck began moving again, I heard whispered curses and murmured prayers. There was little talking amongst us even though we were close together. We were strangers, each focused only on staying alive. The few coats anyone had were being passed around. When one was handed to me, I cocooned inside it, never wanting to come out. After several minutes, I reluctantly passed it on.

And so it went. With each stop, the truck became more crowded and more confused. We took turns passing the coats and opening them and covering as many people as possible. Without being prompted, we took turns shuffling from the outside of the circle to the inside where it was warmer. Sometimes I would squat. I'd close my eyes and try to concentrate on not panicking. Instead, I kept praying to either be let off the truck or for blankets to be distributed. More men shuffled in, each asking the same question I had asked, "Where are they taking us?" Now I was the one shrugging.

The cold air seared my lungs. With every breath, it hurt. My ears, cheeks, fingers and toes were throbbing. My skin hurt to the touch. I blew on my hands, then covered my ears and face with them until my hands were so cold that I had to move them beneath my armpits.

The German soldier's words of assurance before I was forced out of my home played over and over in my mind. "You have everything you need."

Everything I need. If I had the energy I would have laughed at the absurdity of those words.

Throughout the day, the truck repeated its pattern of moving, then stopping, picking up more men until the truck was packed full. At first the stops were inside the ghetto of Radom, then outside. When the truck gained speed, I pulled my head from my shirt and realized we were no longer in Radom. Tears clouded my sight and the lump in my throat was so hard I couldn't swallow. I had been taken from the only home I had ever known. I forced myself to breathe normally, to try to think of something—anything else. I had always been fond of kissing the cheeks of those I loved. Sometimes I was teased about this, but I didn't care. Now, here I was being taken away and I did not even have the opportunity to kiss my mother goodbye. It was the first time I could recall not doing so.

What's going to happen to me … to my family? When will I see them again? Do they even know I've been taken? Did they hear the knock on the door or the soldiers ordering me to leave? Did they want to call out to me but remained silent for fear of the repercussion? Oh, God, please! Protect them! Protect me!

I was overcome with sorrow knowing how my disappearance would torment my mother. Worry and despair would consume her. The last time I had worked for the Nazis, I had nearly died. Mother never learned how close I had come, but she knew enough to be frightened. She would be worried sick about me now, and for me, worrying about her was worse than even the wretched cold.

What will happen to her when she awakens to find me gone? How is she supposed to go on? How are any of them? How will they secure enough food without me to sneak out of the ghetto to get it? God, please protect Abe if he takes risks to get food! They will kill him if they catch him! As I pleaded with God for Abram's safety, I realized my words were the same as the ones Mother used with me when she found me sneaking in with my knapsack full of food that went far beyond our ghetto rations. I told her the truth—how, with my Jewish armband stuffed into my back pocket, I had crept out of the ghetto about four in the morning. I slipped out between two of the taller buildings after the guards had passed. I wanted to be at the market as soon as it was light. Some of the vendors recognized me and gave me extra bread. I was lucky no one ever turned me in—lucky I was never caught. Mother was horrified and begged me never to do it again. I told her that it was a choice I had to make; we were hungry, we needed to eat, and the food rations of the ghetto were not enough.

I had been alternating between standing, squatting, and sitting. Each was miserable. It had been hours since we had been able to relieve ourselves and there was not even a bucket on the truck. At first we tried using a corner, but it was too crowded to reach it. With no choice, we were forced to soil ourselves and stand in our waste. I was horrified by the smell, and for a time it was a constant struggle to force back my vomit. I gagged every time I thought of what was frozen between my bare toes. Eventually I was too cold to care.

The sun offered little relief from the cold. The raw, icy air pierced my skin like knives, slashing and cutting, penetrating again and again. We had been given nothing to eat or drink and I felt hunger like never before.

As we left Radom, I was being shuffled farther into the circle of men and unable to watch our route. I could not stop thinking about my family. I imagined Mother going house to house in the ghetto, then to the Jewish Council to ask if others had been taken, frantically searching for any clue as to where we were. *God, please keep her away from the Nazi soldiers and the German officials.* I had a flash of hot anger at the thought of them striking her for asking about me. I prayed again that they would not harm her. *God, let these machine men remember their own mothers! Remind them that their mothers would be doing the same for them if they were taken. Have mercy on her! On all my family! Keep them safe. Please, God, keep them safe!*

Darkness was coming on now. *Is she searching for me right now?* I knew Mother was praying for me. I could feel it deep in my soul. I could feel her anguish and heartbreak at the thought of losing another child. She had already lost Solomon. I knew she was thinking that she would not survive losing another son. In that moment, more than anything else I've ever wanted, I wanted to stay alive for her. I wanted to see the look in her eyes when we saw each other again.

My thoughts were growing hazy. I wondered if my brain was freezing. My stomach ached for food. *What is my family eating now? Do they have enough? God, please, please let them grasp my thoughts. Let them know that I am still alive.* I knew Mother was not sleeping. She was pacing the floor, praying again.

As darkness settled over us, I begged God that we were being taken somewhere where we could get off the truck, somewhere warm. My body felt so strange, and I wondered if my blood was freezing too, moving slower, making everything seem impossible to move— my limbs, my thoughts, even my lips, which felt too cold to open. I tried to lift my hand. It barely moved. The truck turned toward an unfamiliar town, and my hopes soared. Soon, tall buildings on each side blocked the wind. The truck slowed and then stopped and the engine was turned off for the first time all day. The soldier driving and those in the cab with him opened their doors.

I prayed they were securing the building for prisoners. The word hit me hard—somehow I had begun to think of myself as a prisoner. *How had that happened?*

In the tall buildings on each side of the truck the lights were still on and smoke billowed from the chimneys. I knew the lights would be turned off soon for the blackout. I could see a line of soldiers with the barrels of their guns pointed at the truck. The soldiers standing near the truck moved inside. Darkness and more cold settled in. I kept waiting for the guards to return, to take us off the truck. I was desperate to get to a warm place where I could rest. I stared at the buildings for a long time. As it grew colder, I continued to wait for the sound of the doors to open.

It struck me like a fierce blow when I realized that there would be no leaving the truck this night. I felt tears forming and wondered if they would freeze before they touched my lips. I pressed myself ever tighter against the others for warmth. Grumblings and cursing spread among the men about the cowardly SS who, even with their heavy coats, hats, gloves, and boots, would not stand out in the cold to guard us. Whispers of escape spread through the truck, of trying to leave en masse. We all knew we had two choices and both were terrible: to stay in the truck and fight to stay alive through the freezing night or to make a run for it. We saw the number of machine guns aimed at us from the windows above, covering both sides of the truck. By the time any of us got over the side of the truck, we would be slaughtered. By staying in the truck we knew we had a chance, however small, to live long enough to find another way of escaping. A skinny teenager moved closer to me and whispered that he was going over the truck's side. I asked him if he was prepared to die because that was what would happen. The boy started to cry and made no effort to escape.

We spent the remainder of the night exposed to the frigid air with only the shelter of one another to stave off the biting wind. I could hear laughter coming from the buildings, evidence that they were having a good time. *What kind of human beings can enjoy themselves fully aware that we are out here so exposed? What is wrong with them?* I had heard of people being hypnotized to do things they would not normally do.

Are these soldiers hypnotized? Has Hitler somehow managed to hypnotize an entire nation? What else could explain such madness? But all the soldiers I had encountered appeared to be fully alert. I continued shivering hard, knowing it was not merely from the cold.

Over and over I pulled my shirt up to cover my head, trying to hold the warmer air on my face until my exposed body could not stand it any longer. I was lightheaded from blowing on my hands and rubbing them across my arms, ears, and cheeks. I kept wiggling my toes, no longer able to feel them. My back hurt so badly from shaking that I felt it might snap in two. My mind had become numb along with my body. Sometime in the night, one of the older men on the truck started to yell that he was hot and began removing his clothes. Somebody next to him tried to tell him that he was hallucinating, but the man would not put his clothes back on.

My thoughts and dreams were scattered and confused. I was no longer sure if I was asleep or awake. My mind kept drifting back to a time not long after the Nazis invaded. The terrible time with the man named Dolp.

* * * * *

The time of digging in the trenches seemed so long ago. And yet as I shivered in the truck, the images and sensations were as vivid as the cold steel of the truck. I blinked heavily, my eyes dry and cold.

The soldiers' laughter had stopped. The buildings were quiet. The red glow of a guard's cigarette shone in the window. The smoker must not have been worried enough about a bombing raid to keep his cigarette hidden. Guns were still pointed in our direction. My mind was a blur. One moment I was digging in the trenches with Dolp riding toward me, and the next I was shivering so hard in the dark, cold truck that my teeth rattled. It was becoming increasingly difficult to remember which nightmare I was actually living.

My head hit the back of the man next to me, jarring me awake. He didn't stir. There was still no light in the sky, no hope of daylight coming soon. I was so cold I could no longer feel it. *How long have I been asleep? Why did I answer that knock at the door? Why did they take me? I didn't do anything wrong. Are my toes moving? I can't tell. My eyelids are so heavy. Why am I so tired? Am I still alive? I have to get off this truck. I need a drink. I need to eat … something … anything. Is Mother walking the streets with Abram, looking for me? Is she crying? I think she's crying. The man behind me has stopped whimpering. Is he dead? Where are they taking me? The older men on this truck remind me of Grandfather. Oh Grandfather …* [20, 21]

The Cold Unknown

There was no place to sit. Some were on their knees.
I stood in the corner, trying to keep warm. It was frigid,
terrible. They collected us, and then they left us.
~Joe Rubinstein

As the thin light of dawn appeared in the sky above the buildings, I could see several gun barrels still aimed at our truck. My body was numb, my head spinning. I tried to wiggle my toes and had no idea if they responded. There were a few whimpers from the men crouched around me. I exhaled slowly, saw the white vapor, and was surprised that I was still alive, that any of us were. My eyes were heavy and my thoughts shuffled between wondering how many of the men on this truck were still breathing and how I would kill the Swinehund Dolp if I ever got the chance.

When the guards returned they did not remove the bodies of those few who had died near me in the night. Instead they started the truck, the black engine smoke filling the air. I was so overcome with despair that all I wanted to do was curl up and cry. My stomach cramped, and my throat ached, begging for food and water. *What must Mother be thinking, awaking to another morning with no word from me? Could she be so consumed with anguish that she might make herself ill? Could someone die of worry?* I didn't know. Yet, as I thought about Mother and all she had been through, I realized that she would never give in—she could hold on to a shred of hope in the worst situations. While she had always been tenderhearted, she was a fighter. *No, Mother will not give up searching for me. Nor will she ever stop praying for me.*

We spent another day of torment on that truck before finally passing through the gates of a small prison camp. When at last we were ordered off the truck, my legs and feet were so numb that I could do nothing more than shuffle slowly on stiff, straight legs. I moved around the dead bodies of four or five men, trying to avoid looking at their faces, faces that could easily have been mine. [22]

Toward the Dark

They kept pushing more people in like animals.
They didn't care if we lived or died.
~Joe Rubinstein

"Where are they taking us?" The man in front of me shrugged. I don't know why I asked. It was the same question I had asked on the truck the night I was taken. Just like then, I knew he, too, had no idea where this would all end.

The truck that brought us here the night before had made so many stops, and I had been so numb and tired from the cold, that I had no idea where I was. Once off the truck, we had been given a set of old clothes and shoes. The pants were ridiculously short, ending above my ankles, but the button-down shirt and shoes were a good fit. I was just thankful I had something more to wear than the meager garments I had on when I was taken.

The line of men standing behind me, waiting to board the train, was so long that I couldn't see the end of it. My chest began to tighten with anxiety. Next to me on both sides were lines of people, lines with seemingly no end. *Where had they all come from?*

I was surprised by the number of people standing near the train platform. I searched the crowd of men for a familiar face. I was desperate to see my brothers although the thought of them here made me physically ill. I wanted them safe at home. Everywhere I looked, a sea of exhausted faces met mine.

"Where are the passenger cars?" I asked the man in front of me. He just shrugged. Passenger trains had benches, seats, windows, and even folding beds, yet before us was a long train of wooden boxcars, the kind I had only seen used to transport animals. I kept waiting for this train to pull away and make room for the passenger trains. An officer blew a loud shrill whistle, and my line surged forward. I could see the men walking up the platform, then toward the openings of the cars—the openings for animals. *Why am I surprised?* And yet I was both surprised and horrified.

As I climbed up the platform steps, I saw that the train doors were open only wide enough for the men to enter single file. A man stopped at the entry, then tried to run back. The guard next to him swung the barrel of his machine gun in one swift movement, striking him. I could hear the sickening, muted crush as the metal smashed his skull. Other guards then dragged the man to his feet and shoved him into the opening.

I looked over my shoulder to see if others could see what was happening, my mind screaming, *I can't do it! I can't go in there!*

Guards with machine guns were everywhere. I looked between the cars to the other side of the tracks; more soldiers stood at the ready. If I dove off the platform and under the car, I would be shot coming out the other side. If I stayed under there until the train left, I would be shot once the train passed. I wondered if I could grab the bottom of the train and let it pull me away, but to where? I looked closer at the heavy wheels and knew I'd be dragged to death. More men hesitated at the entrance and were clubbed over the back of the head; others were roughly shoved in by the tips of machine guns and rifles. Every man reached the threshold and then disappeared like a bat into a cave. Frantic, my eyes darted in every direction. If I ran, at least my death would be swift. I would be shot in the back before I knew what happened. *Is my mother looking out the window, searching the street for me? If I run, she will wait every day the rest of her life for a son who will never come home.* I knew I needed to be stronger than my fear. I bit my lip, fought back my tears, and stepped into the darkness, gasping at the putrid air. There were no windows, only two small high slits for air and muted light. Even for livestock, such travel with no air would have been cruel.

I moved as far forward as I could. More and more men were forced in behind me. People were pressing against me and me against them. I felt panic in my gut even before the doors were closed; when they did, we were immersed in darkness. I was completely blind and was so dizzy and thought I might faint. Someone around me was pounding on the doors, demanding they be opened. Others joined in. People stamped their feet and kicked the walls, all begging to be let out.

My eyes slowly adjusted to the dim light, and I could see the outlines of those around me.

I pulled up my shirt, covering my nose and mouth, fighting against the smells of those pressing in on me. Suddenly I heard a distant sound—the train's whistle signaling that we were leaving. It was happening again. I was being taken somewhere unknown.

Where are they taking us? I felt so small standing there in the crowded boxcar, so insignificant. *What has my life meant? How can I be here now? Where is my life?* I wanted to scream, "What happened to my life?"

I had always thought that I had some measure of control over what I did—and my future. But that had been a façade! *I had control of nothing!* The train wheels began to turn, and I did not even have a handle to grab to keep my balance. There was nothing to hold on to. I choked back my sobs.

I could feel the train gaining speed; I was powerless to stop it. In this place, crowded with men, I had never felt so alone.

One man, his voice old and frail, began to sob, each of his wails echoing the silent cries in my head calling out to my family.

We were all being taken together, and yet we weren't together; we were each alone. *Where is my family? Where is anyone I know?* I began trembling violently, and once again, it wasn't from the cold. There was no one to help us, no one with me. *Oh, God! Where are you? I don't want to be alone!*

If hell could be wrapped in a package, it was encased on that train. Chaos, terror, and exhaustion pervaded every moment. While the train lurched and swayed, we struggled to stay awake, then struggled to sleep. There was not enough room to sit so we relied on the pressure of those around us to support one another while we slept. I could think of little else but lying down, and of food and water. I knew the farms we passed had cellars packed with food and wells of fresh water. Even my bones ached at the thought.

Again, someone said there was a bucket in a corner to relieve ourselves, but with so many people crowded in there was no way to reach it. We all just did what we had to do at our feet.

In a rare moment of quiet, I heard a small, frail voice somewhere in the darkness, "I need water. Please … please … does anyone have water … just a sip? I won't take any more." It was another question left unanswered. There had been many voices in the darkness: "I can't stand any longer, please, I need to lie down, make room, make room … I'm so tired … I think the man next to me is dead … I need to sit … I haven't done anything wrong … Open the doors … I'm going to be sick … I know he's dead … Why is there no water … I can't keep my balance … Stay calm! … I don't want to die … I'm going to kill them when they open the doors … God, where are you?"

I couldn't stand it. I wanted them to go away, all of them, all these tormented souls pushing in on me, drowning me, killing my soul.

Occasionally the train would jolt so hard we would slam into one another. My head kept hitting the same man until I had the chance to wiggle further from him. Sometimes the train slowed down, eased into a railroad siding, and stopped. The sound of a passing train was so close I held my breath, fearing that it might collide with ours. I wondered if they were military trains—trains with a much higher priority than ours. The waiting was agonizing. At least when we were moving, there was hope of a destination—hope of getting off.

On one of the stops the train rolled to a halt and the doors to our car were cracked open. There was only a narrow shaft of light but bright enough that the light hurt my eyes. Slowly, the outline of several German soldiers standing along the station platform came into focus. Each one held a machine gun aimed at us. My knees buckled at the thought of them opening fire. If it hadn't been so crowded I would have crumpled to the floor. I sensed others with the same thought: we had to surge forward and charge those guards. They would kill us all but at least we would die trying to defend ourselves. Before we could act, we heard footsteps echoing off the planks and several men in striped uniforms appeared at the opening of our boxcar. Each carried buckets of water. One of them barked in Polish, "Order! One scoop per man or you will be shot!" Several buckets were pushed inside. I braced for the chaos, waiting for the crash of the buckets, of water spilling to the floor. To my relief, each man carefully, almost reverently, handled the buckets as they were passed. As I waited, the back of my throat began to throb in anticipation. When the man next to me offered me the scoop, my hands were trembling so badly that I feared dropping it. I wrapped both hands around the scoop and closed my eyes as liquid trickled down my throat. My lips felt as though they had just barely touched the moisture when the scoop was empty. I lifted it again, shaking off every drop, then looked away before handing it to the next man. Within minutes a second bucket reached me and I was able to take another drink. I wanted more but none came. I prayed food would come next but instead the doors slammed closed. We heard the bolt slide into place with a deafening finality. The men nearest the doors started pounding, begging to be let off. An hour later, the train began rolling and everyone started to weep.

That night as I was drifting to sleep my head snapped backwards so awkwardly I hurt my neck. "Why is he being taken?" I hadn't meant to say anything, but I could not clear my mind of the image of an old man I had passed in the line to board the train. His back was so crooked his gaze was permanently fixed at his feet. He was so frail that I feared he might fall over if I bumped him. My thoughts drifted to a memory of another man I stood next to in the barracks hours before we boarded the train. He was groaning in agony and his feet were so black with frostbite, it didn't look like he would be able to keep them. *Why are they being taken?* I could understand the healthy young men like me being taken to work, but why all the others? They said we were being taken for resettlement, but it made no sense. *Why go to all this trouble to transport old men, sick men? Why not leave them in the ghetto? Why would Hitler waste resources he could use for the war?*

The answer struck me hard. *Taking us has nothing to do with work and the war! They're going to kill us all!* I choked down the stinging bile. My skin felt clammy and cold. I saw the boxcar spin around me. I grasped the arm of the man next to me. My eyes darted through the darkness. *There must be a way, some way! Some way to fight!* I closed my eyes and could hear the drumming that began in Radom, a ceaseless drumming of the German war machine. *How do you stop something like that? Grandfather! You said, "What will be, will be. It's in God's hands." So what am I supposed to do now? Just leave it up to God and do nothing while they kill me? Grandfather! God gave me hands to fight and legs to run away! Is that what I'm supposed to do?*

Out of the darkness I heard a voice cry, "I don't want to die!" For a moment I thought the voice was mine but then I realized it was the man next to me, the man whose arm I held tight. His arm felt strong. I let out a long, slow breath. I wasn't alone. None of us here wanted to die. Somehow, some way, I had to find a way to live. *God, stop this madness!* [23]

The Arrival

*I was dead tired and couldn't think of anything else.
All I wanted to do was lie down. I didn't care where.*
~Joe Rubinstein

Thursday, April 30, 1942

Thump, t'thump, t'thump, t'thump, t'thump. The rhythmic sound of the train and with it, the words, "Food and water," "Food and sleep," "Food and water," "Food and sleep," thump, thump, thump ... repeated ... over and over in my head. I'm not sure when I began chanting the phrases but the rhythm occupied my mind for a long time. My head nodded with each repetition. My eyes remained closed. I no longer took notice of the other sounds of wails, moans, and cries— only food and water, food and sleep, food and wa ... An interruption jarred me from my reverie: metal scraping metal. It took me a moment to realize the train was slowing until it eventually stopped. I heard distant doors sliding and commands shouted in German. Then I heard something new: the movement of masses of people. "I hear them," a voice yelled not far from me. "People are getting off. We're getting off!" With a clank and release, the doors to our train car were forced wide open. Blinding sunlight filled the tomb. I recoiled like a turtle retreating into its protective shell.

I had no idea where I was and I didn't care. I just wanted out. I was standing in the back of the car wedged between men and the wall.

The man in front of me began to sob and others joined him. Someone began shouting in Yiddish thanking God and others whispered prayers of their own. I looked to the ceiling, waiting for my turn to get off. *What's taking them so long?* I was pressing against the man in front of me, forcing him to hurry. Shouts and curses came from men struggling to walk on stiff, weak legs. Several men tripped. I wondered if I would be able to walk. As the weight of people in front of me lessened, I nearly fell. Some did fall and were helped to their feet by those around them. I shuffled forward, through the mess and around the bodies that were lying on the floor, pretending that no one around me had died. I stumbled into something on the boxcar floor and stepped away. I kept my eyes straight ahead, looking down just enough so I didn't trip on the dark shadows that I couldn't bear to see. The wailing of the old man still echoed hauntingly in my head. I hadn't heard him in a long time. I hoped his was not one of the bodies now at my feet.

As I moved and climbed down out of the train car, an inmate in a filthy, tattered, striped uniform emerged from the adjacent car dragging out a body. The contorted face of that stiff corpse horrified me. As I wondered what the inmate had done to deserve such a wretched task, another inmate emerged carrying a dead teenage boy with curly black hair.

How long have I been on this train? I couldn't tell. It was all a swirling blackness of time. The light still hurt my eyes, and I continued to squint against it.

"Schnell, schnell!" barked someone from behind. I felt a hard jab against my shoulder. I knew I had been shoved by the butt of a gun, forcing me to hurry along. My legs did not feel connected to my body, yet I felt them moving as I ran forward to catch up with the men in my line. I was gasping for each breath even though I had only run a few steps. Ahead were rows and rows of identical, plain barrack buildings. *Where am I?* I had no idea but I was relieved that maybe there was room for everyone on the train after all.

I needed to reach a bed. I had to rest. Instead, our line continued to shuffle along. I saw many more of the inmates in ragged stripes. Most were thin and wasted and none seemed to even notice us.

My thoughts were muddled and I feared I was drifting off to sleep while I walked. I had no idea how my legs were still moving. A distant shot rang out, and then another. As I followed the row of men into a large wooden building, the image of the older man, the one with the crooked back would not leave me. I shook it off, hoping that I was only imagining the worst. * [24]

* Author Note: In March 1942, trains began arriving daily at Auschwitz. Sometimes several trains would arrive on the same day, each carrying one thousand or more victims coming from the ghettos of Eastern Europe, as well as from Western and Southern European countries. During 1942, transports arrived from Poland, Slovakia, the Netherlands, Belgium, Yugoslavia, and Theresienstadt. [25]

Marked for Life

We were there to die.
~Joe Rubinstein

I let my filthy clothes drop to the ground and then moved naked to another line, where we were told we would be shaved. I was too tired to be shaved. I just wanted to lie down; I didn't care that the floor was cement. Shivering, I stood and tried to cover myself with my hands, wishing there was somewhere to turn. I flushed when I saw they were shaving not just our heads and beards. When my turn came, I stepped up weakly onto the stool, clenched my jaw, and struggled to remain expressionless before a man with an electric razor. I willed myself to stand still while I wanted to kick him in the face. The shaving tugged painfully at my body hair, which was not accustomed to being shaved.

When it was done, and still feeling the sting of the razor, I was directed to a shower room where an inmate stood holding a large hose before a group of us. Several more newly shaved men came in behind me. When there were about thirty of us standing there naked, cold, and exposed, the inmate switched on the nozzle and aimed it at us. The man began shouting in German, "*Entlausung.*" They were spraying us for lice. We were ordered to turn slowly. The disinfectant chemicals seared my skin, especially where I was raw from just having been shaved. I sucked in my breath, every muscle spasming against the pain. The potent reek of chemicals against my empty stomach was too much. I began to shake and then heave, with nothing in me to vomit. As soon as the spraying stopped, overhead shower heads doused us with cold water. I recoiled from the cold but my thirst drove me forward. I gulped as much as I could, although I feared I might spew all of it back up. The shower was short. I wanted more time to erase the filth, but the water had stopped.

I looked for a towel to dry off. Instead, we were ushered naked and wet outside, and then into another barracks where inmates were handing out heavy, wooden, Dutch-style clogs, striped trousers, a shirt, and a cap. We were given no underwear, and I felt awkward dressing without it. The clothes were several sizes too large, and the cloth was thin, but I was so relieved to have clean clothes that I didn't care. I rolled up the shirtsleeves, made several folds at the waist, and cuffed the extra material at my ankles. Everyone around me wore ill-fitting clothes. I was glad that I could at least button my shirt closed, something that could not be said for many others, and was startled to realize how much we looked alike in our striped uniforms and shaven heads and beards.

I set down the clogs, slipped my feet in, and shook my head. These were not shoes. Shoes were soft, flexible in my hand, designed for comfort, stitched with care—not heavy, rough things carved from wood. Mine were tight at the heel and loose on my toes. I looked around for socks. Others were doing the same. I cursed under my breath when I realized there were none. I had put on socks nearly every day with barely a thought, and now I could think of little else. I hadn't taken a step in the wooden shoes and already my feet hurt.

We walked clumsily in our clogs to another room where an inmate sat behind a long table. He spoke in Polish, obviously his native language. He asked for our name, hometown, birthdate, and the names of our parents before making a few notes. Instead of writing my name, Icek Jakub Rubinsztejn, he wrote "Josef Rubinstein." He handed me a piece of paper with a number on it, then pointed down the hall toward another room where he said we would receive a permanent mark to match the number on the paper. *A permanent mark?* I had no idea what that meant. As I turned to leave, my voice sounded weak when I asked the man, "What day is it? And where are we?"

"April 30, 1942. Auschwitz." When the answer came to the question I had been asking since first being taken, it meant nothing. I had never heard of a place called Auschwitz.

After the man with the needle finished and the needle was resting in the inkwell, I bent my right arm towards me to read the tattooed numbers right-side up. The numbers were uneven and huge, covering most of my forearm, carelessly done—like a child with chalk on a sidewalk. The arrogance of the Nazis enraged me. I wanted to scream, "You mark me like an item to be sold! Who are you to do this to me?" I remember Grandfather telling me that among Jews, permanent markings on the skin were strictly forbidden because they were a sin against God. The Nazis had obviously known this about us and how degrading such a brand would be.

I looked at the number more closely and felt a dark emptiness spread through me, as if the ink that had pierced my skin was now moving through my veins. Like the white sheet covering my father's face, that sheet in my mind had turned black; I was marked for life. A mark—my identity—was nothing more here than a log in a book. To the Nazis, I was no more. I was simply 34207. * ** *** [26]

* Author Note: Only those prisoners selected for work were issued serial numbers; those prisoners sent directly to the gas chambers were not registered and received no tattoos. At Auschwitz II (Birkenau), the SS staff introduced the practice of tattooing in March 1942. Some Jewish prisoners (but not all) had a triangle tattooed beneath their serial number. [27]

** Author Note: April 30, 1942, 606 prisoners sent by the Sipo and SD from Radom receive Nos. 33996-34601. [28]

*** Author Note: On his first day at Auschwitz-Birkenau, April 30, 1942, sixty-five prisoners and two Russian POWs perished—by beatings, starvation, disease, and some by suicide. [29]

Sustenance of the Starved

Pigs would not have eaten that food.
~Joe Rubinstein

My fingers shook as I clenched a black bread roll. I took a big bite of the roll, barely tasting it before swallowing. It was the first food since boarding the train. I opened my mouth to devour the rest but paused when a gruff voice passing my shoulder whispered to me in Polish, "Save some of it … you'll want it for breakfast too." I turned to look at the man but could only see his back, a man in stripes in a sea of striped men. I studied his back for a moment and then stuffed the rest of the stale piece of roll into my mouth, willing myself not to swallow it too fast. I lifted the bowl and drank the last drop of a bitter brew that was supposed to be tea. I wanted more, but already the bread felt hard in my stomach, a stomach that was now unaccustomed to food. Sweat began forming on my brow, and I feared that I would not be able to keep down what little I had just eaten.

Much later that night, a loud snore of someone sleeping below my bunk startled me awake. It was pitch black. It took me a moment to remember where I was. The last thing I heard before falling into an exhausted sleep was the sound of a gong ordering all the inmates in the bunks to silence. My shoulder ached with the weight of my body against hard, cold wood. I was shivering. As my eyes adjusted to the darkness, I saw the silhouettes of bunks stacked around the room four levels high and crowded with men. I was sleeping on the top bunk on a small bit of straw, a thin blanket pulled over me. My stomach knotted with hunger and thirst. I rolled over to escape the hot, foul breath of the man on my left, only to find another hot breath to my right. The barracks were alive with loud snores, snorts, coughs, and whimpers. Several cried out in their sleep. When I'd fallen asleep earlier, I had been too exhausted to notice. Now, I was desperate to stop the noise and the repulsive body smells surrounding me. I covered my face, gagging. My skin still smelled of the chemicals sprayed on me. I wasn't sure which smell was worse—my skin or the men around me. Despite the chill, I began to sweat again. I couldn't breathe. I had to get out. I didn't care if I froze to death; I didn't care if they shot me. *They will shoot me. Is that what I really want?* I closed my eyes and forced myself to calm down and began begging God to take away my panic.

I forced my mind to imagine that I was back in Radom. It was early morning, but Mother was already awake, already cooking. I could almost smell the potato pancakes on the stovetop. Mother always rose early and made us breakfast. At the time I seldom considered how happy I was to have such a home. Now I would give anything to wake in the morning and be there. [30, 31]

Day 2

Our bunks had to be spotless. They would punish us if we didn't do a good job. They would take you out and you would never return. If you smiled or made a mean face, they would take you out.

~Joe Rubinstein

Friday, May 1, 1942

A loud and irritating gong woke me. My eyelids were heavy and swollen. A door opened and light from the hallway seeped in. I opened my eyes, looking directly into the sad, tired eyes of another prisoner who looked more exhausted than I felt. The man sighed heavily but did not speak. I watched him push himself to his elbows and begin arranging the straw berth with particular care. It was not easy, as there was not enough room for him to even sit fully upright. The man continued to work, taking meticulous care that not even a wrinkle was left in his blanket. I looked around and realized that everyone around me was doing the same. When the man saw that I was not working, he whispered something in a language I had never heard before. I looked at him and shrugged my lack of understanding. The man pointed his boney finger at me and then to his berth, then swung his arm, emulating a hitting motion. It was clear: anyone without a tidy bed would be beaten. The more I tried to straighten the straw and the thin blanket, the more I realized the absurdity in trying to make a tidy berth from a straw mattress in such a cramped space.

Soon dark shadows of men collected below, like wasps crawling out of their mud nests. I had no idea how many shared these quarters but knew it had to be in the hundreds.

I climbed down the bunks carrying the wooden shoes that I had tucked next to me while I slept, recoiling as I stepped into them. I yearned for a pair of thick socks and considered tearing my shirt and using the cloth to wrap my feet. I knew that I could be beaten for damaging my clothes. Accenting the point, a stocky inmate with a green triangle sewn on his shirt appeared carrying a long club. He began shouting in German for us to hurry and jabbed at those he did not feel were exiting quickly enough. He was our "capo," another inmate assigned to supervise the rest of us.

The man then began walking through the rows of bunks and poking the ribs of those who had not gotten out of bed. On his clipboard, he made notes and continued counting those who had died during the night.

We were ordered outside while it was still dark. I guessed it must be no later than 4:00 or 4:30 a.m. As the light of day gradually dawned, I could not stop staring at the shadowy, thin figures of the men around me. To an outsider, they all looked dirty and exhausted. Some had open wounds, scabs, and were badly bruised. Some were a sickly yellow color. Nearly all were pale. Over and over I asked myself, "What have they done to these men?"

The night before, I had been too exhausted to notice the condition of the latrines. After a night of sleep, I was mortified. We were ushered into the room containing two long rows of wooden benches with open toilet holes cut into them. I bit my lip as I sat down and cringed when my back touched the back of the man behind me, my legs rubbing against those on each side. I squeezed my eyes tight and tried to pretend that none of this was happening.

Later, sitting at a long table in another barracks, I forced down a rank tea, which more closely resembled brown, foul water. I had been given a small, tasteless roll that was gone in two bites. I watched as several of the men pulled pieces of bread from their sleeves, a portion of last night's dinner. The man who had whispered in my ear had been right. I fought my threatening tears. I had no idea how I would get through the day without eating something more. * [33]

* Author Note: On Joe's first full day there, May 1, 1942, eighty-eight prisoners and one Russian POW would die at Auschwitz-Birkenau. [34]

And Still They Come

Sometimes I think I'm going to die if I think about it.
~Joe Rubinstein

Another day; another train has arrived. Our work crew passed by hundreds of exhausted people who had just disembarked. I thought my train had been crowded but this one carrying even more strangers was much worse. I felt deep pity for all of them. Unlike my train, which had transported only men, these lines were teeming with women and children, too. They all looked so tired they could barely stand as they waited in line for the SS to decide who was strong enough to work and who would be sent to the barracks housing the women, children, and the feeble.

We approached the lines where an SS officer in a black uniform with a horse crop in his gloved hand ordered a teenage boy to stick out his tongue. With a flick of his wrist the boy was directed to go to the line with men close to my age. Behind him, a middle-aged man with his right foot heavily bandaged, limped forward and opened his mouth to be examined. The officer didn't take time to look. Instead, he nodded his head toward another line of mostly women, children, and the elderly, many who stood leaning heavily on their canes. I had no idea how the older people were still standing after their ordeal. Near the front of that line I saw a young man leaning on a pair of crudely carved crutches next to an elderly man who sat huddled in his wheelchair.

One of the older men in the line was holding the hand of a small boy whose pants were soaked with urine. I wondered if it was his grandson. He smiled at the boy, struggling to hide the fear I knew he felt. My heart cried out for the man. Grandfather would have done the same for me. I was relieved to walk past because it hurt too much to think of that sad grandfather. Most of the children clung to their mothers, while others clenched the hands of their siblings. Everywhere children and babies were crying out for something to eat and drink. I passed one little girl wrapped up in her mother's arms. She had huge brown eyes. As I passed, she looked right at me and started to cry, saying she just wanted to go home. I wanted to cry with her. I wanted to go home, too. The girl pressed her face against her mother's shoulder, and I moved on.

Nearly every person I saw carried some of their possessions. Some held bags and pillowcases stuffed full while others clutched small suitcases. Most of the women had scarves covering their heads, and many of the young girls had stylish hats. Many people wore coats and gloves and I noticed some with thin-framed spectacles. Nearly everyone wore the Star of David armbands or had it sewn on their shirt pockets. Many of the men wore yarmulkes, skullcaps, and the holy tallit katan under their shirts, with the tzitzit fringe showing.

There was a rabbi with a long, white beard wearing black clothes. He had a swollen, purple ringed eye. The Nazis hated the religious men more than anyone, openly beating them in the ghetto and forcibly shaving their beards. Most of the men had no beards other than the stubble that had grown since they had been put aboard the train. One of these men, a balding man of about forty, looked directly at me. He wore a heavy coat with a fur collar. His nose was long and straight. Yet, it wasn't his features that I knew I would have a hard time forgetting when I tried to sleep that night. It was his expression. His was a face filled with a fierce rage—a rage that did not fit on the face of a man I sensed was gentle and kind. The Nazis had a way of doing that, of creating a reality that should never exist.

Nearly every parent I saw wore the same strained look of grim encouragement on their faces, smiling weakly at their children. Yet behind the smile, each was etched with the ultimate pain, the realization that they had lost their ability to protect their children.

I passed a grandmother holding a young girl's hand, a grandmother who looked like she wished she had not lived so long.

A pretty teenage girl with long, red braids lifted her eyes just as I neared and smiled. I smiled back, a bit sheepishly. I wondered if she knew that if I could, I would have asked her to go dancing. My line of workers pressed on so I had to keep moving past her, and as I did, I felt my face grow warm with embarrassment.

"Elżbeta? Can you hear me? Elżbeta?" came a man's voice from somewhere in the crowd. "Elżbeta. Elżbeta! Your father loves you! Elżbeta, don't be frightened, Elżbeta! God is with you, Elżbeta!" I hummed so I wouldn't have to hear the pain in his voice—an agony so sharp I felt I had been split clean through just listening to it.

A pregnant woman stood with her hands pressing against her back. I was certain her back would buckle if she removed those hands. She glanced sideways at me as I approached. Her belly was low and immense; dark, puffy skin outlined her tired eyes. Her mouth was tight, revealing her fear. She was in the same line as the old man in the wheelchair. I wondered why the SS hadn't already directed her to the camp hospital. I turned back and stared at the poor woman, incredulous. *She should be in a hospital! Why isn't she in a hospital? She's going to have a baby!* I looked around helplessly at the sea of people and had to restrain myself from shouting. *Every one of these people should be at home ... cooking dinner ... going to school ... reading to their children ... playing soccer ... having fun! These men ought to be out working to earn food for their families, not standing in this Godforsaken line in this Godforsaken place!*

I was suddenly filled with such outrage that I wanted to strike out and hit someone. I would not have been surprised to hear my own teeth crack as I clenched my teeth. *How have they not yet been ground to angry nubs?* Dark spots clouded my vision. I felt I might pass out from the fury building up inside. I was so angry it made me weak. *How can any of this be happening? God! Why is this happening? This is not the way life should be!*

A piercing cry filled the air. My head snapped around to see a young woman screaming as a soldier walked away with a baby. The woman continued to scream. Another soldier raised his club and struck her. Two women ran to her as she sank to the ground. The soldier lowered his club and cursed, calling her a filthy Jew. [35, 36]

A Day in the Life

If you were young or old, you were dead.
~Joe Rubinstein

I sat at a long wooden table sipping a bowl of soup that was too thin to identify. Whatever it was, it was terrible. After nearly dying of starvation aboard the train I didn't think I would ever object to anything edible but, after three weeks of the same foul-smelling food, I fought to swallow it. I closed my eyes, recalling for a moment my mother's chicken soup brimming with vegetables from her garden. When I opened my eyes I couldn't bring myself to look again at the awful dribble in my cup.

The room was crowded with hundreds of men. Some sat on the benches, some stood, and others ate outside, standing in the dirt. I still could not comprehend the number of people at this camp, and the babble of different languages bothered me—not because I couldn't understand them, which was frustrating enough, but I was more troubled because of what it meant. Although most inmates were Jewish, it wasn't just Yiddish spoken here, nor even Polish and German, but rather I heard French, Italian, Russian, Greek, and many others languages I could not identify. *How is it possible that Jews from so many countries are here? How many other countries does Germany control? How many countries are sending their Jewish people here?**

Almost daily I heard whispered fears that there were spies among us and it wasn't safe to trust anyone. One thing was clear: the Nazis wanted us hating each other so we might forget how much we despised them. They searched for the cruelest among us, then rewarded them by appointing them as capos—inmates who were assigned command of the barracks and our work units. The more brutal they were, the more food and power they were given.

My mood was dark. I hadn't wanted to talk to anyone. Terrible rumors had begun circulating about a recent train that arrived— packed full of men, women, and children—rumors that the Nazis had taken everyone off and killed them. All of them poisoned by some sort of gas.

I put down my cup, nauseated.

Ever since hearing the rumor, I had felt like I was in a long tunnel. I heard the voices around me, but they were weak and distant.

"It's a lie!" my mind had screamed. But knew it wasn't. I felt sick. An entire trainload of people slaughtered! Then more rumors of women and children in the barracks being rounded up and killed! *What has happened to all those I saw standing in line? The little girl crying on her mother's shoulder who only wanted to go home ... the grandparents ... the pretty girl with the red braids? Oh God! What of them?*

Why? The same helpless question that had plagued me on the train. *Why have the Nazis gone to all this trouble to bring so many people here?*

As it had once on the train, the answer came to me again—the answer I had since talked myself out of believing. *They're bringing them here to kill them, in a place where no one will see the evil and no one will know what happened.* A knot pressed hard within my chest.

I looked at my tattoo; the skin around it was still red. The people on that train didn't live long enough to be tattooed. My eyes shifted about the crowded room. There were no children, no elderly—only those like me—strong enough to work. Anyone young or old had no chance. I scraped my fingertips across my tattoo. I wanted to dig it out. If the SS were numbering us in order, then thirty-four thousand, two hundred and six people had been tattooed before me. *How many more unnumbered souls have been killed here? How many have been murdered with their families having no idea what has happened to them?*

My head was pounding. The pressure behind my eyes pulsed hot. I felt I was dying along with all the people I could recall from that group—limb by limb, dying from knowing such a terrible truth. *How does one bear the unbearable?* I didn't know. I couldn't breathe. I was numb, tumbling down into nothingness. I thought of the electrified fence that the Nazis had built to keep us all in. Every day since I arrived, every day, I had seen inmates touch the high voltage wire. It was the quickest way to die. I squeezed my eyes and fought against the image and the temptation. I couldn't do it. Doing it would mean letting the Nazis win. Doing it would mean never seeing my family again. Doing it would mean taking something that was only God's to take.

Like a predator circling its prey, the same question had been turning around and around in my mind. *Why am I really here?* The answer came suddenly—rising in me like the soup I had just eaten, threatening to overtake me. *I'm here to work until I die.* ** [37]

* Author Note: The variety of languages listed here is more representative of what Joe experienced in his later years at Auschwitz.

** Author Note: "The first selection among weak and sick prisoners took place on May 4, 1942: 1,200 prisoners who had arrived in the previous month were declared 'unfit for work.' On May 12, 1942, for the first time, a transport of 1,500 people was brought from the nearby town ... directly into the gas chambers." [38]

A Different Kind of Army

We were like an army, only a different kind of army.
~Joe Rubinstein

We marched, lived in barracks, and were forced to do calisthenics every morning for hours. Our heads were shaved often, as were our bodies. Our uniforms had stripes; our boots were wooden clogs. Our drills often began before dawn and ended after dark.

In our army, we worked and we ran. If we did not run fast enough, we were beaten. If we showed emotion, we were beaten. If our barracks were not immaculate, we were beaten. Immaculate is hard to achieve with filthy water in rooms crammed with hundreds of men, with mere benches of rough cutouts for toilets, with men dying every night from dysentery. Immaculate is hard to achieve on putrid mattresses of straw.

In our army we were fed, not to be made stronger, but in order that we would grow weak. Ours was a different kind of army—our army of concentration camp inmates—an army without weapons, without battlefields. In our army our commanders wanted us to die, for in this army we, the inmates of Auschwitz, were the enemy of our Nazi commanders. In our army anyone who engaged the enemy would be killed.

In my own private army the battle I fought every day was a battle within: the battle to stay alive. [39]

Blisters

If my feet got infected, they would kill me.
~Joe Rubinstein

Before coming to Auschwitz I never thought about keeping my feet clean. But in the place where disease, starvation, brutality, and death were everywhere, it became my obsession. If my feet became infected, I would not be able to work and I would be shot. I would not be the first to die from something as simple as blisters.

Without socks and clean water, keeping my feet clean was nearly impossible. I spent every waking hour in the wooden shoes. I ran calisthenics in them, marched in them, and worked in them. Every day my feet were covered in angry, red boils. I continually watched for any bits of rags to stuff inside my shoes. I tried straw, but it would not stay in place long enough to do any good.

Each night I tended to my feet as carefully as I could. I dunked my sleeves into my allotted water and wiped my feet as best as I could. The water was dirty, and illnesses were rampant. I was one of the lucky ones and thanked my mother for it. I'm certain her nutritious cooking gave my body a foundation to fend off the diseases that were killing so many others.

At night, I used to turn the wooden shoes over in my hands, wondering what Mr. Nagel would have said if he could have seen them. His gentle hand knew only how to craft shoes of comfort. I wondered about the Dutch who wore such shoes by choice. I decided the clogs they wore had to be crafted with much greater care than these, which were roughly hewn and never sanded. [40]

The Icy Blanket

We had to carry it in our hands and in our shirts.
~Joe Rubinstein

I hated when it snowed. When it did, they made us move it all—acres and acres of snow. We had no shovels, so we scooped it into our hands. We had no place to carry it, so we carried it in our shirts.

I called Auschwitz "the big camp." The complex was not just big; it was huge, covering many square miles. Sometimes the snow fell while we slept. Sometimes it howled its presence for hours. Half-dressed, half-starved, half-dead, we were marched outside to clear the grounds.

Silently, the white blanket of death greeted me like a mournful friend. I exhaled wisps of white vapor. My face burned against the stinging gale. I pulled my small cap down tighter. I could be shot for losing my hat, even to the wind. They didn't care. They wanted a reason to kill. A missing hat would do just fine.

There were times the snow fell faster than we could move it. I was often so thirsty I tried to suck the snow from my sleeves, but the cold only burned my throat. When the winds gusted, a few inches of snow could form drifts several feet high. Exhausted, we trudged our way through it. Snow accumulated in my wooden shoes so often that I finally gave up trying to dump it out. Sometimes when I lifted my leg from a drift, my foot was bare; momentarily losing my clog in the depth of the snow. On some nights, we shoveled until after dark, with the moon reflecting off the white ground. At those times, I could see my shadow—a shadow that looked big, although I knew I was growing smaller every day, smaller physically and emotionally.

As I shuffled back to the barracks at the end of a day's labor clearing snow, I often could not lift my frozen legs, scraping and dragging them along instead. The Nazis didn't care that we would return to the barracks with our bodies plagued by frostbite. They weren't concerned that some of us would not return at all. There would be no fire to greet us, no heavy blankets, no hot cocoa like Mother often had simmering when I came in from the cold. Instead, a hard bunk in the frigid barracks waited for me and a thin woolen blanket—if mine had not been taken while I shoveled. In bed I pulled my legs to my chest and massaged my frozen feet back to life. I blew on my hands until I became lightheaded, my skin stinging so badly I would cry out in pain. Outside, I could hear the sounds of the snow and ice pellets tapping the roof.

The next day I knew I would have to do it all again. [41]

Hallways of the Dead

We saw them, hundreds of dead bodies, every day.
~Joe Rubinstein

For prisoners at Auschwitz the line between life and death was thin and blurred. It was often hard to tell the difference since living often looked like death animated. This was especially true for those who had been starved to the threshold of death; they were the walking skeletons with their skin stretched taut over their bones, legs, and swollen ankles. They were everywhere, with their vacant, hollowed eyes, lying in their bunks at night, too weak to even roll over.

Every morning before we were allowed to eat we had to drag the corpses of those who had died in the night into the barracks' hallways. [42]

A Question Repeated

I couldn't find anyone I knew.
~Joe Rubinstein

I asked the same questions of every new arrival I heard speaking Polish, "Have you any news from Radom? Do you know my family?"

It was risky asking even such simple questions. We could be shot for asking questions. We suspected some prisoners were Nazi sympathizers disguised as inmates. We knew some were persuaded with food and water to keep tabs on what their fellow inmates were saying and doing.

I heard rumors that there were listening devices installed in our barracks and in the areas where we worked. With these devices the Nazis could pick up any hint of conspiracy or escape. Their tactics worked. There was little trust among us and not much conversation. I was scared, but I was not too scared to ask about Radom and my family.

The answers to my questions were always the same. No one had any news of Radom. No one knew of my family. [43]

Swallowing Hell

Twice a week we moved the bodies in carts.
~Joe Rubinstein

Demons prey on shadows and shapes. I know because I did their work.

It was early morning and the sky was low and heavy, threatening rain. Twenty of us marched toward the trees, our wooden clogs hitting the ground in dull slaps, one after the other, like the applause of a polite audience.

I squeezed my fist to stop the grimace threatening my face. If I made a mean face, they would shoot me. I still had no socks. My feet were raw and chafed against the rough wood. My thoughts were morose—thoughts of another day doing the same job. I swallowed the bile rising in my throat. Breakfast was often little more than weak, bitter coffee. Before dawn that morning our rations included a stale biscuit and a glop of orange marmalade. They needed us to be strong, which meant there were many bodies. I blinked quickly, forcing back my tears. *How much longer can this go on? How much longer can I go on doing the work of madmen?* Work that carved out my humanity bit by bit—leaving me hollow, more dead than alive.

The Nazis never touched the bodies of those they murdered. They left that most despised work to a kommando work unit, a small group of prisoners that included me.

Twice a week we marched to a place tucked behind the trees. From dawn until after dark, exhausted and half-starved ourselves, we moved corpses from outside the gas chambers to the nearby pits where bodies were heaped on top of each other like books to be shelved—precious pages of lives waiting to be destroyed.

We transported them in small wooden handcarts. The adults required two of us—one at the wrists and the other at the ankles—to swing them into the cart. The bodies of infants, we tenderly carried in our arms. We often swung the smaller teenagers over our shoulders. Our capo ordered us to stack as many bodies as possible into the cart. If the corpses were large the cart sometimes only accommodated one body. We could fit a lot of babies and young children in one cart. We had to work quickly because several hundred men, women, and children were killed in each gassing. If we worked too slowly the capos would club us.

I hated when I started to think about my family and the bodies, thoughts that shouldn't be intertwined. Sometimes, though, I was caught by surprise. The arch of a brow, the angle of a nose, or the line of a chin would trigger a memory. Then I prayed and fiercely pleaded with God. *Not these naked, lifeless dolls!* I forced myself to paint a different picture: *My family just spent a warm night in their beds, in Radom. My mother is just now making breakfast for them. Cinnamon is in the air. Chaim has found his way home. Anszel and Marsha have brought the baby. Mother wishes the stove were hotter, the eggs cooking faster, so she can rock the baby—she can hardly wait to cradle him in her arms, just like she did all of us.*

I tried to control my thoughts, to stay in that safe place of home, but the bodies crept back in.

In that place of death, I became an expert at discerning how each one had died. Some had been imprisoned here, like me, for a long time—dying just the day before or even earlier that same day. Some of the bodies had small wounds from the bullet of a pistol; others were torn open by machine guns. Some had welts around their neck—death from hanging. Many of the bodies were already skeletons before they died—death by starvation. Others showed the grisly signs of being tortured, of cigarette burns seared into their hands and eyes, with genitals and breasts cut off. Scores had been worked until their exhausted bodies could no longer continue and they bore the telltale signs of it: their calloused hands were ripped and shredded, the bottoms of their feet covered in blisters.

And some were ravaged by disease. Dysentery swept through the camp earlier that summer. Every morning, heaps of bodies were stacked outside the barracks. For the first time I could roll over in my berth without having to breathe in the hot, foul breath of another man lying inches from my face. The extra space did not last long, as more people were brought in to replace them. The disease left a stench of vomit and diarrhea that seeped into every fiber of cloth, every morsel of food, every breath of air. Some of the dead in my cart simply gave up and had touched the wire. That happened every day.

Most of the dead were the new arrivals from the trains, people who believed they were brought to this camp to work for the Nazis' war effort. They believed that once the war was over they would be allowed to return home. There would be no work for most of them. They had been brought to this camp for one reason: to die where their murders could be concealed. Most were dead within two hours of arriving.

The Nazis didn't care how the deaths of any of the people in my cart occurred, just as long as the result was the same.

I hated that I'd been reduced to thinking of the most efficient ways to push bodies in a cart—calculating whether it was easier to stack a few adults or many children. I hated being a tiny cog, trapped in the Nazi's grinding, heartless machine of death—a cog that had no way to escape.

I hated the impossible, surreal contradictions of that place, of knowing that life could be so good while listening to the sound of bulldozers covering bodies with dirt. I hated the ways I had become like them, the Nazis and their small, petty minds, convincing themselves that because they had taken everything from us—our countries, our homes, our families, our possessions, our clothing, our hair, our everything—having left nothing but the naked shadows and shapes, it was no longer human beings they killed. And yet, sometimes pretending was the only way I kept my mind from collapsing—when faces and bodies faded into shadows and shapes I didn't have to hold my breath. It was easier to grasp the limb of a tree in my hand than the leg of a grandmother.

I tried not to look at the hands of the children that should have been playing instead of stiffly splayed. I turned my head from the frozen grimaces on the faces of the dead, whether their eyes were rolled back or staring ahead, seemingly seeing right through me. I tried to ignore the crack of skulls smacking against one another as they were thrown into my cart and the sound of breaking ribs when I heaved the bodies like sacks of flour into the pit.

I tried not to notice when I lifted a body and the skin was still warm, a body that had been filled with life minutes earlier. I tried to ignore the softness of a child's blond hair brushing across my wrist as I lifted her. I tried not to look too closely at delicate eyelashes against a toddler's perfect skin. I tried to conceal from the capos that I was scanning the bodies, struggling to determine who was the mother of the baby I held in my hands, wondering if I could place them into the pit together. I fought the screams rising inside me when the fragile hands and wrists of the elderly snapped like chicken bones in my grasp. I didn't want to hurt them anymore. I struggled to ignore the arms of a young man hitting my back and legs as I swung him over my shoulder. I masked the stabbing pain in my spine as I lifted the dead weight of a man twice my size and my ineptness as I tried to keep a tight grip on a slippery dead ankle in the pouring rain. I restrained myself from cursing at the bodies that weighed my cart down in the mud after a heavy rain, as I struggled to keep it righted and moving on the slimy paths.

I yelled out in cold reflex at the shocking gasps of the dead when they hit the cart just right and the trapped air in their lungs escaped in loud, deep haunting moans like the wails of a body still yearning for its soul. I grew afraid of that crying of the dead. I also grew to fear getting too close to their mouths, afraid the gas that killed them might kill me too.

I thought of all these things each time I marched toward the pit. I couldn't help wondering whether the bodies would be a little stiffer and easier to lift in the winter. Surely the cold would put an end to the flies that always knew where to find dead bodies. I hated the swarms of them buzzing, landing, and biting, with no more care of the flesh they ate than the Nazis who made the kill. They landed on the faces of the dead, on their eyes, crawling in and out of their open mouths, and then they came to pick at my eyes, to creep into my mouth.

Hour after hour, their mindless pursuit drove me to stand at the edge of the pit and contemplate my own death. It would be easy to jump in with the bodies and wait for death. It would be easier than staying and swatting flies off the faces of dead babies. Jumping would quell the detestable stench of the chemicals sprayed over the bodies to speed decomposition—a scent so vile I gagged in reflex with each breath. Jumping would stop the buzzing in my ears hours after I crawled into bed each night.

Like a volcano threatening to erupt, I wanted to cough it all out— all of it: the putrid, rotted flesh, the chemicals, the blood, the urine, the bile, the dead.

We marched closer. A row of empty carts waited for us like carriages taking patrons to a play. Soon I would be standing before the pile of naked bodies strewn in every direction, one upon another, waiting to be moved.

I tried not to think of how my body would look lying naked in one of those carts. Would the young man helping me carry the bodies one day be the one to carry my corpse the next? Or would I be carrying his? If I went before him, would he say a prayer for me?

Sometimes the guards kicked and stomped their heavy boots against the stomachs and skulls of the dead. They bellowed that all of us Jews were nothing but trash at their feet. They wanted us to believe them.

Because of the prayers, I knew they had failed, at least in this. For each day as I trudged along the path pushing a cart full of bodies toward the pit in their final procession, I would say silent prayers for them—prayers not for shadows, shapes, or trash, but prayers reserved for the people they were and the lives they once lived.

It was all I had to give, the only funeral they would know. * [44, 45, 46]

* Author Note: Bodies that had been buried in mass graves eventually began to putrefy in the hot Polish summers. By the end of summer, 1942, the commandant of Auschwitz, Rudolf Höss, ordered Jewish prisoners to dig up the mass graves, layer the bodies with wood and other combustibles, and then burn them in large open pits over a metal grate. This method was soon replaced with burning bodies in crematoriums. [47]

The Green Grass of Radom

*I used to love to watch Father's horses grazing
in the pasture. Radom was so beautiful.*
~Joe Rubinstein

With all the ugliness that surrounded me, my escape was a place
of peace and beauty. I thought of it often, that green grass of
Radom. I could still imagine the grass dancing, drawn in every direction by the wind as if with an invisible wand.

Sometimes when I closed my eyes I could even smell it, that sweet
grass of my father's horse pasture. As a young boy, I would stand on
the lowest rail of the wooden fence with my arms crossed over the
top rail, my chin resting on the back of my hands, and watch my father
feeding, brushing, and harnessing the horses. I was mesmerized by
the graceful motion of their manes and tails, which mimicked the
swaying of the tall grass in the fields as they blew in the wind.

I thought often of that green grass of Radom when I looked at the
dirty, barren ground of Auschwitz. It was a place where there once
had been lots of green before the Nazis turned it into a concentration
camp of the starved. Hungry men will eat just about anything. Starved
inmates had eaten all of it, down to the bare earth. [48, 49]

Trains in the Night

They had orders to kill people and they did.
~Joe Rubinstein

From my wooden bunk I heard them every night, those trains of Auschwitz arriving at their last stop. I heard their whistles with each arrival, crying out along with the wails of the human cargo they carried.

The train whistles were the same as the ones I loved as a child. From the stillness of my bed in Radom I would lie in the dark and listen for them, counting the number of times the engineer pulled the cord. I used to imagine where the trains had been and where they were going.

I remembered a neighbor who worked at the Radom rail yard. My mother felt sorry for him because he rarely took the time to enjoy a hot meal. Occasionally, Mother would send Chaim, Abram, or me to surprise him by taking him something to eat. Often, it was one of Mother's hearty soups and bread. Just carrying it always made me hungry. Our neighbor was always so happy to see me coming that he would thank me with a crushing hug.

I liked walking around the rail yard, my eyes wide in wonder at the massive engines, cars, and wheels. I would search for trains with their engineers visible in the open windows. If they saw me, they usually smiled and waved back.

Those beautiful memories comforted me briefly, but then the fetid smells and the groans of the sick and starving men reminded me I was not safely at home in my bed. Instead, I was in a place where train whistles resembled screams of terror.

The sound of trains at Auschwitz was the sound of death. [50]

For a Crime I Didn't Commit

After fifteen lashes, I couldn't feel any more pain.
I had to save myself. I had to get in that pit.
~Joe Rubinstein

I didn't even know who he was, but he nearly cost me my life. One of my Auschwitz bunkmates told the capo supervising our barracks that I had urinated during the night and that my urine had leaked through the wooden slats to the levels below. There were two levels beneath me, with three men to a bunk. I didn't know which man made the accusation or why he would have done so. Most of us kept small metal water containers near us when we slept so we could sip from them during the long and unbearable nights. Sometime during the night my basin had spilled.

I tried to plead my innocence, but it made no difference. My sentence was decided before I had time to wipe the sleep from my eyes. Twenty-five lashes. It was a common punishment. In my cart, I had carried the bodies of others who had died from twenty-five lashes.

I had seen it often. Some men survived the initial beating and returned to the barracks only to bleed to death. Some died because of infection festering in their wounds. After the brutal lashing some were deemed unfit for work and gunned down on the spot. Some were sent to the hospital, never to return. We all knew what happened once at the hospital: they were sent to the gas chamber.

I couldn't stop myself from considering all these horrors as I followed the capo into the hallway. We passed the bodies of three skeleton-thin men who'd died during the night. I knew that other inmates had dragged the bodies to the hallway where the corpse-collecting truck would collect them during its morning rounds. Their bodies would end up in the pit. I wondered if my slashed and beaten body would be next to theirs.

The unspeakable routines of Auschwitz had long since numbed me. I wasn't sure I was still capable of feeling anything. However, as I walked past the three bodies, I realized that wasn't true. I felt something I hadn't felt in a long time—fear. It began rising in me from the moment I saw the outstretched finger of the capo pointing at me in my bunk and heard his raspy voice call out "34207."

My number—34207—was one number I had prayed I would never hear from my bunk. Anyone whose number was called rarely came back.

My stomach twisted as I continued to follow the capo, knowing what was waiting for me outside. *So this is how it's all going to end … every last bit of me that hasn't yet died in this place. Memories that I hadn't thought of in years flashed through my mind like pictures in a book: Mother making her special stuffed cabbage because she knew how much I loved it; Tatte carrying me on his shoulders as we walked to the barn; my daily treks with Grandfather to the synagogue; Grandmother patting my head as she always did after I'd carried heavy buckets of water several blocks to her apartment so she would have water to do the dishes; the hours of soccer with my siblings; the fun tricks Chaim and I played on those who couldn't tell us apart; the stolen glances from Mr. Nagel's daughter as I worked sewing shoes; the long hours in the lumberyard; the days of standing with Mother on the corner selling vegetables … all of it is going to end … my life, my future … all of it was going to end because of a bit of spilled water and the barbarians who thought because they could that they had the right to take the innocent life of another human being.*

As I stepped through the outside door I saw the smirk on one of the SS guards. Raw, flaming anger flashed through me. He knew where I was headed. I set my jaw and turned my gaze, determined not to give him the satisfaction of seeing any fear on my face. I would not show them a scared or a mean face. Straightening my shoulders, I moved toward the man waiting for his next victim. He was filthy. Sweat beaded on his upper lip, even though it was still early morning. I saw the way his shoulder muscles bulged beneath his striped shirt, a shirt that was too small for his frame. His pants and shirt were stained with dried blood.

I tried to catch his eye as I walked toward him, searching for some trace of the man he might once have been before he came here, a fellow prisoner. I could not tell his nationality. He could have been French, German, Polish, or Czech.

Many of those ordered to conduct the punishments were hardened criminals before ever coming to Auschwitz. I couldn't tell if that were true of this man. I could see no evidence that he derived anything from the task he was about to perform—no pleasure, no disgust, no guilt, nothing. *When I move the bodies, does my face hold the same lifeless expression as his?* I couldn't help thinking the question: a question to which I didn't want to know the answer.

Several SS officers stood by the man, waiting to ensure my beating was brutal enough. If not, the punisher would be shot and another brought to replace him. The man lifted a long, thick whip from the ground. Extending from the grip, the end of the weapon was covered in a jumble of wire and shreds of thick leather that twisted through the dirt like a writhing snake. I felt the blood rush from my head before I was ordered to bend over. The capo barked at me to lower my trousers and lift my shirt, my pants dropping around my ankles as I bent over. I closed my eyes, sucked in my breath, and waited.

I felt the impact of the first blow before I felt the pain. My knees buckled and I struggled to stay on my feet. Searing heat and brilliant light exploded in my head; before I had time to think, another blow came. *Can there be two parts of me now?* I wasn't sure. My body felt split in half. I knew the skin across my back had ripped open. The next blow hit the same wound.

I remember counting the blows as they came—three, four, five, six, seven, eight, nine, ten, eleven, twelve, thirteen, fourteen. After fifteen it didn't hurt anymore. I couldn't feel the blows but I could hear them. I could hear the whirl of the wire through the air before it hit my flesh. I could hear the dull thud of the club against my ribs. I could hear the jangle of wire as it was pulled back off my skin after the blow, before the one that came next—twenty-four, twenty-five.

And then, silence. My panting was the only sound I could hear. I opened my eyes, aware that I was still on my feet. Blood pooled in my wooden shoes. I was bent so low that the ground was only inches from my face. Sweat dripped off my nose. I remember thinking that I just had to walk away and I could not let myself fall. If I did, they would shoot me. I wasn't sure how to move. There seemed to be nothing connecting my desire with my ability to move my limbs. I was surprised when my legs began to respond. I tried to straighten my back, but I couldn't. Bent and broken, I shuffled my feet through the dirt, wondering if I would even hear the shot if it came. I was beyond caring. If I was dying, I was not going to do it in front of these men who were hoping for it.

With the primal instinct of a dying animal, I just wanted to get away. I could feel the blood streaming down the back of my legs. I was leaving a trail of it. I could feel the slap of the open skin from my back against my side as I moved. I considered walking to my barracks, but I couldn't stand the thought of the pressure of the straw against my back, of lying there waiting to die with filthy men and their stench surrounding me. I had to keep moving. I shuffled with no thought of where I was going. I moved behind the long rows of barracks, and then another, and another, until I saw it. If I had seen it before, I hadn't noticed. Now, like a man lost and dying of thirst in the desert with an oasis within his grasp, my only focus was on what was before me.

It was an odd color, that dumping-ground pit of slimy, greenish-black, thick muck. It reeked of chemicals and of things on which I did not dwell. I didn't care. My only thought was that it would be cool and soft on my back.

In this place, there was no hospital or doctors to care for me. The only doctors here were ones who sentenced us to death. Today, there would be no doctor or nurse to stitch my wounds, no mother to wash away the germs and filth, no grandmother to rub balm for the hurt. In this place, and only with God's help, I would have to heal myself. I slipped off my clothes and crawled into the hole. I cried out, my skin stinging as fiercely as if burning embers of coal were being pressed against me. I knew my back was torn open. I was nauseated. My head whirled. I was losing consciousness and wondered if I might drown. Slowly, the fire began to quell and the spinning ceased. I sank lower in the mud. Submerged up to my neck in the green darkness, I somehow managed to keep my head up against the muddy side.

If there was a search for me, I was not aware of it. I don't recall hearing through my hazy stupor any blaring sirens or barking guard dogs. I didn't see any of the SS search units deployed to scour the grounds whenever there was a suspected escape or an inmate missing roll call. I don't know why the guard or the capo who brought me to be lashed did not follow me. Maybe they knew I was too sick to run away and assumed I had crawled off to die. If there had been a search, it was half-hearted. I don't think anyone walked to the back of these barracks, and no one searched the pit. If I had been found, I would have been shot for failing to report or for being too sick to work. I didn't care. I only knew that I had to stay in that pit, and that's what I did.

I'm not sure how long I stayed there. I remember trying to crawl out and then the burning began again, so I slipped back in. Later, when I wasn't lying in the muck, I was curled beside it, praying for some way out of my hell.

I'm certain I would have bled to death without the black, slimy balm. When my desire to eat grew stronger than my desire to stay in that pit, I limped back to the barracks. Covered in mud, I crawled face first into my berth. Somehow, I had managed to survive twenty-five lashes.

I never did learn who had turned me in, or why. *Were they bribed? Was he a spy?* I suspect it was none of those. It was simply a fellow inmate, probably a Jew, angry that he had gotten wet during the night. I don't know why he reported me, but in the end it didn't matter. I had become accustomed to betrayal. [51]

The Missing Half

*The only way Mother could tell us apart was
by the mole on my ear.*
~Joe Rubinstein

Our capo yelled at me, ordering me to run—our morning calisthenics. I forced my legs to move. Despite the early hour, it was warm. It was the kind of weather that would have made Chaim and me eager to finish our chores so we could go outside to play soccer.

For months I had tried to keep Chaim from my mind. Every time I allowed him in, I started to hurt all over—especially my chest. It tightened and clenched now as the thought of him came to me. I knew it was not from the burning in my lungs, having to run when I was still barely awake. The part that hurt was the part that realized I didn't feel whole without him. Like one-half of an apple—sliced, wounded, incomplete. I would never be whole, not really, without the one who looked just like me. *Where are you Chaim? Why can't I sense you?*

Chaim and I were close in a way that only those who have spent nine months together in a womb could ever know. We knew each other so well that we seldom needed words to convey what we were thinking and often finished each other's sentences. When I looked at him, it was like looking at a mirror image of me. As we grew older, few people could tell us apart. It didn't help that when we were young, we usually dressed alike. We did so, not because our mother made us, but rather, because we wanted to. Sometimes we fooled people, even when we didn't try.

My aunt "Nanny" lived with her two small children in the cramped apartment with Grandfather and Grandmother. Nanny was never able to tell us apart. I loved her and would see her a couple times a week when I appeared at their apartment, sweating and breathing hard from navigating their second-story stairs carrying two heavy buckets of water balanced by the yoke around my neck. Each visit, my aunt asked me who I was, and each time I would make her guess.

There were times when it wasn't so funny to be mistaken for Chaim. On at least three different occasions, a group of three or four boys ambushed and beat me as I walked down the street—believing that I was Chaim. I would cry out, "I'm not him!" It never stopped them from hitting me anyway.

When I get home tonight, I would think angrily, wiping the blood from my nose after a hard punch, *I will ask him what I always do, "What did you do now?"* I already knew the answer. *He'll tell me that he was just defending himself.* Once, it was over a game of soccer when the boys' tempers got the better of them. At least two other times the reason was more sinister—a slur against Chaim being Jewish. Whenever anyone made a slur at me, I walked away. Not Chaim. He would say he had to defend himself, and so an occasional fight would ensue. Later, the gang of boys would mistakenly come after me.

I had no way of knowing then that a few years later I would be beaten again for a crime I didn't commit, for a bit of spilled water. Like the teenage boys in Radom being conditioned to hate the Jews, the Nazis didn't care either that their assumption had been wrong.

A few months before the war I met a girl at one of the Radom dances and we went on a couple of dates. Soon, Chaim started to date her—only she thought Chaim was me! He had not bothered to tell her the truth. It wasn't until she started seeing Chaim on a regular basis that I learned what he had done. I wasn't mad at him after he told me how smitten he was with her. I didn't care. She wasn't the girl for me. I was happy for Chaim and told him, "If you like her, then it's okay to date her. But the next time you go on a date, you'd better make sure she knows that it's you!" Before the ghetto was closed, Chaim confided to me that he planned to marry her. I had been so happy for him and couldn't wait for the wedding.

Thinking of that wedding as I ran calisthenics—a wedding that never happened once the ghetto closed—made my chest hurt even worse.

Each day I scanned the new arrivals of inmates, searching for the one who looked just like me, praying I wouldn't find him there; praying I would. I so wanted to feel whole again. [52]

A Precious Gift of Warmth

I had never seen Mother happier.
~Joe Rubinstein

The oven had been the gift from our next door neighbor, Mr. Scholski,* when I was about eight. He was a bricklayer by trade, and brick by brick, he built us an oven in our dilapidated apartment. He refused to let mother pay him for it, saying his reward was bringing her a little joy. Although he did not accept our money, he savored the food that Mother baked for him in it.

The oven had been a gift more precious than gold and it showed in my mother's face, her eyes brimming with joyful tears, her shoulders shaking as she stood before the oven. It meant that she could bake breads, meats, casseroles, and pies, not on her stovetop, but in an oven. The oven seemed to encapsulate the warmth of my mother's love, filling the air with much more than the sweet aroma of great food. That oven helped her feel complete—a widowed mother who had little else to give to her kids.

If I concentrated hard enough, even through the most foul of smells from my bunk at night, there were the briefest of moments when I imagined I could still smell it—my mother's bread baking in that oven. Then, my sweet musings of home would quickly be poisoned by the wretched images of the new ovens at Auschwitz, ovens which had a very different purpose than baking bread; ovens that burned flesh. Instead of simply burying the dead in pits, the Nazis had begun incinerating them. In that terrible place of death, ovens no longer held the same precious meaning. The Nazis had taken that from me too. [53]

* The spelling of Mr. Scholski's name is unknown.

Shattered

He said, "Your family is gone and so is mine."
~Joe Rubinstein

October 1942

"They sent everyone to Treblinka." His voice was hushed and hurried. We knew we had little time before the gong would sound and we would have to leave.

He had arrived at Auschwitz two days earlier. I overheard him speaking Polish while he stood in line for food. He was from Radom—the first person who had answers to my questions about home.

"What does that mean? Where's my family now?"

He continued as if I hadn't spoken. "I was living in the smaller ghetto in Radom, the one they call Glinice, working at the nearby ammunition factory. Two months ago, my supervisor stopped a small group of us leaving and ordered us to stay at work. I didn't understand it until the next morning when we went back to the ghetto." He looked at me quickly and then averted his eyes. "There was no one left," the man turned pale as he spoke, "except those that had been shot. They were just there … on the ground … in the street … dozens of them … women … and children, too!" His breathing was forced. "My wife and my three children were with me in the ghetto … and they were simply gone. I found a police officer who told me that everyone in that ghetto had been loaded on trains. Those who refused to leave were shot. They sent me to the big ghetto … and two weeks later … it happened again. They wouldn't let me leave from work … for three days. When

I finally went back, it was empty. The big ghetto, thousands and thousands of people ... they were just gone."

Before I had a chance to understand what he was saying, he continued. "Many of the front doors to the homes were wide open, blocks and blocks of them, swinging on their hinges, like they were waiting to greet the people back. My supervisor at the plant told me everyone in both ghettos ... everyone ... was put on trains and taken to Treblinka."

"Where's Treblinka?" I needed to know. I had to find a way to get there.

The stranger pursed his lips. "Treblinka is not a concentration camp."

"What is it then?" I hated the panicked sound of my voice.

"People go there ... for one thing ... only one thing ... to be killed."

The man's words were coming in gasps; his eyes looked straight at me. "If your family was in Radom, your family is dead. So is mine. They're all gone."

Even before he said the words, I had known. Maybe it was my bond with Chaim; maybe it was the sense that something in the world had changed—a shift, a movement, of something that wasn't as it should be. I don't know exactly when I knew, but I had known. Deep in my heart, I had known it for a while. It wasn't until now that I allowed myself to believe it.

I have no idea how I remained standing with no air left in me. I wanted to ask if he had seen Anszel and Chaim. Was it possible that like him, they too weren't there at the time of the raid? *Maybe he is wrong! Maybe he is wrong about all of them! Maybe at some point he saw my mother and Abram and Laja. Was Mother searching for me? Did they have enough to eat?* I had so many questions I was ready to ask, but no sound left my lips. The questions didn't matter. *How can anything matter without my family?*

A gong sounded. The man put his hands on my shoulders, then wrapped his arms around me. I felt nothing. He pulled away, turned to leave, then looked back over his shoulder at me. I knew he wanted to say something, but he too had no words. *How was that shell of me still breathing, when everything inside was gone?*

I never slept that night. Deep into the night I allowed myself no thoughts of my mother and siblings; instead, over and over I whispered through clenched teeth, "I'm never going to forgive them for what they've done to my family. Never."

Saying it was the only thing that kept me from running to touch the wire. [54]

Night

Nights were always the worst.
~Joe Rubinstein

Nights were always the worst. The reality of what had been, of what I had been forced to do, of what I would be forced to do the next day, had time to work on my soul. Nights were when I knew that beyond the cold and hunger there was something worse, the knotted something that had formed deep within me, crying out that this was not the way life was supposed to be.

Often, it was a loud snort of someone sleeping near me that startled me awake. It was always pitch black, and I had trouble remembering where I was. It was usually my aching shoulder against the unyielding boards that brought me back to the nightmare that was my life.

At night, I felt my lungs expand as I inhaled. I had to think about what I had seen, and breathed, and consumed, and I wondered if everything about this place had burrowed itself so deeply inside me that it had become like the cancer that killed my father—a cancer that had eaten away everything that was good.

How could I sleep when my arms ached from the weight of dead bodies I had just carried, when my stomach cried out for food, when my body was ravaged with illness? How could I sleep when my mind was so full of outrage and so many questions for God? How could I sleep when everyone I loved was gone?

It came to me in the dark one night on a crowded berth. The one thing they had no control over, the counter to their hatred and my fear was prayer. It was my last solace. With the sound of a hundred men crammed into the small space surrounding me, their snores, moans, and cries became the mantra of my prayers—prayers that begged and pleaded with God. Pleading to find a reason to live. 55

An Experienced Prisoner

I was an experienced prisoner. I knew how to live,
and I knew how to die. I told the man,
"Tell them what you are."
~Joe Rubinstein

Walking back to the barrack, I saw an SS officer standing over an older prisoner who was cowering on the ground. The guard was yelling, "What are you?"

The prisoner looked bewildered and replied, "German."

The SS officer raised a long club and struck the man across the back. He then asked the same question. Again the man replied, "German."

I knew what the guard wanted. I fought the urge to shout it at the man, "Why won't you say it? It's what you are! It's who we all are!" Instead, I said nothing. After two years here, I had become an experienced prisoner. I knew how to live, and I knew how to die.

My fist clenched as I watched until the man being beaten finally answered in a voice so quiet I could barely hear him, "Jew. I'm a Jew." The guard lowered his club and walked away.

I went to him and helped him to his feet. I was angry—angry at the guard, angry at the inmate, angry at this place, angry at the world. I told the man as he steadied himself and then began walking away, "Next time, tell them who you are." [56]

For the Sport of It

They just killed them, all those kids, for the fun of it.
Of all the things I saw, that was the worst.
~Joe Rubinstein

It haunted my dreams and my waking hours alike. I wanted to close my eyes and not see their faces, but I couldn't. It was one of the things that nothing could erase. I replayed it over and over in my mind, wondering if there was something I could have done to stop it, to stop them. It was different with the bodies in the pit, for they were already dead, but these children—these were children I had to watch cross over from life to death.

The first time I saw it happen, I had just finished running calisthenics. It was their laughter that caught my attention; laughter was something I almost never heard here. A group of SS officers were standing in front of a line of about twenty young children. All of the children looked no older than ten. Several were mere toddlers. About half were girls. There was no sign of their parents. Behind the children was a large inmate holding a club.

The SS were pointing and motioning to the man with the club, saying, "Yes, yes, that one first." One of the older boys who had a full head of black curly hair looked at the man holding the club. I could see what he was thinking: they had been brought outside to play a game. I knew this was no game. I didn't like the way the SS were laughing. It was unnatural laughter, devoid of any joy. The man with the club pointed to the boy and then motioned for the boy to look toward the SS. Then, without warning, he swung the club, whacking the child across the back of his head. The boy fell face first in the dirt, his arms dangling backwards at his sides. The boy was dead. The group of soldiers laughed harder. The man hauled back and hit the next child, a little blond-haired girl of about three. And then he hit the next. The club dripped with the blood.

I stood there with tears of hot rage streaming down my face—my mouth open, screaming with no sound coming forth. I could do nothing to save them, and I couldn't bear the shame of such helplessness. I couldn't bear to hear the cries of the other children as they realized what was happening, the flashes of understanding and fear emanating from them. A boy of about eight tried to run, with urine streaming down his legs. An SS man reached out with his club and struck him over the top of his head. Other youngsters started screaming in disbelief. Several of the toddlers looked around, crying out for their mothers. One girl dropped to the ground sucking her thumb. I could still hear her whimpers.

They were babies really, every one of them young, innocent, beautiful children who bore no blame—children who had trusted those who were now killing them—children whose young minds could not comprehend what was happening.

Remembering their young faces left me gasping for breath— young faces so unaware of the existence of hatred, unaware that anyone would want to harm them.

After all I had seen, all of it terrible, it was the killing of the children that created a hollow pit deep inside me that never left—a dark pit holding everything in hell's despicable arsenal.

Of all the evils at Auschwitz, nothing was worse than the evil killing of children for the sport of it. Such evil has no explanation. Such evil is ultimate darkness. [57]

Stars of Hope

*What happened to the German people who were
so brilliant that they would kill people just because
of their religion?*
~Joe Rubinstein

It was a rare night of clarity in that place of death—a place where ovens burned the bodies of the dead. Seldom ceasing, smoke choked out everything, even the night skies.

In the darkness that night, the chimney smoke had stopped. I knew it would begin again soon. In that momentary reprieve, I was shocked by the clarity of the sky, of the stars and constellations long obscured; shocked that they looked the same there as they did in Radom. They were just as bright, just as brilliant, just as magnificent. Their patterns had not altered. But the eyes looking at them were different. The boy had changed. His eyes had seen things that never should have been seen.

How can they look no different when everything under them has shifted? Hasn't the universe changed, too? Is there anyone anywhere looking at these same stars who knows or cares about what is happening to us? Are we alone? Am I alone?

It bothered me somehow, the unaffected night sky—a reminder perhaps of everything that the boy in Radom had lost. Radom, where life was so full, so rich, so innocent. The unaffected night sky was a haunting reminder that the Radom of my old life was just as far away from me as the stars.

That sky stirred something in me, something I once knew as hope. I hadn't thought of that word in a long time. I wasn't sure it still existed. I prayed it was hope that I felt—hope that I'd found something—one thing that even the Nazis hadn't been able to change, one thing in God's creation that still reigned.

I wished I knew how to climb my way to them, to grab hold of the stars, of anything that was as I knew it before—before the war, before the hell, before I lost everyone I loved. [58]

One Stroke for Life

*He said I didn't look Jewish. He wasn't giving me
the Jewish mark.*
~Joe Rubinstein

I held out my right arm and looked at the stranger holding the tattoo needle. We had been brought into a large, unfamiliar barracks to be tattooed again. Most inmates ahead of me in line were walking away with a new, small triangle tattooed on their arms just below their numbers—a triangle signifying they were a Jew. I had never heard of inmates being brought back in for additional tattoos. I had seen many of the more recent arrivals with the symbol, but originally my arm had just been tattooed with the number. When it was my turn, the capo doing the tattooing squinted up at me over the top of his narrow, wire-rimmed glasses, and said, "34207. You don't look Jewish to me. I'm not giving you that mark. I'm giving you something else." He then proceeded to make an upside-down V under my tattooed number and told me that I was now a political prisoner and that I should exchange my shirt for one displaying a political triangle badge.

I had no idea why or how he made that decision. My sense was that it was done with barely a thought. As the inmates filed out of the barracks, mine was the only incomplete triangle I saw. I knew that it was uncommon to have the political prisoner status and I had no idea how this would affect me. I only knew that in the pecking order of Auschwitz, none was lower than those with the simple symbol of the Jew. I had no way of knowing that one stroke—one simple line of ink would mean the difference in whether I lived or died. [59]

Beyond the Gates

I can't say all Germans are bad … they aren't.
~Joe Rubinstein

Vernichtung durch Arbeit, "destruction through work," was the Nazi goal, and we all knew it. Every day we marched under the entrance sign that proclaimed in bold letters: **ARBEIT MACHT FREI**, "Work makes you free." From the first time I saw the mocking sign, I hated it. We all did. Work did not make you free here. Work killed you. Every time I passed under it, I vowed to find a way to hold them to it—to find a way to let work make me free.

It was a crack, a small opening. They were taking strong, fit teenagers and men of small stature to work in a nearby coal mine. I knew what working the mine would mean. I had seen the returning workers, filthy and exhausted. Every night some of the bunks that had been occupied by the mining crews remained empty. I didn't care. For me, working the coal mine would mean leaving Auschwitz for hours every day, leaving the piles of dead bodies outside the barracks each morning, leaving the air, thick with human ashes. I was dying there, both in body and spirit. Every day I lost more control of both. If I didn't find a way out soon I would die, and the legacy of my entire family with it. I wanted to live. I knew my mother and my siblings would want that for me.

For once I was grateful I had not inherited my father's height, or I would not have been selected to work the mine. The days were long, starting about four in the morning, with our labor detail leaving the camp in the dark, marching in our wooden shoes for nearly two hours to reach the coal mine. Once there, I was given a helmet and a light that I would keep with me for the rest of the time. My helmet was number fifty-eight, and its light was my guide in the darkness. Some of the tunnels were so short and narrow there was often no room to stand, so I would spend my days digging coal and loading it into small railcars while on my knees. Some of the days I helped with the pipe ventilation lines, which was a strain on my neck and arms but a relief from the constant shoveling of coal. Many of the workers in the mine were civilian coal miners, hired and paid for the work they did. We were not supposed to interact with the civilian coal miners, but working in such close proximity, it was often not enforced. Some of the civilians kept their distance from us, while others were more curious.

The SS would accompany us to the mine and then turn us over to the German civilian supervisors, whom we called "Meisters," to oversee our work. Some of the supervisors were nearly as cruel as the SS, hitting inmates over the head with shovels if they didn't work fast enough, spitting in their faces or shooting them outright. Others were exceedingly kind. One of our Meisters was a German named Apt. He would bring food into the tunnels and hand it out. Once, after I thanked him for giving me a sandwich, he said to me, "You're a young kid. I don't want you to die here." Those few words of kindness and concern from a German supervisor nearly brought me to tears. They were some of the only tender words spoken to me by anyone since the war had begun, words I knew I would remember for the rest of my life.

After several days of walking to the coal mine and back in the wooden clogs, I could not take it anymore. I asked our capo if I could exchange them. I knew I was risking getting shot by even asking, but suspected that with my new political prisoner designation, there was a chance to finally be rid of the dreadful clogs. It was a chance I was willing to take it. To my great relief, I was given a pair of well-fitting leather shoes.

The work was strenuous, tedious, cold, and loud. One afternoon I was digging coal in an especially difficult seam, and the next thing

I knew I was thrown to the ground, covered in dust. There was blood coming from my left ear, and I could not hear anything. There had been an accidental explosion of dynamite. As I coughed out dust, I looked around, certain the mine had collapsed. It hadn't, but everyone around me had also been thrown to the ground.

Some of the other inmates were terrified of the dark tunnels. Many of the young teenagers would tremble and weep as we descended in the elevator cage deep into the dark mine shaft. I wasn't afraid. After working in the pits with the dead bodies, nothing seemed scary. The coal mine was a relief. At the end of each long day we marched back to Auschwitz, taking turns carrying the bodies of those whose deaths were another victory for the Nazis in their quest to kill us through work. Some had been shot for not working fast enough; some had been beaten, but most died from illness and exhaustion.

One morning, as we prepared to begin the long trek to the mine, we were instead loaded into a large truck and driven to the mine. At day's end we were relocated to the barracks near the mining camp. I had no idea when I drove through the metal gates earlier that morning that I had left Auschwitz for the last time.

Because of my new status as a political prisoner, I was assigned to supervise our small barracks. I was allowed to take a warm shower and had a separate area for sleeping. There were showers at Auschwitz; we took them the first day I arrived. After that, our only means of bathing was when we were ordered to jump into one of the dirty ponds on the complex grounds. Dirty ponds were of little help.

After showering at the coal camp, I was given a set of clean clothes. That night my rations of food were enough that for the first time since coming to Auschwitz, I didn't finish eating, still feeling nearly as starved as when I started. When I saw where I would be sleeping, I was overcome with emotion. Instead of being crammed on a wooden bunk, I had my own cot with a real mattress.

As I closed my eyes that night, it was the first time the thought occurred to me that I might have a chance at surviving. I knew it was slim, for dozens of young men like me who were too exhausted to work were being loaded into trucks each day and taken away. I knew they were being taken to the gas chambers. The work I was doing at the mine was very dangerous. The guards could shoot me at any time, but it was the first time I had any inkling of hope. Because of my new status as a political prisoner and being allotted more food, I would have a better chance at surviving, and maybe, by some miracle, I could live long enough for the war to end.

I could not sleep that first night outside of Auschwitz. I kept thinking about my prayers, of crying out to God in the pit of mud after being beaten. It occurred to me that maybe my prayers had been answered by being taken from one pit of mud to another; only this pit was made of coal. I wasn't sure my prayers were actually being answered, but I promised myself that I would never again take such small things like clean clothes for granted. The next morning, I was given a pair of wool socks and leather boots. Heaven sometimes arrives in the smallest of packages. [60, 61, 62]

Crumbling Stone

I had to do what he said or I would die.
~Joe Rubinstein

Jawischowitz (Sub-Camp of Auschwitz)

Just when I had experienced a glimmer of hope, my world was shattered. I had seen it before, guards abusing the female prisoners and guards abusing the men. Usually it was done in private, where they thought no one would see—but in this place, few things went unseen. Many of the toughest of inmates who had somehow found the strength to overcome daily beatings, torture, and starvation were driven to touch the wire once they were sexually abused. For them, having to live with the images of the sexual abuse perpetrated against them was more than they could bear.

I had been one of the fortunate ones, to have escaped Auschwitz sexually unscathed, both from my captors and from other inmates. The same could not be said for many who had spent time in wards full of hundreds of men, each clinging desperately to life.

Between moving the bodies, watching children being beaten to death, learning the fate of my family, and facing unimaginable deprivations, I thought that when I left Auschwitz, nothing could be worse than what I had already endured. I was wrong. I would soon find that nothing was worse than losing your self-respect.

My abuser was the most powerful inmate in the coal mining camp—the record-keeper—a man even the SS guards feared. Once this man wanted something, there was no saying "no." No one could. And for a time, what he wanted was me. It did not matter that I had been assigned supervisor of one of the barracks. I was still an inmate of little significance. I had a choice—comply or die. There was no other.

After the first night, I stood in the shower—alone and sobbing. As the water pooled at my feet and washed down the drain, I envisioned my body washing away with it—anything, if it would make me clean and whole. *Will I ever be either again?*

Death would have been easier than the foundation of my life being torn away, my innocence and dignity shredded. Death would have been easier than spending the rest of my life trying to forget and forgive myself. Every night, I thought about killing myself instead of having to face the brute again. The only thing that kept me from taking my life was the realization that my death would have been the final victory of evil, taking every last morsel of my being and that of my family. Someone had to live through this. Someone had to beat them.

Every day I awoke with the same decision—a decision to let the memory of it destroy me or to fight through it and allow myself peace and joy. Every day, I chose life. [63, 64, 65]

A Good Shine

He told me it was heartbreaking, even for them.
~Joe Rubinstein

He liked the way I shined his boots. The German officer lived just outside the coal mining camp, and two days a week, I was given a reprieve from working the mine to work for him. As an inmate, being singled out is rarely a good thing. I had worked hard at making sure I never stood out. Never making mean faces, never talking too loud, and keeping mostly to myself. After first coming to the coal camp, a group of us were ordered to shine the boots of the German officers as they stood on the street. We were each given a rag and polish. I was accustomed to shining the boots in Mr. Nagel's shop and knew how to make them gleam. When I was finished, the short black-haired officer with a square jaw kept looking at the shine of his boots. I saw his gaze pause at the red triangle on my shirt chest. I could see that he was taking note of my political prisoner status. He requested that I come back the next day and clean not only his boots but his quarters as well.

All night I worried if he had heard about what the record-keeper had done to me. *Please, God! Not this man too!*

The following morning, I looked uneasily at the guards positioned at the gate. I had been given permission to pass, but I was afraid. The guards were famous for killing people at their whim. I took a deep breath and prayed that they would not shoot me. I was able to leave without incident.

To my great relief, it quickly became apparent that I was there only to work. Several times a week, for several months, I left the camp to clean his private quarters. I had the sense from the start that he had a gentle nature. You can tell that about people. He never raised his voice or threatened me in any manner. Instead, he politely directed me to do different chores. He thanked me often and told me repeatedly that his shoes and boots had never looked better.

I learned at Auschwitz that I had a quick mind for learning other languages. From the start, I realized that the difference between living and dying was the ability to follow orders. Out of necessity, I had learned to understand German, although I was still poor at speaking it.

While I worked, the officer generally remained at his desk, reading and writing as I cleaned. One morning, just as I had finished mopping his floors, he said to me, "You're a nice kid. You don't belong here." Then an odd expression touched his face, as if he had been pondering something and had reached a decision. "You don't look like a Jew to me, so I'm not going to treat you like one."

I didn't say anything, but after that, he began offering me extra food and he asked about my family. I told him a little about being a twin and my widowed mother raising five children on her own and left it at that.

Inmates were always required to remove their caps when greeting or passing an officer, so one afternoon, as was customary, I had just removed my hat to bid him farewell when he said to me, "You shouldn't be in this place."

I couldn't stop myself. I spoke before thinking. "I'm here," I cried angrily, "because your people put me here!" The officer's eyes narrowed. I held my breath, knowing he could easily shoot me for such a remark, but I was glad I'd said it.

His smile faded. "I don't like it … you know … what we're doing to you Jews … because of your religion. I can't believe Germans are doing this. It's not right."

I knew he meant it—for he, too, could be shot for uttering such words. No one could speak against the Führer and survive.

He looked me straight in the eyes and said, "Sometimes, it's heartbreaking. Even for us soldiers." [66]

A Chance at Freedom

He wanted to bring me clothes and help me escape.
~Joe Rubinstein

Brzeszcze Coal Mine near Auschwitz

I didn't even know his name, but he was willing to risk his life for me. He was a poor man, a worker in the mine, a short, stocky Polish man of about thirty-five, with sandy brown hair and thick eyebrows that melted together. He wore a thick chain with a small tarnished cross around his neck. He made the sign of the cross every time before taking the first bite of his lunch. He ignored the standing orders not to interact with the inmate coal miners, and several times, he had shared his sandwich with me, asking about my family and telling me about his as we ate. It was obvious the man was poor, and giving such precious food away must have been a great sacrifice. He had been a coal miner all his life, like his father before him. He told me that he was appalled by the condition of the inmate miners and could not believe what he was witnessing. He felt helpless to stop it.

I had been working in the mine about a month. We had just emerged from the mine elevator for the noon break. I had just removed my helmet. His wife had made me a tomato and cucumber sandwich, and as he handed it to me, he paused. "Tomorrow," he whispered, "I will bring you clothes and you can walk out with me. You can hide in my home."

I wasn't sure I had heard him correctly. "What?"

He nodded his head and whispered, "Tomorrow."

My first thought was of my shaved head. "I can't," I said touching it. "They will know."

"No, I will bring you another helmet, one like mine. They won't know."

I knew the man was sincere and I believed I could trust him. But I couldn't chance it. It was too risky for him and his family—and too great a risk for me.

I shook my head. "I … I can't."

"You must. I've seen it before. They come strong like you, and soon they are not and then poof," he put a pretend gun to his head, "they are gone."

"But your wife … your family?"

"They've already agreed. It's what we must do."

My eyes darted in each direction, making sure no one could hear us. How could I explain to him that I could not be responsible for his family being killed? How could I make him understand that while I knew I could trust him, eventually others would know, others who would betray us?

"In Radom," I whispered, "when the Nazis came, they went to our neighbors and friends, people we had known all our lives, and asked them to name all the Jewish families. They had no choice … I knew this. If they didn't comply, there would have been retribution against them, but I can still see my mother's face when she learned that our friends were betraying us. How can I trust the strangers here, when I could not trust those whom I had known all my life? No, I can't do it. It's in God's hands. I will take my chances in the camp."

The man's expression was grim, "If you change your mind, come to me. My offer stands."

I shook my head. "I can't, but thank you, and please," I whispered, "please, pray for me … for all of us."

Before the war, I never considered that working in a coal mine could be a way to the light, but when what surrounds you is only darkness, even a small light in a tunnel shines bright. That man, with his promise of freedom and through his witness of God's love, became a warm light within me, a beacon of hope to follow. [67]

Pierre

Inmates helped each other.
~Joe Rubinstein

"You'll be shot if they catch you." Honesty was one of the things I liked most about Pierre. He had just returned to the barracks carrying a towel freshly doused with cold water. Folding it carefully, he laid it across my forehead. I'd had a pounding headache ever since I woke up that morning, and working in the mine all day had made it worse. It was dark outside, and we were given a couple of hours with nothing to do before being required to go to sleep. Pierre was my friend at a time when I really needed one. My only friend since coming to Auschwitz. Two years older than I, Pierre had a dark complexion and dark eyes to match. He was French and a Jew. He worked in the mine with me and lived in the same barrack. We had become fast friends, speaking in Yiddish. Pierre had trouble pronouncing my name, so he called me Upe.

Pierre looked around uneasily, afraid someone might have heard our conversation. He was always worried that I talked too freely. He was convinced we would be overheard by spies waiting to turn us in for any offense. I had just told him that the night before I had stolen some potatoes from the kitchen storeroom and offered one to him now. Even though I was in a position of helping to oversee these barracks, Pierre was right; if I was caught, I would be shot.

The night before, as I stood in the dark waiting to make my move to the storeroom, I had listened to the sound of the chorus of men snoring, and I kept thinking of the nights when I waited to sneak out of the ghetto to get food. Like then, my heart was pounding so hard I could feel it. Eventually, I pretended to go to the bathroom, and instead, retrieved a few of the oldest potatoes, the ones least likely to be missed. I ate a couple of them and then saved a few to give to the men who looked in most need of them within our barracks.

I told Pierre I took them because I was hungry, and that was true. Even more than that, I took them because I wanted to know that there was still a part of my life where I had some control.

I wanted my headache to go away so I could play cards with Pierre. He had made a deck out of discarded pieces of cardboard that he had collected over several weeks. He wrote in the numbers and suits with small pieces of charcoal. We had to rewrite them often, trying to compensate for the smudges. It was not the only game Pierre had devised. His favorite game was checkers. He made the board from cardboard and charcoal, and gathered pebbles for the markers. The first time I played it with Pierre I realized that I was laughing. I stopped in wonderment. I had no idea when the last time was that I had heard that sound coming from me. I knew it was before I was taken. I had forgotten how good it felt.

Then I thought about my family.

Pierre saw the change and asked me what I was thinking. "How can I enjoy myself when they are dead?"

"Upe," he said, reminding me suddenly of Anszel, "you owe it to your family's memory to keep your laughter and your happiness. God does not want you living in sorrow, and neither would they."

I knew it was true, but believing it in my heart was another matter. Pierre had spent less than a day at Auschwitz before being sent directly to the coal mine camp. He asked me if I'd ever played games there. I nearly choked. "Auschwitz is not a camp where you play games. Auschwitz is a destroyer camp."

A week after my headache, Pierre and I stood waiting for the elevator car to drop us into the mine shaft, when he whispered that he was certain he had seen Allied planes flying over the camp the day before. He said that he was saying to himself, "Drop the bombs!" We all knew that at some point these camps would be bombed by the Allies; it had to be only a matter of time. Although it meant that we would likely be killed, there wasn't an inmate who wouldn't welcome it. If a bomb could stop the next train from coming to Auschwitz, it was worth it. What none of us could understand was why, as massive a place as the Auschwitz complex was, it hadn't yet been bombed. They had to have known about this coal mine being used to help the Nazis. *Why hasn't it been bombed, or even the rail line? Aren't those usually one of the first targets in a war? Surely by now somebody on the outside knows what is happening here!* The only explanation I could think of was that maybe the Allies mistook the coal camp for prisoner of war camps, and they didn't want to kill their own men.

The mine was closed on Sundays, so we slept in an extra hour. I was sipping my coffee in the food barracks when Pierre sat down across the table from me. His eyes grew wide. "Merde!" he swore in French, and then in Yiddish he said, "You're yellow!"

I looked down at the skin of my arms and hands and realized he was right. Pierre then went on to describe my yellow face and dark-circled eyes. An SS officer walking past our table took one look at me and told me I was to report to the Artzmeldung, the camp hospital. My heart sank; I knew what getting sick here meant. Pierre knew it, too. His stricken expression said it all. He shrugged his shoulders and smiled weakly at me. I did the same. As I walked away from my good friend, I had the same sinking feeling I'd had when I left my family for the last time. [68]

Sickness and Salvation

The Gestapo watched us and told the doctor,
"You're not going to help that guy." They would
only let us treat the younger ones.
~Joe Rubinstein

His name was Dr. Stephen Bozchski, a Catholic surgeon from Poland, and he saved my life. The man was short, blond, and handsome with an easy smile. He put the stethoscope to my chest and listened to my lungs. I could see the lines in his face were deeper than I first imagined, and he looked tired, too tired for his forty-something years.

I explained that I didn't feel sick. After listening to my history since being taken, he explained his theory: that because my body was so accustomed to being overworked and deprived of adequate food and sleep for so long, when I was quite ill, I was not aware of it. He gave me some foul-smelling medicine to sip and then walked out of the room. He left, telling me that I was to spend the night there.

It was a long night in the infirmary, with sounds of carts being rolled around and feet shuffling up and down the hallways. Sometimes I could hear moaning and coughing coming from another room. I kept wondering if in the morning I was going to be told that I had been "selected" to go back to Auschwitz. That would mean being sent to the gas chambers. I kept telling myself that I felt well enough to work. I didn't realize how poorly I felt until the next morning when I tried to push myself off the hospital cot. My head was throbbing and my chest hurt.

When I saw the curtain open to my room, my heart nearly stopped. I imagined the Gestapo waiting for me. Instead, it was Dr.

Bozchski. He was carrying a long bulb syringe and explained that he was going to suction fluid from my lungs. It was a terrible ordeal that left me gagging, sweating, and inwardly begging him to stop. When he was finally finished, he sighed deeply and said, "I'm from Poland. You're from Poland and you're a nice kid. If you go back to the mines, you will die either from this infection in your lungs or they'll declare you unfit for work. Either way, you're dead. I talked to them about you. I need an assistant. I explained that you're a political prisoner and I am short-staffed. They've agreed to my request."

I looked at him blankly, having no idea what he was talking about.

"You're to stay here at the hospital and be my assistant. You have my word you're never going back in the mine. I'm going to make sure of it."

My learning curve had to be fast. The doctor was true to his word in taking me under his wing and teaching me what I needed to know to help him. It took a few weeks, but I gradually regained my strength and health. Over time it became clear I was not the only one the doctor had saved. While it was a hospital designated to treat primarily the coal miners, we were frequently told by the SS whom the doctor could or could not treat. If the SS thought they were too old, or too ill, they would be "selected" and taken out to the truck. One day the doctor was ordered not to bother with a man who had just come in with a bad gash to his leg. I followed the doctor into the room. The doctor waited until the guard left. Then he quickly cleaned the area, opened the skin as far as he could, dusted a sulfa drug into his wound, and stitched it closed. In all, it took less than a couple minutes. The doctor told the man to leave or he would be sent to Birkenau to be killed.

Several months after working with the doctor, he told me that he thought the final permission for me to stay might have been granted by someone with great authority at the mining camp. I knew only two possibilities: the man who had abused me and the German military officer who liked the way I polished his boots. I never found out who had made the decision, and whether or not my political designation had any influence. Whoever was responsible for the decision, it saved my life. To my greatest relief, I never saw either one of them again.

I was grateful that most of the patients we treated had minor coal mining injuries. I spent most of my time cleaning bits of embedded coal from their knees. The hospital was small but tidy, efficient, and busy. At night, I slept unattended on a cot in a storeroom no larger than a closet. I was allowed to eat meals with the staff and was quickly gaining back some of the weight I had lost since being taken. The doctor examined my left ear and determined what I had feared— my hearing was lost for good in that ear. It was yet another piece of me the Nazis had taken. [69]

On the Move

They took me again.
~Joe Rubinstein

They came for me again, just as they had before, like monsters in the night. I awoke to two SS soldiers standing over my hospital cot, ordering me to leave. I had heard reports from the doctor that the war was not going well for Germany. I showed them my badge and my tattoo and explained that I was a political prisoner. They told me I was still a Jew.

I saw my clothes on the stool and my shoes on the floor. Without asking, I grabbed them and slipped on my pants and shoes before walking out into the hallway. I pulled my shirt and jacket over my night undershirt and followed the men with the guns. I was determined to take what I could.

It was summer, but the air was still cool. I felt the air leave my lungs and my head grew lightheaded and dizzy as I ran through the possibilities of where I was being taken. I could not go back to Auschwitz! *Oh God, please! Anywhere but that place!*

There were only a handful of men in the truck with me as we rolled away from the hospital. My thoughts were dark as I was forced to leave without being able to thank Dr. Bozchski or say goodbye. As I looked toward the barracks, I wondered about Pierre and where he was. I hadn't seen him since my illness several months earlier. Both men were the closest thing I had to family. I felt my throat swell with sorrow. Just like the time I was forced from my home in Radom, once again I was devastated at being taken without being able to say goodbye. [70]

Laja's Tears

It's how I remember her still.

~Joe Rubinstein

The hum of the truck's tires was rhythmic, reminding me of another time when the sound of railcars rang in my head. As I left toward another unknown, I couldn't stop thinking about all those people I had seen that day standing in line just after they got off the train—the pregnant woman, the man on crutches, the boy who had wet his pants, the little girl with the haunting brown eyes. I knew in my heart that she and everyone else in that line that day never left Auschwitz. I forced back the sick emptiness and sorrow threatening to consume me. The teary eyes of that little girl, like the eyes of so many of the children I watched being murdered, embedded their way deep into my soul, reminding me of another's tears …

I never knew why she cried.

I was a teenage boy, becoming a man, and I was irritated by her tears.

When I thought of my younger sister, it was always her tears I recalled. To me, she was "the cry baby." Being the only girl, maybe it was as simple as being spoiled, using her tears to get her way.

I wondered sometimes if she even knew why she cried.

Maybe she cried over the loss of a father she would never know. Mother had told us that Tatte had always wanted a daughter, and when he finally got his wish, he grew ill and died. He had no chance to get to know the little girl he had longed for. Maybe Laja's tears were really our father's coming through her.

If Laja had lived, perhaps she would have joked with me over her childhood antics of using tears to get what she wanted. I would have liked that.

Sometimes I envisioned what she would have been like, the young woman she would never become. I think she would have grown to be very pretty, like Mother.

Maybe Laja's tears were the tears of all of us: our family, the Jews, the blighted countries of the Nazi's terror, the soldiers fighting them, and the plight of all that was to come. Did some part of her know?

I prayed that one day I will find Laja in Heaven. I yearned to see her, smiling. [71]

An Inattentive Teacher

He didn't teach, he slept.
~Joe Rubinstein

Buchenwald Concentration Camp, Weimar, Germany

I was covered in sweat and dirt. My one good ear rang from the deafening explosions of dynamite every few minutes.

After leaving the hospital, I had been taken to the Buchenwald Concentration Camp with a sign at the entrance proclaiming: *Jedem das Seine*, "To Each His Own." Every day our haggard crew of inmates was taken to a quarry to dig, carry, and break rock. We rotated using picks, shovels, and wheelbarrows. The work was exhausting. My back and shoulders ached constantly. The dust that the explosions created was worse than breathing the dust of coal. It was so thick it clogged my nostrils and left a thick paste in my mouth. We weren't given enough water while we worked, so the dust lingered in my throat. I was constantly trying to spit it out. It was a losing battle. The dust particles scratched my eyes and hurt every time I blinked.

The rations and the quality of food were better than at Auschwitz, although nothing compared to the food in the hospital. I was quickly growing thin again, but after a few weeks of moving rock, my muscles were strong. My skin, which had been badly sunburned after first arriving, had turned a dark brown. I fought a constant battle with my sore, sunburned lips. Sometimes I couldn't help but smile when I wondered what Anszel would say if he could have seen me moving rock until my hands bled. He never would have believed his lazy brother capable of such work.

Despite my own fatigue, another amusing memory came to me when I remembered another who was truly lazy. The man had been my teacher at the religious school I attended in Radom. He was a young rabbi in his twenties with a long beard, and he slept more than he taught. While his classroom of nearly fifty students was quietly reading, he slept. When we solved arithmetic equations at our desks, he slept. When we grew fed up and went outside to play, we would return nearly an hour later only to find him still asleep. I had no idea why he slept: a medical issue, a problem with alcohol, a night job? Was he simply bored? I had no idea.

Mother, along with several other parents, complained to the school administrator, but nothing happened. Over the years our teacher continued to sleep, and I quickly grew tired of school. When the man was finally replaced, I had lost all interest in a formal education. After that, I cared only about the knowledge that I could acquire on my own.

The only bright part of my school days was the fun Chaim and I had with those unable to tell us apart. Even our closest school friends couldn't figure it out. We could have wreaked havoc in our classroom and against our teacher who never knew who was who. There was no need, as the daily confusion was enough to keep us fully entertained. [72]

Far from Home

It was so fortified I wondered if Hitler was hiding there.
~Joe Rubinstein

The truck rolled to a stop. We had been riding for hours and I was stiff and sore.

I looked around. Nothing but barren fields surrounded us on the dirt road. I had no idea where we were or, for that matter, where I had spent the past several weeks. The guards left the truck and took turns relieving themselves. I needed to do the same.

Until the previous day, a large group of us had been housed at an underground bunker compound. The cement bunkers were massive and the perimeters of the complex were surrounded by heavy artillery. We slept on cots and ate in chilly bunkers. We were rarely permitted to leave the bunker. On the rare occasion when we did, we stood watching as massive missiles were being loaded onto trucks. I could not fathom the damage such bombs would deliver. There was nothing for us to do but stand idly by, stomping our feet to try to stay warm, and watch the machines do the heavy lifting. It was one of the few times I yearned for more work, for at least it would keep me moving. It was odd to have us there doing nothing. It made no sense, but I had long ago given up trying to understand the Nazis. I no longer cared. Then, one day and without explanation, we were boarded on a truck and taken away.

As I looked down the lonely lane waiting for the guards to return to the truck, I remembered something I had long since forgotten. I had not even been old enough to go to school. Father had ridden up our street on one of his draft horses. Mother and I ran out to greet him. It was rare to see him riding a horse instead of driving a wagon.

While I loved to watch Father's horses from a distance, up close I was terrified of them. Tatte knew about my fear and was determined to cure me of it. I was hiding behind Mother, trying to peer from around her skirt, and the next thing I knew, Tatte leaned toward me, grabbed my coat collar, and hoisted me in the air until I landed in front of him, my small legs sticking straight out left and right, straddling the huge steed. I was terrified, and it must have shown on my face. Mother turned a funny scarlet color that spread from her neck to her face. She pulled me off the horse so fast I hardly knew what had happened and scolded Father in a tone I had never heard her use before, telling him never to do that again.

I ran back into the house, relieved that Mother had rescued me. Much later, I realized it was the only time I ever rode a horse with my father. I have a lot of those sweet memories of being with my father, my mother, and my family that I wish I could relive again. Moments I want back.

I never had the benefit of seeing my father grow old. I wished he could have lived at least long enough to see me through my teenage years—to teach me how to become a man, to help me prepare, some-how, for all that was to come.

I wished I were standing outside on the busy street with my mother selling produce and watching as Tatte rode toward me, perched high up on his wagon behind his team of horses, reins threaded in his thick fingers. I imagined hearing the musical tapping of his horses' metal shoes ringing against the cobblestones. I wished it were so. I wished Tatte could ask if I'd like to hop aboard, to ride with him for a while. I wanted to answer him, "Yes, oh yes." [73, 74]

And Then It Was Over

Something in Heaven opened. I said, "I'm free!"
~Joe Rubinstein

*Theresienstadt/Terezín, Czechoslovakia May 6, 1945 *

"It's a trick," Herman spoke with certainty. "If we walk out, they're going to shoot us." My new friends, inmates Herman Finkelstein and Max Manheim, had good reason to feel that way. We had all seen it before, tricks like guards grabbing an inmate's cap, tossing it outside the gate, ordering the inmate to retrieve it, and then shooting him for attempting to escape when they did. Then, with the sound of the gunshot still echoing in the distance, the SS guards would laugh openly. Everyone knew it happened.

I looked overhead at the line of guard towers surrounding the Theresienstadt Concentration/Ghetto Camp where I had been imprisoned for the past few weeks. We had seen the SS leaving the camp the day before. I wasn't certain they were all gone. The towers appeared empty, but Herman was not convinced that the SS weren't hiding somewhere, ready to mow us down as soon as we took a step outside.

On the open gatepost a flyer telling us in German that we were free to leave flapped in the wind. The Red Cross had arrived a few days before; but now, there was a lot of confusion as to who was in charge. We could hear the sounds of fighting in the distance and were told Soviet troops were coming. A few Czech gendarmes wandered the grounds but showed no interest in preventing us from leaving. Many of the inmates were too sick to leave, and there was talk of the camp being quarantined. If that happened, I would be one of them. I was sicker than I had ever been in my life. My body was weak, exhausted, and ravaged by coughing fits so severe I wasn't sure how much longer I could live. Every day it felt like another part of me had shut down. I wondered if this was what it felt like to die a slow death, piece by piece. I had to get out of there. I grew queasy just thinking of being taken to the camp hospital, even if it were run by the Red Cross. I couldn't bear the thought of lying there among the dying. I had done that for far too long.

I wanted to walk out those gates, but I too found it impossible to believe that we were truly free to do so. We had been hearing talk for the last few days that the Soviets were very close. Another inmate said he heard the camp's SS commandant, Karl Rahm, had been given the order to kill all of us but that he had refused the order. I didn't know what to believe.

Unlike Herman, Max was adamant that it wasn't a trick, not after what we had seen the SS guards do earlier in the day. We had just walked out of our barracks, and I heard Max exclaim, "Look what they're doing!" Three of the SS guards were standing near the gate, pulling civilian clothes over their uniforms. I had no idea what they were up to, but Max whispered, "It's over. They're leaving so they won't be arrested." I couldn't believe it. It sounded too good to be true.

Hours later I looked at the open gate and said weakly, "I don't know if I'm strong enough to walk."

Max put his arm around my shoulder. "We'll help you." And so, just like that, we walked out. Just like that, it was over. Just like that, I was free. *But free to do what? Free to go where?*

For six years since the invasion of Poland, I had yearned to be free. I had prayed for it continuously and wished and hoped and longed for it. Yet, once it came, I was too weak and sick to really care. If I were stronger, I might have been gripped by fear and trepidation, afraid of that freedom—afraid it wasn't real and afraid that it was.

The three of us walked in silence, hearing only the sound of our breathing. No one else left with us. I had listened for gunshots. *Might they come from the tower or behind a tree, or perhaps from a nearby home? What will the civilians think when they see inmates in striped clothing walking free of the guards? Will they shoot at us?* We had no idea; we simply continued walking. Eventually we crossed a bridge, then into the center of the nearby town of Litoměřice. [75, 76]

* Estimated date.

From Ashes to Alive

He said, "Take whatever you want.
We owe you more than that."
~Joe Rubinstein

Litoměřice, Czechoslovakia*

"Take whatever you want. We owe you more than that." The shopkeeper spoke quickly, his eyes shifting nervously about the store. He was a small man with thinning, brown hair and his gray suit was sharply pressed. The man's shock when we'd stumbled into his shop moments earlier had quickly transformed into fear. No matter what the shopkeeper knew of the concentration camps during the war, he was no longer able to ignore their existence, not with three of their inmates standing before him in the entrance of his shop. We were half-starved wearing our filthy, rank, striped clothes. It was obvious that neither the shopkeeper nor the three of us knew what to do. Staring each other down, like animals in the wild, we couldn't decide whether to fight or flee. The shopkeeper made the first move and offered for us to take anything in his store.

I had not wanted to go into the shop, but Max was determined, and he was mad. He said that we needed help and we were going to get it. He said the local citizens would be so afraid right now, that they would do anything to help us. I wasn't so sure they wouldn't try to kill us. By the shopkeeper's reaction, though, I had to admit that Max may have been right.

Did the owner tell us to take whatever we wanted because he was afraid of us frightening away his other customers? Or was he fearful that we might seek our revenge on him? Revenge for his compliance with what had been happening so near his home? Or was it out of his sense of remorse? I suspected it may have been a little of each. But whatever his motive, all I wanted to do was to get away from him and his pathetic look of sympathy. I was shocked when I caught my reflection in his full-length mirror. *It's no wonder he's afraid of us!* I was a filthy mess. I had the same expression I used to describe the starved, emaciated people at Auschwitz when I said that they were "down to their bones." It was how I looked. Even more surprising than how thin I was were the sad, penetrating eyes looking back at me. *What has happened to that happy, innocent young man who was taken from Radom?* I could see no trace of him staring back at me.

I found a suit that looked like it might fit. When I let my striped inmate pants and shirt drop to the floor, I felt like a snake shedding its skin. I left them in a heap but gave the pile a kick before exiting the dressing room in a loose-fitting brown suit. I found the smallest belt I could, pulled it to the narrowest notch and saw that it was still too loose.

The owner opened his register and offered each of us money. I didn't even want to look at him. I was suddenly very angry at him. Moments later as I heard the shop door close behind me, I clenched my jaw and pulled at my new hat, setting it low on my brow. All I wanted was to get out of that town and leave behind all the venom that had poisoned me since the day the Nazis marched their way into my life. I would not let them have any more of me. Their taking was over.

Max was right about the people. Everyone we met was afraid of us and offered to give us anything we wanted. Max secured us a room for free in a small hotel. I nearly cried when I looked at the bed with a mattress and clean sheets. After showering, I collapsed on its softness and was asleep before I had time to consider all of what had happened that day. I slept for nearly twelve hours. When I opened my eyes, my gaze traced the hotel's uneven ceiling. I kept listening for the sounds of the Nazi sirens screaming down the street, their guns at the ready, forcing me back. If they did, I would not go. They would have to kill me. I had nothing left to give. [77]

---

* We believe the clothing shop was in Litoměřice, but it may have been another village near the Theresienstadt Concentration/Ghetto Camp.

View of the railcar on display in the permanent exhibition of the United States Holocaust Memorial Museum.
Washington DC, June 19, 1991. Photo provided to the museum courtesy of Polskie Koleje Panstwow S.A. Caption and photo courtesy of The United States Holocaust Memorial Museum (Photo Archives).

Members of the Ordedienst (Jewish police) give assistance to prisoners boarding a deportation train in the Westerbork transit camp.
1945. Auschwitz, Poland. Photo provided to the museum courtesy of Mark Chrzanowski. Caption and photo courtesy of The United States Holocaust Memorial Museum (Photo Archives).

View of the main entrance to the Auschwitz camp:
"Arbeit Macht Frei" (Work makes one free).
Instytut Pamieci Narodowej. Friday, May 11, 1945 – Tuesday, May 15, 1945. Auschwitz, Poland. Caption and photo courtesy of The United States Holocaust Memorial Museum (Photo Archives).

A view of the Auschwitz concentration camp after liberation.
Friday, January 19, 1945. Auschwitz, Poland. Unknown Russian archive. Caption and photo courtesy of The United States Holocaust Memorial Museum (Photo Archives).

A view of the Auschwitz II camp showing the barracks of the camp.
Monday, January 29, 1945. Auschwitz, [Upper Silesia] Poland. Photo provided to the museum courtesy of National Archives and Records Administration, College Park. Caption and photo courtesy of The United States Holocaust Memorial Museum (Photo Archives).

View of Auschwitz-Birkenau under a blanket of snow immediately after the liberation.
Friday, January 19, 1945. Auschwitz, Poland. Unknown Russian archive. Caption and photo courtesy of The United States Holocaust Memorial Museum (Photo Archives).

Survivors lie in multi-tiered bunks in a barracks in the newly liberated Buchenwald concentration camp.

Wednesday, April 11, 1945. Buchenwald [Thuringia] Germany. Photo provided to the museum courtesy of Robert A. Schmuhl. Caption and photo courtesy of The United States Holocaust Memorial Museum (Photo Archives).

**Jews from Subcarpathian Rus await selection on the ramp
at Auschwitz-Birkenau.**

*May 1, 1944. Auschwitz, Poland. Photo provided to the museum courtesy of Yad Vashem
Panstwowe Muzeum Auschwitz-Birkenau w Oswiecimiu. Caption and photo courtesy
of The United States Holocaust Memorial Museum (Photo Archives).*

**Jews from Subcarpathian Rus await selection on the ramp
at Auschwitz-Birkenau**

*Monday, May 1, 1944. Yad Vashem. Caption and photo courtesy of The United States
Holocaust Memorial Museum (Photo Archives).*

Jewish women and children from Subcarpathian Rus await selection on the ramp at Auschwitz-Birkenau.

1944. Auschwitz, Poland. Yad Vashem. Panstwowe Muzeum Auschwitz-Birkenau w Oswiecimiu. Caption and photo courtesy of The United States Holocaust Memorial Museum (Photo Archives).

Jewish men from Subcarpathian Rus await selection on the ramp at Auschwitz-Birkenau.

May 1, 1944. Auschwitz, Poland. Yad Vashem. Caption and Photo courtesy of The United States Holocaust Memorial Museum (Photo Archives).

Jewish brothers from Subcarpathian Rus await selection on the ramp at Auschwitz-Birkenau. Pictured are Israel and Zelig Jacob, ages nine and eleven. They were gassed shortly after arrival.
Monday, May 1, 1944. Auschwitz, Poland. Yad Vashem. Caption and photo courtesy of The United States Holocaust Memorial Museum (Photo Archives).

Jewish women and children from Subcarpathian Rus who have been selected for death at Auschwitz-Birkenau, walk toward the gas chambers.
May 1, 1944. Auschwitz, Poland. Yad Vashem. Caption and photo courtesy of The United States Holocaust Memorial Museum (Photo Archives).

Jewish women and children from Subcarpathian Rus who have been selected for death at Auschwitz-Birkenau, wait to be taken to the gas chambers.
May 1, 1944. Auschwitz, Poland. Yad Vashem. Caption and Photo courtesy of The United States Holocaust Memorial Museum (Photo Archives).

Jews from Subcarpathian Rus who have been selected for death at Auschwitz-Birkenau, wait to be taken to the gas chambers
May 1, 1944. Auschwitz, Poland. Yad Vashem. Panstwowe Muzeum Auschwitz-Birkenau w Oswiecimiu. Caption and photo courtesy of The United States Holocaust Memorial Museum (Photo Archives).

Jewish women and children from Subcarpathian Rus who have been selected for death at Auschwitz-Birkenau, walk toward the gas chambers.
May 1, 1944. Auschwitz, Poland. Yad Vashem. Panstwowe Muzeum Auschwitz-Birkenau w Oswiecimiu. Caption and photo courtesy of The United States Holocaust Memorial Museum (Photo Archives).

Jewish women and children from Subcarpathian Rus who have been selected for death at Auschwitz-Birkenau, walk toward the gas chambers.
May 1, 1944. Auschwitz, Poland. Yad Vashem. Caption and photo courtesy of The United States Holocaust Memorial Museum (Photo Archives).

Jews from Subcarpathian Rus undergo selection at Auschwitz-Birkenau; in the background is a group of Jews headed towards the gas chambers and crematoria.

Monday 1, 1944. Auschwitz, Poland. Vad Vashem. Caption and photo courtesy of The United States Holocaust Memorial Museum (Photo Archives).

The entrance to the gas chamber in Auschwitz I, where Zyklon B was tested on Soviet prisoners of war. The building in the background is a hospital for SS members.

Instytut Pamieci Narodowej Auschwitz, Poland, date uncertain. Sunday, April 1, 1945. Photo provided to the museum courtesy Instytut Paieci Narodowej. Caption and photo courtesy of The United States Holocaust Memorial Museum (Photo Archives).

**German soldiers of the Waffen-SS and the Reich Labor Service look on
as a member of an Einsatzgruppe prepares to shoot a Ukrainian Jew
kneeling on the edge of a mass grave filled with corpses.**

*1941-1943. Vinnitsa, [Podolia; Vinnitsa] Ukraine. Photo provided to the museum courtesy
of Sharon Paquette. Caption and photo courtesy of The United States Holocaust Memorial
Museum (Photo Archives).*

Gravediggers unload bodies from a cart into a mass grave in the Warsaw ghetto cemetery.

September 19, 1941. Warsaw, Poland. Photo to the museum courtesy of Guenther Schwarberg. Caption and photo courtesy of The United States Holocaust Memorial Museum (Photo Archives).

Suitcases that belonged to people deported to the Auschwitz camp. This photograph was taken after Soviet forces liberated the camp.

Auschwitz, Poland, after January 1945. Photo provided to the museum courtesy of National Archives and Records Administration, College Park, Md. Caption and photo courtesy of The United States Holocaust Memorial Museum (Photo Archives).

**Shoes confiscated from Majdanek prisoners and quote in English
displayed on the third floor of the permanent exhibition.**
*Friday, November 3, 1995. Washington, DC. Caption and photo courtesy of
The United States Holocaust Memorial Museum (Photo Archives).*

German civilians view a wagon piled high with corpses in the newly liberated Buchenwald concentration camp.

April 1, 1945. Buchenwald, [Thuringia] Germany. Photo provided to the museum courtesy of Patricia A. Yingst. Caption and photo courtesy of The United States Holocaust Memorial Museum (Photo Archives).
Note: Photo has been cropped.

View of a wagon piled high with corpses outside the crematoria in the Buchenwald concentration camp.

April 1, 1945. Buchenwald, [Thuringia] Germany. United States Holocaust Memorial Museum, courtesy of Patricia A. Yingst. Caption and photo courtesy of The United States Holocaust Memorial Museum (Photo Archives).
Note: Photo has been cropped.

A pile of corpses in the newly liberated Dachau concentration camp.
Friday, May 04, 1945, Dachau, Germany.
Photo provided to the museum courtesy of Muzeum Niepodleglosci Dokumentationsarchiv
des Oesterreichischen Widerstandes United States Holocaust Memorial Museum Zydowski
Instytut Historyczny, courtesy of Jack Moses. Caption and photo courtesy of The United
States Memorial Holocaust Museum (Photo Archives).
Note: Photo has been cropped.

The corpses of prisoners laid out for mass burial in the Nordhausen
concentration camp.
Wednesday, April 11, 1945 – Sunday, April 15, 1945. Nordhausen, [Thuringia] Germany.
Caption and photo courtesy of The United States Holocaust Memorial Museum
(Photo Archives).

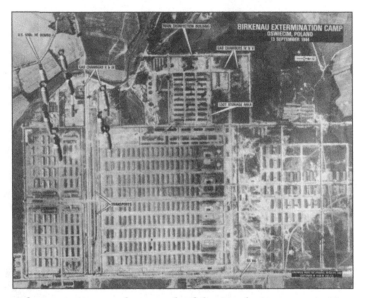

**An aerial reconnaissance photograph of the Auschwitz concentration camp
showing the Auschwitz II (Birkenau) camp with bombs descending
over crematoria II and III.**
Mission: 464 BG:4M97; Scale: 1/23,000; Focal Length: 12"; Altitude: 23,000'.
*September 13, 1944. Photo provided to the museum courtesy of National Archives and
Records Administration, College Park. Caption and photo courtesy of The United States
Holocaust Memorial Museum (Photo Archives). .*

**General Dwight Eisenhower and General Troy Middleton tour the newly
liberated Ohrdruf concentration camp. General Troy Middleton is
commanding general of the XVIII Corps, Third U.S. Army.
Thursday, April 12, 1945. Ohrdruf, Germany.**

*Photo provided to the museum courtesy of National Archives and Records Administration,
College Park. Caption and photo courtesy of The United States Holocaust Memorial
Museum (Photo Archives).*

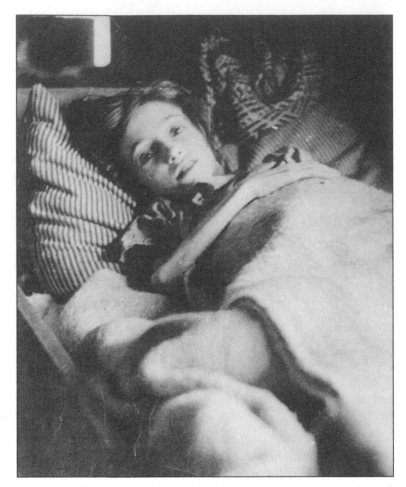

A twelve-year-old Jewish girl lies in bed after her liberation in Bergen-Belsen. Pictured is Helena Rabbie. She was born in Amsterdam on September 8, 1933, and died in Bergen-Belsen on April 24, 1945, eleven days after the liberation.

Photo provided to the museum courtesy of Maurice Raynor. Caption and photo courtesy of The United States Holocaust Memorial Museum (Photo Archives).

PART THREE

I waited patiently for the Lord.
He inclined to me and heard my cry.
He drew me up from the desolate pit,
out of the miry bog and
set my feet upon a rock, making my steps secure.

~Psalm 40:1-2

Which Way?

When I was set free, I felt I was born again.
~Joe Rubinstein

Litoměřice, Czechoslovakia

I was twenty-five years old. I had no family, no money, no home, no possessions, and I didn't know what to do. I was standing on the street corner in a country I knew nothing about. In the nearly six years since the Nazi had invaded Poland, I'd had no control over any aspects of my life. I had been told what to wear, what to eat, and where to be. Suddenly, I had nothing but choices. I felt paralyzed by them.

It's strange how the simplest of decisions can have the biggest impact on our lives. For me, the choice was Herman or Max. That one brief moment in time would determine the course of my entire life.

Both men argued that I should go with them. Herman was headed to Frankfurt, Germany, and Max was going back to his hometown of Duisburg-Hamborn, Germany. I thought about returning to Radom, but I couldn't bear the thought of standing before the places we had lived—the places where my family should be. I grew lightheaded and could not breathe every time I thought of it. There was nothing for me in Radom. Going there was not an option. I simply could not endure such heartache. Doing so would kill me. Of that I was certain. My only chance of survival now was finding a way to move forward. There was no going back. So complete was my dread and aversion of returning to Poland, that, at that moment, I was willing to consider the unimaginable: willingly moving to Germany. Facing the heart of the beast—a beast that had devoured so much of me and my life that there wasn't even enough fear left in me to be scared.

Herman, who was slightly younger than I, was brilliant, having been a mathematician before the war. He had no money either, but he had some big dreams of starting his own textile business like his father.

Max was a gregarious older man of about forty who had lived his entire life in Duisburg-Hamborn, Germany. He wanted to start a shoe factory there, arguing that war-weary people were going to be in the mood for quality shoes. He said he had extensive business experience and was convinced that with my shoe design knowledge and his background in business, we would make a good team.

A small seed of an idea had begun to take root in my thoughts. The idea of going somewhere far away from Europe, somewhere where there had never been trains leading from its cities to Nazi concentration camps. With no money to my name, I had no idea how I could make that happen. Some part of me felt I had something to prove—that I wasn't going to let fear stand in the way of my future. I had spent too much of my past living that way.

I needed to find work quickly, any work, and decided that Max was my best hope. Herman was very upset with my decision. While Max was talking to the bus driver about securing us a ride, Herman whispered to me, "Why are you going with that old man?"

I shrugged and told him that I liked him and that he had a good plan for me. Herman argued that I was making a mistake. He was still grumbling when we shook hands and promised to keep in touch. Then I followed Max onto a bus, headed for western Germany, near the city of Dusseldorf. As we drove away, I watched Herman standing at the curb, growing smaller and smaller. I wondered what would become of us, our lives having been ripped apart. *What would become of all who lived through such darkness? How could we ever heal?* [78]

Picking Up the Pieces

I just wanted back the good life God gave me.
~Joe Rubinstein

The United Nations Relief and Rehabilitation Administration (UNRRA) provided relief food and shelter for those of us who were just out of the camps, and they coordinated survivor registrations in an effort to help reunite families. There was no record of any of my family on any of the lists. At each turn I was given the same answer: my family was believed to have been killed at Treblinka.

I was assigned to a small apartment and given some money for food, and it was there that I slowly began to physically recover. I wanted to stay in contact with Max to begin the process of setting up the business. Every time I brought it up, he would say, "I'm working on it."

Eventually, it became clear that Max's interest in starting a shoe factory had lost out to his interest in his new girlfriend. I looked for work at every turn, with no luck. Duisburg-Hamborn, like so many other European cities, had been decimated by war, with many of the buildings having been damaged or destroyed by Allied bombing raids. Businesses that had thrived before the war were gone, and with large numbers of soldiers returning, there were more people than work. No one was eager to hire a Polish Jew with little formal education whose German was poor. Many German civilians feared getting too close to any of us Jews, believing we might come after them. Others wore heavy expressions of guilt and remorse. I began wearing long sleeves to cover my tattoo. It just seemed easier that way.

The documents from the concentration camp listed my name as Josef Rubinstein. I liked the name Josef, so that is what I began using.

There was a German man who lived in an apartment next to mine. He knew that I had been at Auschwitz, and he stopped me one day to ask what it had been like. I looked at him blankly. *What was it like? Where would he like me to begin?* It was obvious the man was sincere, but I found I simply had no words, so I just told him the truth. "It was hell."

The gentleman looked at the floor, then back at me. "I'm so ashamed of what we did." He paused, then added, "We aren't all killers."

I knew this, of course, and was glad to hear him tell me. Still, I could think of nothing to say. [79]

Beyond Words

Life was never supposed to be this way.
~Joe Rubinstein

I had a long time to think about the fate of my family in Treblinka, and over time to gather more details about the liquidation of the Radom ghettos. "Liquidated." The term was such a clean and tidy word; just the way the Nazis liked things—clean and tidy on the outside with the stench of death within. It's a word that made me sick.

Chaim, Anszel, Marsha, and their infant son were likely taken on August 5, 1942, from the smaller ghetto in Radom, along with nearly 6,000 others. They boarded a train bound for Treblinka, where they were gassed within two hours of arriving.

Abram, Laja, and my mother were likely taken from the larger ghetto between August 16 and 18, 1942, along with approximately 20,000 other men, women, and children. Both ghetto roundups were scenes worse than any hell imaginable—with dogs barking, shots ringing out, people screaming and crying. I couldn't bear to think of it. As bad as that was, what awaited them on the train was far worse, worse even than my experience. Their train was more crowded. That thought was unbearable.

The stranger from Radom had been correct. Treblinka was created for only one purpose: extermination. And they needed it done as quickly and neatly as possible.

Their train would have arrived at the train station with fragrant potted plants swinging in the wind. With details rivaling a Hollywood set, the mock station was staged to look like a train station hub, complete with a ticket window, a painted clock, and postings of other destinations and fake train schedules. Some arriving by train were greeted by friendly, smiling SS officers telling them that they were going to get a warm shower, clean clothes, and a hot meal before being taken to their barracks, where they would work for the German war effort. My mother would likely have believed them, thinking that she would stay there for the duration of the war, after which she could take her family home.

As they left the train, their legs would have been weak and wobbly; children aboard would have been crying, asking to be carried. Even though they had barely enough strength to walk, mothers and fathers would have lifted their children into their arms.

They would have been told to mark their belongings and remember where they put them and then undress. Mother and Laja would have been mortified at their nakedness before others. They may even have been given a fresh bar of soap.

Once in the shower room, they would have looked up at the shower heads, waiting, eager to be clean. Just before the doors were closed, many more people would have been shoved in, more people trying to cover their nakedness. If there was no room to stand, the children, who had earlier been pulled aside, would have been thrown on top of those standing. They would have heard strange noises, wondering if it was the sound of water filling the pipes. Eagerly, they would have waited. For a moment, they would not have understood what was happening. Until the moment the gas began filling their lungs, they would have had no idea they were victims of a façade. Soon the suffocation would have begun, amid the screams, the shouts, and the prayers. People would have crawled on top of one another, trying to get to the remaining clean air. People underneath them would have been crushed to death. After it was over and the gas fully dissipated, the doors would have opened.

There are other accounts, too, of those arriving when the Nazis were in more of a hurry, of whips lashing them as they ran toward the gas chambers, of men being gassed first while their mothers, wives, and children could only stand naked, listening to their screams, knowing they were next.

I would come to learn that the Treblinka gas chambers were capable of killing 3,000 people every two hours with a maximum of 22,000 people in a twenty-four-hour period, death from suffocation and carbon monoxide poisoning. The chambers were so crowded that when the doors to the chambers were opened, many of the dead were still standing. Dead mothers were reported to be still embracing the bodies of their dead children—mothers like mine.

When I moved the bodies in Auschwitz, they were buried in massive pits, covered with soil. Later, the killings there became even more organized. The bodies were burned in the pits and later, in crematoria. At Treblinka, the bodies of my brothers, sister, and mother would have been thrown into massive pits of wood, covered with petrol and burned. Twelve thousand people could be burned in one massive, fiery inferno. The pits at Treblinka burned twenty-four hours a day. Afterward, the human ashes were mixed with sand and spread over several square miles, ashes of my beloved family.* [80]

* Author Note: There have been many attempts to accurately calculate the number of victims of the Treblinka death camp. Since the Nazis destroyed most of the relevant data, it is doubtful if a definitive figure will ever be established. However, based on the most recent research, it is estimated that a total of nearly 900,000 Jews were murdered in the camp between July 1942 and August 1943. [81]

Dancing It Away

I wanted to dance the horror away.
~Joe Rubinstein

I called him Sig and he called me Upe. Siegfried Kline was the best friend I had ever known, yet I shared nothing with him of what happened during the war. Sig's mother was from Norway and his late father was German. They had lived in Germany throughout the war while Siegfried was in school. When I met him, he was working for the government. Sig lived with his widowed mother who, once she learned about my family, had taken a keen interest in my well-being and invited me to join them every Sunday for dinner. She occasionally dressed in her native Norwegian clothing and served authentic food from her homeland. Eating with a family was something I never thought I would experience again. It meant more to me than I had words to express.

I knew there was much Sig wanted to ask me about what I had experienced in the camps. He also knew that I was not ready to share the details. Siegfried was the kind of friend who cared more about me than his curiosity. I really liked that about him—that and the fact he was great fun. I was ready to have fun. I wasn't alone. Young people everywhere were trying to shake off the horrors of war. Ours was a generation that had spent much of our teenage years and early twenties knowing mostly tragedy. We were tired of it and ready to laugh and forget.

Our favorite place was a dance club called the Rinehoff. Friday and Saturday nights its dance floor was packed with young people frolicking to the sounds of a live band. Sig and I were usually among them, dancing with a different girl each night.

At times, when my gaze moved about the crowded clubs, it struck me as peculiar that there we were, young men and women from opposite sides of the war together having fun. There was great excitement at the clubs and plenty of pent-up energy being expressed. We all seemed to sense it—a feeling that there was nothing we could do to change the past. It was our mission to get back a little of the careless fun of our lost youths. We all had a lot of making up to do.

I considered dancing a frivolity of life, but it was impossible to suppress my joy when doing so. Dancing became my personal release and victory, my proof that although the Nazis had taken so much of what I loved, somehow my joy and my innate love of life remained. Siegfried said to me often that he thought dancing was the best thing I could do, and I think he was right.

I was happy to have a friend like Siegfried. Never before had I known such a bond with anyone other than my brothers.

I danced the fox trot, jitterbug, and my favorite, the Viennese waltz.

Everywhere I went, girls were eager to dance with me, and every night Sig would laugh and say the same thing, "Upe, what do you have that I don't?"

"I have no idea," I respond, "but whatever it is, I'm glad!"

"Smiling Joe," chuckled Sig. "You know that's what people are calling you."

"I know … and I like it." I grinned. I did like it, very much.

"I don't know how you do it," he said, his expression suddenly serious. "How you can still smile after all that time in the camps."

I told him the truth. "If they take my joy, they'll have taken everything. I can't let that happen."

One Friday evening, instead of dancing, I accepted an invitation from Max Manheim to go out for dinner. After our meal, as we were leaving the crowded restaurant, we walked past a table of rowdy, young German men, all of whom looked like former soldiers. I could always spot them. I'd had a lot of practice.

It was obvious they had been drinking for a while. The biggest one of them, a broad shouldered man, belted out, "So, Jew boys, you see this fine duck here," he picked up the platter that the waitress had just set down, with a beautiful untouched duck finely garnished with boiled potatoes. "I have a question for you and you need to think real hard." He grinned, then winked at his friends. "I'm going to let you do anything you want with this fine duck here. But here's the catch: anything you do to that duck, I'm going to do to you! So what's it going to be?"

It was a stupid question, obviously trying to belittle and intimidate us. I think he was waiting for us to say something like, "Ignore it," and then we'd cower and walk away.

Max was in no such mood. He moved in close to the platter, looked the man who was holding it right in the eye, then stuck out his tongue and licked the duck.

The man threw the platter on the table with disgust. I sucked in my breath, waiting for someone to start punching, but suddenly I couldn't contain my laughter, nor could Max. He threw his arm around my shoulder, and we walked out of the restaurant howling. I heard the man exclaim, "Once a Jew always a Jew!" I didn't care. Never again was I going to be intimidated by such brutes. Those days were over. [82]

A Night That Changed a Life

I kept thanking God for my new life.
~Joe Rubinstein

Siegfried and I were talking outside a restaurant on Wesiler Street when I felt a light hand on my shoulder. I turned to see an older man with thinning dark hair wearing round, wire-rimmed glasses and a gray suit. "I couldn't help noticing your accent," he asked excitedly. "Are you from Poland?" It was a question that would normally cause me to draw away. Even after all that had just happened, many still showed open hostility toward anyone from Poland. In this man, I recognized a familiar accent.

I said yes and introduced myself. He laughed and told me he liked my name, for his was Joe as well. Joe Gusenda was born and raised in Kicgow, Poland. He had a kind face and a gentle demeanor. I immediately liked him.

We talked briefly. He asked about my background, and I told him that I had spent the war in the camps. His expression grew solemn. "And your family?" he asked. I sensed that he already knew my answer.

"All gone." I still could not believe the truth of those two simple, terrible words.

His expression melded into a mixture of pity and sadness; yet, there was seething anger there too. It had been there all along, I just hadn't realized it until that moment. I wondered about its source. "Josef," he said hoarsely, "I'd like you come to my home tomorrow evening. My wife, well ... she's a great cook." Sensing my hesitation, he wrapped his arm around my shoulder and said brightly, "Besides, I have a very pretty daughter."

He quickly wrote his address on a piece of paper, and the next night I found myself knocking on the door of a beautiful, first-floor apartment at Number 11 Gillo Street.

The man was wrong. His daughter wasn't just pretty, she was gorgeous. I couldn't stop looking at her and I couldn't stop smiling. I tried glancing at her parents, at the floor, at the ceiling; no matter where I looked, I couldn't stop smiling. And she noticed. She smiled back at me—a radiant smile that shone through her beautiful brown eyes. Irene was twenty years old, with long, wavy, dark hair pulled back at the sides. She had on a black skirt and a white blouse that wouldn't stay tucked in the back despite her repeated efforts. Her face was open and kind.

I knew I was in trouble when I saw her red shoes, for anyone who would wear these stylish, intricately woven red-leather sandals was my kind of girl. With long legs and arms, everything about her was sophisticated, graceful, and yet, unpretentious and friendly.

I called him Mr. Gusenda, but he insisted I call him Joe and his wife, Anna. They had a beautifully furnished apartment with a glass china hutch filled with fine crystal and porcelain figurines. It was a warm and inviting home.

I loved the sound of Irene's laugh, and she laughed a lot. It was clear how proud her parents were of their lovely daughter and how much they loved her. We spent the evening sharing stories. All three were fluent in Polish, German, and French, with Irene also having studied English in school.

Irene's father had been an excellent swimmer when he was young, and he instilled this love in Irene. When she was a young girl visiting her grandmother in Poland, there was a large lake nearby, and young Irene used to regularly swim the length of it. That scared her grandmother and the first time she caught Irene doing so, she reprimanded sharply, "I'm going to tell your father what you've done!" This caused Irene to chuckle, knowing her father was the one who challenged her to try it in the first place.

At my urging Joe and Anna told more stories about Irene. When she was twelve, she had been standing on the shores of the Rhine River with her father when a boy upstream fell in and was being pulled under by a strong, circular current. Without hesitation, Irene jumped in and grabbed the boy, but she was not strong enough to swim with him to shore. Very quickly, they were both in trouble in the fast-running water. Irene's father jumped in and was able to get hold of Irene as she held on to the boy, and together they were able to kick their way to shore.

I was amazed at what I was hearing, for that boy could have been me. When I was about six, I waded out into a deep pond filled with large lily pads. I'm not sure why I did it, because I didn't know how to swim, and when I felt the roots of the plants tangle between my legs, I panicked. I couldn't believe how quickly I felt myself slipping below the surface of the water. If it hadn't been for the quick actions of an older neighborhood boy jumping in to rescue me, I would have drowned.

Irene's parents shared another story about something incredible that Irene had done when she was only about thirteen and a member of an organized swimming club. Arrangements had been made for them to attempt to swim the English Channel. She had covered herself in a thick, black oil to protect her skin from the cold seawater. Irene had made it more than halfway to the English coast before she was so exhausted that she was forced to climb into the rescue boat trailing them. One young woman in the group was successful in the crossing. After hearing this story, I knew immediately that Irene was my kind of girl—fun, bold, and unafraid. The stories about Irene kept coming, and I couldn't get enough of them. Anna shared what had happened during one of the bombing raids as they were huddled in the apartment house basement, crowded in with all the other tenants. Irene was convinced she smelled smoke. No one else could smell anything, and they were not about to leave the safety of their basement shelter on the word of a teenage girl. Undeterred, and much to the dismay of her parents, Irene ran upstairs and found the building in flames. The apartment building next door had been bombed and had started a fire in their building. Irene ran back to the basement, yelling for everyone to leave. Anna said that had it not been for Irene, it was unlikely any of them would have survived. As it was, everyone was able to get out safely.

Looking around the home filled with photos and family mementoes, I welled up with emotion. The camaraderie here reminded me of my family. I had forgotten how it felt, especially the laughter and banter that flowed with ease between a close family. I missed and yearned for the closeness that comes with such love. Sitting there, I realized I wanted to be a part of it again—a part of a family, a part of life. I needed more than the frivolity of dancing to fill the deep void of my life. I needed love.

We spent several hours weeping and laughing. I told them about my family and a few of the details I hadn't revealed to anyone about my time in the death camps. They were shocked and horrified.

Irene's father told me more about his growing up in Kiegow, Poland. He was eighteen when World War I broke out. Poland had been split into several territories that were annexed by Germany, Russia, and Austro-Hungary. He was pressed into the German army during the Great War, where he was later injured when a bullet passed through his foot, leaving him partially disabled. After the war, he had been unable to find anyone willing to hire him. He read a newspaper article about a coal mine in northern France that was recruiting workers. He had recently been married to Anna Naskrent, and they made the decision to move to Lallaing, France, near the Belgium border. It was there that their children, Walter and Irene, were born.

Irene's father had long dreamed of becoming a tailor but had no money to do so. He took a second job in an electrical plant. He spent his days working at the coal mine, his nights at an electrical plant, and his evenings drawing sketches of clothing designs. After several exhausting years of working two jobs, the family had saved enough money to open a tailor business and decided their best opportunity was in Duisburg-Hamborn, where Irene's mother was born. They moved to Germany in 1930, when Irene was five and Walter seven.

Things were going well for them until the Nazi party began gathering strength. From the beginning, Joe and Anna had distrusted the Nazis but believed they were in the minority and that cooler heads would prevail.

When he was old enough, Walter enrolled at the university in Beuten, Poland, near the German border. When the invasion of Poland came, Walter was ordered back to Duisburg-Hamborn. Joe and Anna were devastated at the news of Germany's invasion of Poland, but not completely surprised. Anna had visited her family in Poland not long before the invasion. She came home and told Joe that she had seen German soldiers in Poland, disguised in civilian clothing. Her husband had asked how she knew they were German. She said she didn't know exactly, she could just tell.

The war had been terrible for Irene and her family. Two of Irene's cousins enlisted as pilots in the Polish Air Force. Each was shot down on separate missions, captured by the Germans and executed.

Anna eventually brought out a picture of Walter and handed it to me. They hadn't yet shared anything of what happened to him. I knew by their expressions that it was bad, and I realized Anna shared the same look of deep anger and sorrow I had seen on her husband's face when I met him the previous day.

In the picture, Walter was a handsome, dark-haired teenager who looked a lot like Irene. As I studied the picture, I realized Irene had grown silent. Her eyes had filled with tears and she would not look at the picture of her brother.

Joe then began to tell me a story that was eerily familiar, so familiar that my stomach began to tighten and the palms of my hands began to sweat. The family had been living for several years in a noisy apartment above the Herrkommer Restaurant. In 1943, a knock at their door changed their lives, as it had mine. Like me, Walter opened the door. I wondered, as I looked at my hands now, if his had been trembling like mine as he reached for the handle. Two Gestapo men in black uniforms asked if he was Walter Gusenda. They told him he was under arrest and being taken to Berlin. I could imagine it clearly. Irene had been away at the time. I was thankful she never had to see Nazi soldiers standing in the doorway of her home. Joe demanded to know the charges against his son and was told that Walter had been seen talking to a young man who was suspected of spying against the Nazi regime. Walter was being arrested, accused of being a spy.

For the next year, Anna and Joe fought a tireless, agonizing campaign to secure Walter's freedom. Since she was the only German citizen in the family, Anna was the only one permitted to visit Walter in jail. She was allowed to do so twice. One night, the Gestapo knocked again at their door, this time informing them that Walter had been sentenced to execution. Anna was given permission to visit him and rushed to the Berlin prison. By the time she arrived, she found him hanging from a tree in the jail courtyard. He was twenty-one years old.

Irene shared with me later that Walter's death had nearly destroyed her parents. She said that my first night with them had been the happiest she had seen them since.

As I walked away from their apartment later that night, I felt overwhelming emotion. I couldn't stop thinking about Irene and all that her family had been through. And I couldn't stop thinking of the blessing her father said before we ate. He thanked God for the lives of our lost loved ones, and he thanked God for sparing my life. As he spoke, I opened my eyes and looked at my hands folded in my lap, hands that had endured more than I thought possible. For the first time it really hit me, that my life being spared was reason to celebrate. I had been trying so desperately not to think of any of it. Now, through Irene's family, I realized that I was thankful for more than just having survived. I was thankful for the chance at a new life.

I had no idea how or why I was still alive. There were so many times when I should have died. So many little things happened to save me—like the man deciding on a whim to draw a "V" on my arm instead of a triangle. Even being taken from the ghetto had, in a twisted way, saved my life when almost everyone else in the ghetto died. Moving the bodies and working in the coal mine had allowed me to have a little more food, finding the pit of mud after nearly being beaten to death, getting sick in the coal mine—and finding the doctor who would save my life by keeping me from returning to the mine. All these things and more saved my life. So many little things, one after the other, nearly every day since I was taken, had to have come together for me to survive. Was it all blind luck or miracles at work? If miracles, why for me and not others? I didn't deserve to live any more than anyone else. I had no answers.

Grandfather used to tell me that God's ways are not for us to fully understand, but that no matter what, everything was in His hands. As Irene's father prayed over our meal that night, his prayers reminded me of my grandfather's prayers. It struck me for the first time that the war was truly over, every aspect of it.

And so began my journey back to life and my courtship with Irene. What I hadn't expected was how much fun she would be and how much she loved to dance. [83]

From Despair to Love

He told me I'd been a prisoner for so long,
now I needed to live.
~Joe Rubinstein

"You can't get married! You've finally gotten yourself free of the camps. You need to enjoy life a little longer ... with me ... having fun!" Sig laughed at himself. Seeing he wasn't getting anywhere, he decided on another tactic. "And what am I going to do on Friday nights? And besides, all the girls are crazy about you!"

"I'm serious, Sig. I need your opinion. I'm Jewish. She's Catholic. What if ..."

"Joe," Siegfried had put down his beer and looked directly at me, "if you love each other, it won't matter. You'll work it out." Siegfried had known Walter before the war but at that time had never met Irene. Despite his humorous protestations, he had been happy about our match from the start.

Two years earlier, shortly after the night I met her family at dinner, Irene and I had gone to the club with her chaperone in tow, a neighbor from her apartment building. On our first date, Irene wore a light-blue dress with a wide, flared skirt and a dark satin ribbon tied at the back. She had on matching high heels with a slender strap across her ankles. Siegfried and his date had joined us there. When the ladies went to the powder room, Siegfried leaned over to me, flashing a broad smile, "Joe, seriously, how do you do it? She's beautiful. She can dance, and her legs ... well ... they're beyond gorgeous."

I took a sip of beer and couldn't stop the grin I knew was consuming my face. "I know. And I'm telling you right now, I am going to marry that girl!"

And so I did. With the blessing of her parents, Irene and I were wed in Duisburg-Hamborn on September 27, 1947, with Siegfried as our best man. Since neither of us was converting to the other's religion, we were not allowed to be married in a synagogue or the Catholic Church. It was not the wedding either of us had imagined when we were young, but war had a way of changing things. The priest at the Catholic Church said that since Irene was marrying a Jew, she was being discharged from the church. She was heartbroken. That did not stop Irene's parents from joining us at the courthouse, which they adorned with beautiful white flowers. Siegfried's mother was there, and some of Irene's family and friends were able to join us. Irene looked beautiful in a gold dress, her long, flowing skirt sweeping the floor.

Before the ceremony I stood in front of the mirror in the restroom, wearing a black pin-striped suit that Irene's father had hand-tailored for me. I barely resembled the same pale and thin man who had walked out of Theresienstadt two years earlier. The terrible cough and fatigue that had plagued me since my imprisonment had finally been resolved, thanks to Irene's father. Shortly after my first dinner at their home, he had arranged for me to be treated by a specialist who determined that I had been suffering from tuberculosis.

How is it possible that I survived to see this day? So many times I should have died. So many times I should have ... I blinked back hot tears, trying not to go there. Instead, I raised my eyes to God and prayed a prayer of gratitude for my life. I prayed for my mother and wondered what she would have thought if she could see me now. She wouldn't have been happy about me marrying outside the Jewish faith, but had she met Irene, I know she would have loved her and been happier still that I had found love.

I looked at my reflection and could see the sorrow etched deep into my eyes, sorrow that I had never been able to even dance away. I leaned closer, studying the eyes that had seen too much. In them,

I could not see which part held my sadness, and yet, each time I leaned back, that sadness was there looking back at me. I smiled at my reflection, hoping that when Irene looked at me she would see only happiness.

As I turned to leave, I was stopped by a momentary flash of hope that when I walked through the doors I might see Chaim standing there as my best man. Abe would be there giving me a warm hug of congratulations, and Anszel would pat me on the back, telling me that I would make a fine husband, now that I had gotten over my laziness. Mother, Marsha, and Laja would all be there, brimming with happy tears. I closed my eyes and forced back such thoughts. I wanted no trace of disappointment on my face when I greeted my bride.

As Irene and I spoke our vows, we both knew that we had a choice. We could live in the sorrow, anger, and despair of the past, or we could move forward with joy. We chose joy. After leaving the courthouse, we all made our way to the Rinehoff where we dined, celebrated, and danced.

Our union was a new beginning for both of us—a rebuilding of family out of the ashes of our lives. It was a lovely fall day, just the kind my mother would have loved. Everywhere, I felt her presence and that of my brothers and sister. Irene later said that she felt Walter there, too. I knew God was with us as we stood holding hands, for only He could have brought together such an improbable couple, a German Catholic and a Polish Jew binding their lives with such love and grace in the quiet space between night and a new dawn. [84, 85]

Touché!

I knew right away who he was.
~Joe Rubinstein

I knew who the seller was, or rather, "what" he was. I knew it the moment I saw him walking toward me. I saw it in the way he walked, in the way he pursed his lips, and by the look of brazen superiority embedded in his gaze. His shoulders were straight but not as much, I suspected, as they once were.

I wished Herman Finkelstein had been with me, seeing that arrogant stranger. Herman would have loved witnessing where his generous gift had brought me. He never would have believed it. Herman had come to visit us in Duisburg-Hamborn several months earlier to meet Irene. We had only been married a couple of months, and I was eager for the two to meet. I barely recognized Herman. He was no longer the thin, frail inmate who helped me walk out of the concentration camp. He had gained weight and in his suit and expensive fur coat, he looked sharp. He was all smiles. Herman was eager to let us know that he had made good on his promise of starting a textile factory in Frankfurt and had already made a fortune. One of the first things he said after he gave me a warm embrace was, "Why didn't you listen to me? You could have been a wealthy man by now!" It was true. If I had gone with him I would have been wealthy in money, but then I would never have met my wife. I had no regrets. Though we had little money, I was rich beyond measure in my life with her.

Irene had learned the art of cooking from her mother. Over a delicious meal of lamb, Herman tried to convince us to move to Frankfurt and work for him. I explained that we weren't ready to leave Irene's parents yet. As he did just after the war, Herman tried to persuade me to change my mind. When he realized that I could not be dissuaded, he pressed a wad of money into my hand, and despite my protests, he would not take it back. He told me that he heard there was a great demand for silk stockings and a shortage of them ever since the war. He gave me the name of a garment factory in Frankfurt and told me to go there, use the money to buy stockings, and then sell them in Duisburg-Hamborn. And so I did. Door to door, wearing a suit and hat, carrying my satchel of supplies, I knocked on the doors of strangers.

Herman's instinct proved invaluable. The demand for stockings was so great that I soon found I needed a car to sell them more effectively. I had no driver's license, so when I saw the posting for a car, I went to inquire about it, taking a hired chauffeur with me.

It was one of the nicest cars I had ever seen, reminding me of Mr. Kiekleski's Opel in Radom. I could not believe that I had made enough money to buy it. The irony above ironies was that when the seller emerged, I had an immediate understanding of why it was so well priced. In the man's line of work, times had become challenging to say the least. Many of those in his occupation had fled or been imprisoned. I wondered if he was being forced to sell the car because he was leaving the country.

As I drove away that day in my new car, I grinned wide, thinking about the look on the seller's face when I signed my name to the paper. He had looked up quickly, I think realizing for the first time that he had just signed his precious car over to a Jew.

As the car moved away, the thought of Max licking the duck came to mind. I started to laugh and couldn't stop. Despite his best efforts to destroy us, Hitler had failed. I only wished Hitler had lived long enough to see the day when a Polish Jew drove away in a car he had just purchased from one of his former generals—a gleaming black Mercedes shining in the sun. [86]

Anywhere but Germany

The German government offered us money to stay.
~Joe Rubinstein

"Anywhere but Germany," was what Irene and I decided when the doctor confirmed she was pregnant. We would not raise a child in Germany. As joyful as we were with the prospect of having a baby, we were apprehensive. We had only a little money. Yet we knew we could not let that keep us from leaving. Money had kept my mother from leaving Poland before the war. I didn't care what I had to do. Money or not, I was going to find a way to protect my family.

Despite everyone's assurances to the contrary, we both knew that it could happen again. History, we'd learned, had a way of repeating itself. The seeds of hate against the Jews were planted deep in Europe's soil, and seeds have the ability to lie dormant, undetected for a long time before springing back to life and spreading their roots. Sometimes it takes thousands of years for history to repeat itself, sometimes only a short while. In our case, we weren't willing to take the chance on when it would occur again.

I had pledged never to live my life in fear. Neither would we be foolish with it. I had been spared. Irene had been spared. It was up to us to go to a place where our new family could have a fresh start. We both agreed to raise our child anywhere but in Germany. UNRRA found an opportunity for us to relocate to Australia, but Irene and I had our hearts set on America.

Siegfried had decided to return to Norway. Although he asked us to come with him, we told him we were awaiting news of our application to live in the United States. The wait for news of our relocation petition was lengthy. In addition to selling stockings, I was eager to make shoes. Irene's father knew someone in Dusseldorf who sold leather skins. Her father let me share the space in his home office to design and make boots and shoes. In his spare time, he helped me with the stitching. Soon, we had more orders than we could handle. I realized that if I wanted to stay in Germany making shoes, I would be able to carve out a good living.

The year 1949 was a year of miracles. In May, our son was born. We named him Chaim-Moni in celebration of the lives of my twin and my grandfather Mendel. We called him Mannie. The first time I held him and looked into his eyes, I had trouble seeing him through my tears. I was in awe and disbelief that this little child was my son. Irene and I wept and prayed prayers of thanksgiving and gratitude that somehow we had both survived the war and been spared to live this moment. I would have given anything for my mother and my siblings to have seen our son. They would have loved him, and he them.

The year 1949 was also when we received the news that our petition had been granted to go to America. Our joy was complete. We would not be processed to leave for many more months, but we were un-daunted—we had a destination, a land of our dreams. Upon learning of our impending departure, the German government offered us money to stay. No amount of money would have changed our minds. [87]

Changing Tides

I couldn't believe he was there. I told him,
"You saved my life."
~Joe Rubinstein

I looked up, squinting against the glare of the sun on the ocean waves, and there he was—a man from another time and place, a man who had saved my life. There are coincidences in life that are so improbable they defy belief. Such was the case on the ship bringing Irene, our son, and me to freedom.

Three months earlier, we had said a tearful goodbye to Irene's family, promising to send for them as soon as we were settled in America. Irene and I traveled to Wentorf, Germany, to await transport with many other designated "displaced persons." Though the wait was long, nothing could dim our excitement; not even being housed in a tiny apartment with another young couple. The only means of separating our sleeping quarters from theirs was a thin sheet hanging loosely between the rooms.

When the day for our departure finally arrived, it was a beautiful fall morning. The air was unseasonably warm when twenty-six of us boarded the ship. With Mannie in my arms and Irene at my side, we stood against the rail of the *USAT General R. M. Blatchford*, an American military ship that, until recently, had transported soldiers instead of civilians. With the blast of the ship's horn ringing in my ear, I was lightheaded and thrilled at the prospect of living in America.

After several days in Bremerhaven where our paperwork was processed and more passengers brought aboard, we watched in silence as Germany grew smaller on the horizon. What a contradiction she was, that country—a country of immense beauty and some of the most brilliant minds the world had ever known. *What had come over its people? How could so many have lost their humanity? Did Hitler somehow manage to hypnotize nearly the entire German population into ignoring God's commandment—to love one another? Will the human race ever learn?*

Grandfather told me once that within each of us are two opposing inclinations, one toward good and one toward evil, and that God bestowed on us one of the greatest gifts we could ever know—the freedom to choose.

At times, I had seethed with rage at God for His seeming indifference and for not stopping the Nazis sooner. As Germany was fading from view, some clarity was forming in my mind, and with it, a peace I hadn't felt in a long time. Goosebumps rose across my arms, and it wasn't because I was cold. I had a sense of what Grandfather had been trying to say. *How could I blame God for His gift of freedom? I had always believed that our fate is in God's hands, that what will be will be, and I saw that was especially true when He gave us the freedom and the power to choose.*

The price of the Nazis' choice was the death of my family and millions of others—the death of goodness in so much of the world. There were times when I let terrible thoughts invade my mind, thoughts of God not loving my family enough to save them. *Grandfather was right, wasn't he? Because God loves us, he allowed even bad to happen, for without freedom, there is no life. Didn't I learn that in the camps? So then did my prayers even matter?* Suddenly, the answer was clear. From the fiber of my being, I knew that God had heard my prayers. Every one. And every prayer from all of us. From the prayers of my siblings; from those starving in the ghettos and camps; from the men, women, and children packed together in a boxcar designed for cattle; from a grandfather suffocating in a gas chamber; from a young man spending a frigid night on an open-air truck wearing only in his pajamas; and from his mother who would die waiting for a son who would never come home. Though none of us had been spared from the consequences of the evil choices of others, we had never been alone.

Did God permit Hitler and the Nazis to survive as long as they did as a lesson for the world? So the world could witness, on the grandest and most terrible of scales, what happens when a whole society chooses evil? So that once and for all, we could see that at its core evil breeds only one thing: death? And that the only conqueror of both evil and death are God and His love? I had no way to know those answers but as I looked down at the baby in my arms, I wondered.

The Nazis had been the extreme—but what about our small, everyday decisions and choices? God had made it clear that when faced with choosing right from wrong He wants us to turn to Him. He gives us the answers, in part, through our consciences. Is that why the Nazis succeeded for as long as they did, because they had learned to kill more than just people; they had learned to ignore the alarm of guilt that is woven within each of us? Some had ignored their feelings and others had justified their guilt by giving it another name—hatred of the Jews. But the result was the same: the Nazis perfected the art of killing their own guilt, their own sense of the moral. Before I knew I was doing so, I was praying for the people of Germany. *Never again. Never again.*

A few days into our voyage, Irene and I stood at the ship's rail, scanning the water in search of whales. We had spotted several of the mammoth sea creatures since leaving, and we were eager to see more. The women and children aboard the ship were housed separately from the men. Irene told me what happened just after she had tucked Mannie into his crib the night before. She was laughing so hard trying to tell me that I had to wait between her laughing fits to hear the story. Strong waves had tossed the ship all evening, and we were still a bit green and queasy from it. As one particularly large wave rolled the ship, Irene said the crib tilted so far sideways that Mannie, still swaddled tight in his blanket, slid right out of it and across the floor.

The following day, I was walking along the ship's deck in search of Irene. I was still chuckling at the thought of Mannie being rocked out of his crib and looked up and saw a familiar face walking toward me. We saw each other at nearly the same moment. My eyes grew wide in recognition. It took him longer to remember; for I was not the thin, hairless inmate he had known at the coal mining hospital.

Dr. Stephen Bozchski and I never expected to see each other again, and yet, there we were, standing together on the deck of the ship, both fleeing a life that now seemed very far away. We were so overcome with surprise, we were speechless. When our words finally came, we could not speak fast enough.

How is it possible ... after all this time ... of all the ships ... that we should find each other here ... now ... both making our way to freedom? It was simply unfathomable.

The doctor told me he had been crestfallen when he returned to the hospital and heard that I had been taken. He sent inquiries trying to determine what had happened to me. To no avail he had feared, and assumed, that I had not survived the war. I told him that I wouldn't be alive if it weren't for him, and we both knew this was true. It was a tremendous reunion and one that allowed me to thank him, something I had wanted to do properly for a long time. An hour later, I had never felt more proud as I did when I introduced my wife to the man who had saved my life. I asked him, hoping for another miracle, if he had any word of what had happened to Pierre from the coal camp. The doctor had never heard of him and had no idea what might have become of my friend.

As we journeyed, the doctor and I stood watching the waves swell in the distance, reminiscing about our time in the hospital, working under Nazi rule. *Did it all really happen?* It was beginning to feel like some far, far away time and place, a surreal memory coming in bits and pieces, a nightmare swirling on the fringes of my mind. [88, 89]

Out of Darkness

*I could not believe that I had lived to stand
on American soil.*
~Joe Rubinstein

We kneeled to the ground and pressed our lips to the soil of freedom. The kiss was the first thing Irene and I did when we stepped off the ship. Neither of us could believe that we were standing on the American shore. We were giddy with delight.

Our first night in America, Irene and I secured a babysitter, a friend from the ship. We then walked from our hotel on 27th Street to 42nd Street to see Times Square. With our legs still unsteady from our journey at sea, we could barely take in all that was before us. As we walked, I couldn't help but think back to all that had happened since the day the Nazis invaded my life.

How is it possible that I am here, in New York, with a wife and a son? As I looked around at the faces of the strangers we passed on the crowded streets I realized that they were no different really from the faces of my youth, of those in a city far away, a city called Radom, a beautiful place that had been torn apart by hatred and evil. As we walked, hand in hand, I found myself praying for each of the people we passed—praying that such evil would never find them.

When we arrived at Times Square, Irene and I gazed in wide-eyed wonderment at the skyscrapers towering around us. We started whispering, then giggling, "We're free. We're free!" Soon our voices were shouts of joy. We didn't care how we looked or sounded, nor did we give any thought to the tears streaming down our faces. Soon our shouts of happiness turned into dancing. [90]

For Just One Picture

*They took me from my home. I never saw
my family again.*
~Joe Rubinstein

They line the walls, refrigerators, and shelves of every home I
enter. My grandchildren exchange them using phones and
computers. My son and his wife have albums filled with them. Those
that can't fit on their walls or in albums are stored in boxes. People
everywhere have them, thousands and thousands of photos, memories frozen in time of those they love, of times shared together, of their
children, of their mothers and fathers, grandparents and siblings,
documenting nearly every day of their lives. They're grateful for them.
They have so many that they scarcely glance at them before filing
them away for some future viewing. We have them, too, of Irene and
her parents and her brother, of our son, of our three grandchildren.
Precious photos of the life we have built together.

The photograph I think most about—the one I would give nearly
anything for—is the one that never was. It's a photo of my childhood
family, one I wish I could share now with my son and grandchildren.
I often imagine what it would look like, if ever there had been such
a photo. Its edges would be worn from holding it, staring at it,
memorizing every texture and tone of that moment, capturing my
family as we were, back in the days when we were unaware of what
was to come, when our greatest worry was whether we were going to
play soccer or hide and seek after dinner. I imagine such a photo of
my family, standing together outside our cottage, of my mother's dress
as it blows in the wind. Anszel, with his handsome face and white
teeth, would be filling the camera with the charm of a Hollywood

movie star. Chaim, looking just like me, would be smiling, but on close inspection, I would see that his eyes hold a more serious gaze than mine. Abe would be poking his finger against Laja's shoulder, seeing if he could make her scowl. Laja's eyes would be red from crying.

When I think about the photo that never was, I yearn to feel again what it was like—that love within our family, that laughter, that innocence. I get angry sometimes when I imagine looking at that photo—a frustration so deep, a feeling that goes beyond words. I want to yell at that young me, to warn myself, to warn all of them, so that we would run back into our home and grab everything we could carry and leave Poland, even if we had to walk.

In that imagined photo, I am looking sideways, my gaze slightly off Chaim's shoulder. *Why can't I see what is coming at us? Why am I not listening to the screams that now rage in my head? What's wrong with that young boy, the boy that was me? Listen to me! Wipe away your smile. Leave. Leave. Leave!*

Mr. Nagel tried to warn us, but I was happy go-lucky. If only I had known! If only I had known that when I was forced out of that cottage, I would be closing the door on a part of my life that would not and could not ever be reopened.

They're gone now: my childhood, my innocence, my family from the photo that never was. My hands are empty, with no photo to grasp. All that is left are the memories—memories strewn together in bits and pieces from my ninety-four-year-old mind. Some memories come in fragments, some in totality, and some are simply gone, dangling just beyond my consciousness, teasing me, letting me know they are there, unable to be recalled.

There are many things I wish I could remember more fully, and many I wish I could forget altogether. It's a puzzle, my mind. For the things I most want to forget I can't, and the things I most want to remember, I can't do that either. Like my mother's face—I can't believe that I can't remember its details. I've spent years trying to remember, and yet I can't see her face clearly. She was pretty; I know that, very pretty. Her silky, long hair was coal black, and she had soft, dark-brown eyes. But the images of her that come are more of the warmth she created than of her actual face: bread baking in our oven, the potato latkes on her stove, the wholeness of her warm embrace.

What I wouldn't give for just one picture of her, of any of them, of my family. [91]

Nightmares and Dreams

I still have nightmares that I am back there.
~Joe Rubinstein

Sometimes even now, I wake—my eyes wide as they search the darkness. My heart pounds so fast I can feel it pulsating against my chest. I'm not certain if I am awake or dreaming. The screams I've just heard still echo in my head. Then I feel Irene's warm hand covering mine. She whispers, "It's okay, Joe. You're safe. It was just a dream."

I breathe deeply, trying to ease my trembling. I am chilled by the sweat pooled across my skin. It seemed so real, my nightmare—they all do—so real I can feel my stomach aching for food, still smell the stench in that place called Auschwitz where death was everywhere. I still hear the screams and moans of those around me, unheard by anyone who could have helped, in a place where reality was far worse than any nightmare my mind can conceive.

Nearly seven decades have passed, and still I dream of that terrible place and time. Of late, the nightmares have become fewer. In their place are happier dreams—the ones where I am back in Poland with my family, where their faces are so close to mine. I wake to find myself reaching out to touch them. [92]

The First Light of Dawn

What really is life? It's family. That's all you have left.
Today you're here; tomorrow you never know. You have
to remember what life is ... it is in you ... you have
nothing else. You have pictures in your mind. You have
to remember the good things. What else do you have?
You have to memorize the good life you had. You have
to make a good life. If someone goes from the family,
they leave behind the things to remember, and that
is what you live by. The good things.
~Joe Rubinstein

On a dark, frigid winter morning, a lone truck rolled out of the ghetto in Radom, Poland, taking a shivering young man in his pajamas and undershirt from the only home he had ever known. That boy was me. The boy never returned to Radom, and since the war, has never returned to Poland. I never had a desire; there was nothing to go home to. My family was my home, and they were all gone.

Fear has kept me away, too. I have survived by trying to keep those memories at a distance, to protect my heart and mind from collapsing under the weight of my pain; and yet, I don't want to forget my family. I don't want the world to forget. I don't want my son, my grandchildren, and their children for generations to come to forget the family, the history, and the connections that were taken from them, too.

I wonder what I would see and feel walking down the streets of Radom today. My body is old now. The legs that once ran through the fields of my father's pasture have grown weak. My heart does not beat as evenly as it once did. Dark spots speckle my skin. But still I wonder

... Is my father's pasture still green? Does anything remain of any of the places I once knew, of the streets where I played soccer? Could I find the corner where my mother stood at her stand, selling produce from our garden? Is there any trace of a familiarity in the faces of the people I would see? Any hint of anyone I used to know, of their love, their friendship, their betrayal?

Could anything be as it was when I was a boy? Would the stars look the same?

If I were to go back, I don't know if I could handle all of what would come—the torrent of *"if onlys." If only the Nazis had been stopped before they built their war machine ... if only we had left Poland earlier ... if only I could have warned my family ... if only Mother and my siblings could have found somewhere to hide ... if only I hadn't opened that door ... if only ...*

Could I handle the torrent of questions that would come— questions I quit asking long ago? *Why did any of it happen? Why did I survive when my family and so many others were killed?*

Questions and "if onlys" I've packed away until the day I stand before God and receive the answers. Until then there are no answers, so they have remained, buried deep within me, dormant, sealed from eating away at me until nothing remains, like the bones of those left in the pits at Auschwitz.

Walking the streets of Radom, would I be filled with longing and yearning so strong that my body would break? Would my head burst from the surge of memories? Would I feel the torture of fear rising in me as it did when I heard a knock at the door, a knock that changed everything?

Or, might I hear laughter in the wind, the laughter of my brothers, my sister, my mother and father—laughter that once filled in that space and held me through time—reminding me that evil did not win.

I imagine standing over the graves of Solomon, of my father, and of my grandparents; graves that must still be there, graves on solid ground, marked by the gravestones that my mother saved so long to buy, graves in a place that was, and is, real—a place where names are etched in stone, a permanent reminder, a place to grasp, a place to know that it all wasn't just some faraway dream. To know that my childhood was real, my family was real, that it wasn't all erased by the monstrosity of what swept us apart.

It's strange somehow, knowing there's a place that marks the life of a brother I never knew, and yet, there is no such place for my mother, Anszel, Abram, Laja, and Chaim. I wonder sometimes where their ashes have traveled. *Have they found their way to a grassy pasture in Radom, or a Colorado mountain meadow, or a towering forest of trees? Or are they in the air I breathe, with me, a part of me, even now?*

I go there sometimes in my mind, to that cemetery in Radom, to pretend they're all laid to rest there, to tell them I have not forgotten them, to tell them that despite the death that separates us and the events that tore us apart, we have triumphed. We have triumphed because the love we shared, the light of their lives, survives—it survives in me and the love I have for Irene—it survives in our son and his wife Julie—and it survives in our three grandchildren. The love of our family will survive for generations.

I tell them, the family whose faces I have not seen in decades, but they already know. Long ago they were pulled into the same gentle arms of the One who stayed with me while I was in the pit of death, weeping with me, healing me; the same arms that heard the prayers of a broken boy crying out for the dead he pushed in his cart; the same arms that were there, carrying each of them home. Our unfathomable grief is His, too.

I like to imagine my family with me in that cemetery in Radom, celebrating the good times of our lives together, not through tears and heartache, but restored through the embrace of God's grace, purity, and joy … His love.

I like to imagine my family with me in that cemetery, watching me, lighting candles of love on their graves—love enough to keep us all warm. [93]

Epilogue

Threads of Gold

It's a miracle that I'm still here. Sometimes if I think about it, I still can't believe it myself. I'm so happy I'm still here and have such a beautiful wife and family.
~Joe Rubinstein

When I arrived in New York, I spoke virtually no English. Irene had studied it in school, but her German accent was so strong that most Americans found her difficult to understand. Our first apartment was provided to us by the UNRRA. We were grateful to have a roof over our heads, but the small, rundown apartment on Sackman Street was so close to a railroad line that trains shook our beds and rattled our windows, making it challenging to sleep. After a few nights in the apartment, Irene begged me to take her back to Germany. I felt terrible for her, so far from home, struggling to adapt to both being a young mother and to a new place where everything was so strange and foreign. I knew how much she missed her parents and how homesick she was, but I was determined that we could never move back.

We were able to find one of my mother's brothers who had moved to New York years earlier; the other had passed away. Elliot and his kind wife, Norma, had three sons. All three had fought in the war, including Sol, who quickly became a great friend of mine. I was ecstatic to meet any relatives from Poland. I had written to them after the war, telling them the terrible news of my family and asking if they had kept any of the photographs my mother sent them of my family before the war. I was devastated to learn that they could not recall ever having received them. Elliot and his family had been my last hope of finding one tangible memento of my family.

Despite having reconnected with Elliot, times were tough for us. What little money we had when we arrived quickly evaporated. When a job finally presented itself, working at a factory making army bags, I jumped at the opportunity. To my great relief, I was hired, and because of my quick fingers with a needle, I was able to turn out bags much faster and of better quality than most of the other workers. I was given a raise and high praise for my work. I thought of my mother's insistence when I was young that I learn to make clothes, telling me that someday I would be glad I had the skill. At the time, I had been irritated at her for making me learn. Now, I wished there were some way I could thank her and tell her how she had made such a difference in my life, in a place far away from Radom.

I had overcome so much in my life that there were few things I now feared; facing death every day makes most other worries pale in comparison. Taking chances was not something I feared. It was one of the reasons I found myself in an upscale high-rise office of a luxury shoe design company called Gero Brothers, sitting before the Greek owner.

He asked me to call him Richard, and after learning that I had experience in Poland making shoes, he offered me a job in the production department. I thanked him, accepted the job, and then just as I turned to leave his office, I told him that not only could I make shoes, but that my passion was designing them. He cocked his head skeptically. "Okay. Show me what you got." He handed me a pencil and a blank tablet. I opened to the first page and began drawing, first one design and then another. When I looked up, his face was alight with a huge grin. He put out his hand and congratulated me, saying that I was to report the following day as one of his lead designers. I was so surprised it took me a moment to respond. "But I barely speak

English," I managed to say, demonstrating the obvious. I wanted to make sure he knew what he was getting in hiring me.

He slapped me on the shoulder and laughed, "Neither do I! You're in good company! And besides, Joe, your work speaks for itself. You don't ever have to worry about speaking English." He picked up the sketchpad and exclaimed, "You just need to design shoes."

Thanks to Mr. Nagel, I was able to teach other shoe workers how to be more efficient in their work. The job at Gero Brothers afforded us the opportunity to move to a beautiful apartment on Park Place and permitted Irene to quit her housekeeping job and stay home with our son. And it allowed her time to excel at her cooking. She was an extraordinary hostess, running a catering business for fun, making extravagant meals. As our confidence grew with our English, we began entertaining friends and coworkers in our home. Respecting the importance of my heritage, Irene learned to cook in the Jewish tradition. I have said often that if it hadn't been for marrying Irene, I would have been six feet under long ago, and that was no exaggeration. Like so many other miracles in my life, none was more important to me than Irene.

Much to our great joy, Irene's parents were eventually granted permission to move to the United States, where they lived near us. Herman came to visit us in New York. He was still prosperous and doing well in the textile industry. I tried to pay him back for the money he had given me for the silk stockings, but he continued to refuse to take it.

My lack of fear helped me as I strove to make an even better life for Irene and our son. After nearly two years of working at Gero, I was hired as a designer at the renowned Nina Shoe Company, working for Stanley Silverstein. I worked for Nina for several years designing high-fashion shoes. When one of the Nina offices closed, I found myself interviewing with the famous Beth Levine of Herbert Levine, Inc. During the interview, Beth asked me what I wanted for a salary, and I told her. She had seen my work at Nina and laughed when she said she would not negotiate with me, that anything I wanted, she would pay. They had been having trouble with efficiency and production levels at one of their factories. Beth asked me to visit the factory, review the production and operations, and make recommendations. The first change I recommended was to have the workers paid by the number and quality of shoes they produced, not simply by the hours they worked. To help them, I coached every worker at that factory on ways they could improve the speed and quality of their work. The change was dramatic, with the workers making more money, the number of shoes produced increasing, and the quality of the shoes much improved.

I met with each worker and taught them the techniques I had learned from Mr. Nagel. He had no way of knowing it, of course, but his craftsmanship lived on in many of the most splendid, high-priced, and sought-after shoes in the world; shoes that frequently lined the display cases of Neiman Marcus, Saks Fifth Avenue, Lord & Taylor, and others. Shoes designed by Herbert Levine, Inc. were worn by first ladies and movies stars alike.

Beth asked me to design bows and ornaments for a line of shoes about to be unveiled. I did, and one of those shoes, a pump with an intricate bow over the toe, became the company's most popular seller. About a year after working for Beth Levine, one of our new design staff members complained to her that I had left early one Friday afternoon. He came to me later to apologize and told me of Beth's response. She had said to him, "Don't you ever, ever say a negative word about Joe Rubinstein! He can do anything he wants. The man's a genius. He's the man with the golden hands. If you ever speak another bad word about him, you can keep walking … straight out the door!"

I laughed at the thought of the verbal lashing I knew the man had endured and told him not to worry. Beth had always been very protective of me. Throughout my years there, I worked closely with

Beth and her sister and was sad when Beth's sister passed away. Irene and I attended a reception at the Levine home. We had never seen anything like it. It was an estate equal to many of the finest villas in Europe. I could not believe that I was working for this great lady and her company.

Of all the things that happened since our arrival in New York, nothing was more gratifying than the day, five years after our arrival, when Irene and I became citizens of the United States. It was one of the happiest moments of our lives.

To our great sorrow, Irene had two miscarriages after coming to America and was never able to get pregnant again. When our son was old enough, he moved to California, where he met and married Julie Wilson, a beautiful girl from Florida, whom we love like a daughter.

In the early 1980s, Irene and I decided to make the move to California to be near our son and his wife. I was grateful when the Sbicca Footwear company offered me a job as their General Manager in Southern California. Irene's father had since passed away, but her mother was able to make the move with us. As Irene and I left our beautiful colonial home in Poughkeepsie, New York, I thought back to the day we had stepped onto the American shore. I never dreamed that someday I would be designing some of the most expensive shoes in the world and living such a blessed life. I was simply pursuing my passion and trying to take care of my family, the way I had always tried to do for my mother.

Irene, her mother, and I settled into new life in Redondo Beach, where we basked in the warmth and sunshine of the California coast. I found my new job tremendously rewarding. One of my designs, a sandal made of buffalo skin, became one of the company's bestselling shoes. However, it was teaching young men and women the art of shoe design that I found most rewarding.

In America, I changed the spelling of my name from Josef to Joseph. In time, our son changed his name to Dan—a strong Jewish and biblical name. Irene's mother loved the name, and I know my mother would have as well.

After nearly twenty-five years in California, Irene and I moved to Colorado to again be near Dan and Julie. Our three grandchildren, Mark, Jeff, and Kelly, live near us, and we are able to be with them often. Kelly is a forensic scientist, working in a police department crime lab. Jeff is in college, majoring in construction management. Mark is an attorney who was recently married to a lovely young woman named Adrienne. For several years, Mark was a member of the United States Army National Guard. I am so very proud of his service and will forever be indebted to all the branches of the military of the United States and its Allies that fought against Nazi tyranny, liberating Europe and the concentration camps.

Irene and I spend our days now enjoying family and friends and going to the mountains. I still enjoy gardening and have always loved to walk, and do so every day. I tell my elderly friends, "Life is precious! You have to keep moving."

On paper, Irene and I were an odd match—a Catholic girl coming of age in Germany during the war, marrying a young Polish Jew recently liberated from a Nazi concentration camp. As I look at Irene, now nearing ninety years old, she is still beautiful. I can remember the way she looked the first day we met as clearly as though it were yesterday.

It is gratifying to know that at least some part of my life before the war, my knowledge and love of designing shoes, was not lost, and it has afforded our family a wonderful life. But nothing has compared to the times Irene and I have had with our son, his wife, our three grandchildren, and now, our granddaughter-in-law. They have filled our lives with love and laughter; something I never dreamed possible when I staggered out of the Theresienstadt gates nearly seventy years ago—a man who had nothing left but his life. I am an old man now—a man filled with true joy and contentment.

By the grace of God, Irene and I have both been blessed with the gift of longevity. I can't stop smiling whenever I think of the recent wedding of our grandson in June of 2014, a day filled with love. Our family is growing. I'm so happy that it is. My mother and family would have been so happy, too. Joyfully, we did something at the wedding reception we hadn't done in a while. We danced.

We've recently learned that our granddaughter, Kelly, will marry Zach in the fall of 2015. Another joyous event. With an impending marriage and, I suspect, even great-grandchildren in our future, my goal, God-willing, is to be there for as much of it as possible. [94, 95]

In Joe's Words

I fight for my life, all my life. I'm a fighter to the last minute.

I don't give up. The only one who can take away my life is my God, nobody else.

Life is God's blessing. You can't take any part of life for granted.

When you're God's child, you have to help yourself.

All my life people have called me "Smiling Joe." It wasn't an act. I smile because I am happy, because I love life. I love people. All my life I've tried to help people—that's what I do.

I will be Jewish until I die. Once you are born to something that is who you are. I believe in the Torah. Irene and I respect each other's religion … and we celebrate with each other … she learned to cook in the Jewish tradition, and we keep a menorah in our home. I go to church with her and celebrate Christmas with her. My church is in Heaven.

We are all God's children. How could anyone kill people just because of their religion? I don't care what religion you are or what color you are.

There is only one God. We are all praying to one God.

My father died in December. It was frigid. He was lying on the floor. We were all around him. My mother begged him not to leave her. She asked him, "Where are you going?" He pointed his finger to the sky. He said to her, "God is with you, you're in His hands now." It was heartbreaking. In the grave, they covered his body with two boards.

In the truck, there was no place to sit. Some people died. If you left the truck, they would shoot you. The teenager next to me said he was going to get off the truck. I told him then he needed to be ready to die today because they would kill him.

In the truck, they collected us. Then they left us. They left us out all night; it was terrible. It was frigid. They left us the whole time. They went in to have a good time. They didn't care about the prisoners. They were watching us through the windows. You couldn't go out, or they would shoot you. People died on the truck. Then the next day we traveled to little camps to collect more people. They let us off at camp, and then another bigger truck would come. We didn't know where we were going.

I never thought I would be warm again.

At Auschwitz, the men and women were separated. Some went with the kids. They gave orders and pointed … go there … you go there … you go there.

It was really warm on the train. The train was running for miles … town to town … collecting people. One time they opened all the doors and the Gestapo gave us water. One time. I don't know how long we were on the train. Some people didn't survive. Sometimes I shake my head. How did I survive? How?

Of all the camps, Auschwitz was the worst, the worst. It was a death camp. They had orders to kill people, and they did. If you were young or old, forget about it. You were dead.

The train was close to the barracks. They made us get nude, they sprayed us; then they made us take a shower, then put on a uniform. Then get shoes. Some got good shoes, others bad. You couldn't say, "I don't like these." The worst were the wooden shoes. Later, I had to walk two miles to the coal mine in them. You cannot complain …

what could I do? Later, I told them, I can't work in these anymore. I can't. I wasn't afraid anymore. They told me to go to this place to get different shoes. And I did.

After they gassed the people, the bodies went right away to the mass graves ... big ones ... huge ... when I say huge ... huge were the graves ... already prepared for the dead bodies to dump them there. In the beginning, we used carts; later they changed that. Every day the trains came. I saw people going in there. They didn't know they were gonna be gassed; thousands of them, every day. It was our job to pick up the bodies. Sometimes it took two of us to pick up a body together, one at the legs and another at the wrists. It was our job. Later they changed all that ... they got more organized with the killing, and we didn't have to move the bodies any more.

The food was terrible at Auschwitz. Food that pigs wouldn't eat. That's what they gave us in the concentration camp. Vegetables weren't even cooked. What you gonna do? You have to eat what they feed you. Only on Sundays we got a little better food ... cheese, some better bread ... a little better meal. Otherwise, the food was terrible.

He came into camp on his horse. His name was Dolp. He looked to be in his late thirties. He took his gun out, and he just mowed them over; then he went back. I saw that. He just killed them, the people working, digging the trenches. Click, click, click, click, and then he went home. He went home. Don't blame me, but I cannot talk about it. It's terrible. I don't know what kind of people they are. I can't imagine what they have in their minds. I'd say they are sick in their minds to go out and kill people. Then they felt good? Some people feel good when they beat up someone. But this wasn't beating up. This was killing them. Click, click, click, click. People digging, they stick their head up ... click, click, click, click. They kill them and then they go home, just like that. That's what they do. Terrible things go through my mind when I remember. I said, "My God!"

It was very dangerous to go out at night in Auschwitz if you had to go the bathroom; a lot of people were watching you. They were watching everything … if they saw something, they would kill you. You know, they didn't care. They didn't want you to live; they wanted you to die.

I pray to God every day, to something up there. Even when I was in the concentration camp, I prayed to God a lot.

That stuff. That terrible stuff they sprayed on the bodies in the pit to make them decompose or something. It was the worst smell ever. Ever! They sprayed it from big trucks.

In the mornings, a lot of people were dead. We had to pick them up and carry them out into the hallway and other people put them in the trucks. There were terrible things going on. We had bodies every day, all over. All over were bodies. How they died, I don't know. Maybe they killed themselves or maybe someone killed them. There were thousands of people, so we couldn't see everything. But you had to get ready for work, and we saw them, hundreds of dead bodies. Every day.

They killed them, the children … hundreds and hundreds of them. They just killed them because they didn't have any use for them. Those kids that didn't go with their families, they got separated. They beat them. They killed them. Just like animals … that I saw with mine own eyes what they did. The guys that worked there … heavy guys with their clubs. They hit the kids on the back of the neck; they died instantly … thousands of them. I don't know. I was crying every night. How can they do it? These are innocent kids. Ten, nine years old. How they got separated from their parents, I don't know. Usually they gassed the families together. But sometimes they got separated … and a lot of kids in the camp … they had no use for them; they just killed them … hundreds every day. The trucks came and they loaded up the bodies. They did. Young, beautiful kids, out in the open. EVERYONE, everyone can see it. I passed by and said, MY GOD!

It's heartbreaking if you reach an age ... you can die if you've seen that. It's really true ... you can die to see that. That's what they did to young kids. How many of those Nazi guys got caught? Some they hunted down. What kind of a person could do this? What sort of men?

Even after I was free from the camps, I thought they would come and take me back.

If I hadn't gone to the coal mine, I would have been dead. The coal mine saved my life. Not too many people left Auschwitz alive.

Siegfried laughed and said I was marrying a shicksa ... someone of a different religion.

When we were on the ship, I couldn't believe my eyes that the doctor was there. He told me he couldn't believe I was alive. I told him I was alive because of him.

When we got to New York, we couldn't wait to walk to Times Square. We could not believe that we were out of Germany and we were free. I felt like a million dollars. I kept thanking God for this whole new life.

I was designing the most expensive shoes in the world. Beth Levine said I was a man with golden hands.

Shoes that had bows on them were Irene's favorite. Irene said that Beth Levine had a shoe named after me called, "Joe the shoemaker," but if there was a shoe by that design, I don't remember it.

I was never afraid of change if it meant making a better life for my family.

It is a blessing to tell you my life story of what I went through; it's something unbelievable; still, it's all in my body and mind what I went through. I NEVER wanted to talk about this. People asked me about it, but I didn't want to talk about it to nobody, nobody. If people see the tattoo, maybe they think I was some sort of a bad guy. I never like to wear short sleeves ... when I go to walk around, people look at me and they think maybe I'm some sort of escaped prisoner.

I don't think people would understand. Some people have heard about Auschwitz, maybe from their folks or from school, but they don't really know. They know terrible things that went on with the German regime, but they don't know. It was hell. Hell.

The terribleness of what I went through is in me, like cancer. I can't get it out. A person could die from seeing what I saw. Sometimes I think I'm going to die if I think about it.

I say to my children, "Aren't you glad your folks are still here with you?" I can't believe that I am. I've told my grandkids, "You should never be afraid if you want to make a better life." I tell them that they can do anything they want; they should never be afraid to try.

And as long as 'mine' eyes are open, I will never forget my family.

Everybody has a heart and soul. Our soul never dies.
God is helping us, guiding us, forgiving us.
I pray every day for my heart and soul and for my neighbors and my family.

I don't want to live forever. But as long as I'm alive, I'm going to love life, love my family, and love God. That's the way I am.

My God is Almighty, the creator of the world.

~Joe Rubinstein
Amen and Shalom

KL: Weimar - Buchenwald   Jude   Häftl.-Nr.1
                                                                    117.666   P

Häftlings-Personal-Karte

Fam.-Name: R u b i n s z t e i n   Überstellt   Personen-Beschreibung:
Vorname: Juzek   am: 22.1.45   an KL   Grösse: _____ cm
Geb. am 15.10.20 in: Radom   Buchenwald   Gestalt: _____
Stand: ld.   Kinder: _____   am: _____ an KL   Gesicht: _____
Wohnort: Radom   Augen: _____
Strasse: Pereca 12   am: _____ an KL   Nase: _____
Religion: mos. Staatsang.: Pole   Mund: _____
Wohnort d. Angehörigen: ___ Mutter: am: _____ an KL   Ohren: _____
  Reska R.   Zähne: _____
  w.o.   am: _____ an KL   Haare: _____
Eingewiesen am, Juni 1944   Sprache: _____
durch: _____   am: _____ an KL
in KL: Auschwitz   Bes. Kennzeichen: ____
Grund: Polit.Pole - Jude   Entlassung:
Vorstrafen: _____   am: _____ durch KL: Charakt.-Eigenschaften: ___

                                  mit Verfügung v.: _____
                                                             Sicherheit b. Einsatz: ___
              Strafen im Lager:
   Grund   Art: Bemerkung:

       MIL.GOV. QUESTIONNAIRE EXISTS   Kö I.T.S. FOTO
                                                             No 007275
                                  LIBERATED BY U.S. ARMY
KL.S/11.44 500.000
                                                                            1981

Buchenwald Form.
Document courtesy of The United States Holocaust Memorial Museum.
*(See Timeline note ** regarding Joe's date of birth.)*

USS General R. M. Blatchford.
Date of photo unknown. Public Domain.

Joe several months after release.
Document courtesy of Joe Rubinstein.

Irene.

Photo courtesy of Irene Rubinstein.

Irene's brother, Walter Gusenda.

Photo courtesy of Irene Rubinstein.

Irene and Walter.

Photo courtesy of Irene Rubinstein.

Joe, Irene, and her parents, Joe and Anna Gusenda.
Photo courtesy of Irene Rubinstein.

**Joe and Irene celebrate their wedding at the Rinehoff with best man,
Siegfried Kline, Anna Gusenda, and a neighbor.**
Photo courtesy of Joe and Irene Rubinstein.

Newlyweds Joe and Irene.
Photo courtesy of Joe and Irene Rubinstein.

Joe and Irene.
Photo courtesy of Joe and Irene Rubinstein.

Joe in Germany selling women's stockings.
Photo courtesy of Joe Rubinstein.

Irene and a driver showing off Joe and Irene's new car in Germany.
Photo courtesy of Joe and Irene Rubinstein.

Joe and Irene with their son.
Photo courtesy of Joe and Irene Rubinstein.

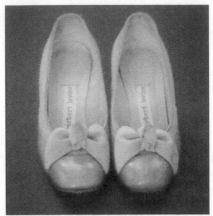

Herbert Levine, Inc. shoes. Bows were Joe's specialty.
Photo by Crystal Geise, www.crystalisphoto.com.

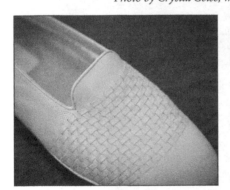 

Photos by Crystal Geise, www.crystalisphoto.com

Joe holding Herbert Levine, Inc. shoes.
Photo by Crystal Geise, www.crystalisphoto.com.

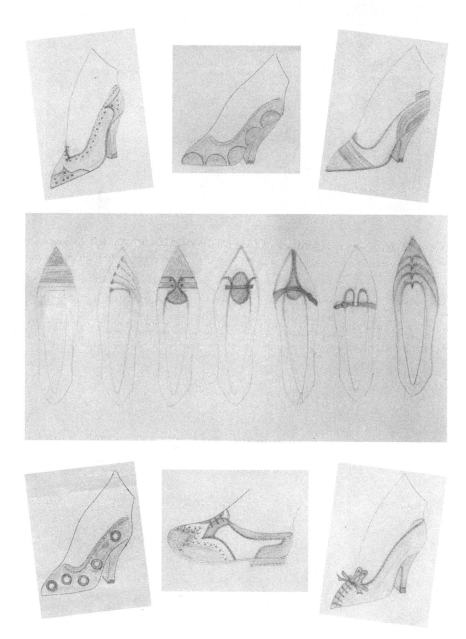

Sketches of shoes designed by Joe.
Photo courtesy of Joe Rubinstein.

Joe and Irene celebrating their 50th wedding anniversary with their son, his wife and three grandchildren in 1997.
Photo courtesy of Joe and Irene Rubinstein.

Joe and Irene, June 2014, at the wedding reception of their grandson.
Photo courtesy of Sarah Rose Photography,
http://sarahroseburnsphotography.pixieset.com.

Joe and Irene, June 2014, at the wedding reception of their grandson.
Photo courtesy of Sarah Rose Photography,
http://sarahroseburnsphotography.pixieset.com.

Joe and Irene, 2014.
Photo by Crystal Geise, www.crystalisphoto.com.

Chapter Endnotes

Part One

1. Source: Fordham University, Modern History Sourcebook: Adolf Hitler: *The Obersalzberg Speech*. August 22, 1939. http://www.fordham.edu/halsall/mod/hitler-obersalzberg.asp.

Prelude

2. Author Note: Joe said whenever the workers saw Dolp coming, someone would whisper, "Here comes the Swinehund, someone's gonna get hurt." Thus, the description of the man next to him is a compilation of those men. Joe described watching as Dolp rode to where they were digging trenches, removed his gun, and shooting those who lifted their heads. Some of the men that were shot were in other trenches near where Joe was working. Joe described the sound of Dolp's gun: click, click, click, and how he simply then turned his horse and rode away. Source: Joe Rubinstein.

3. Author Note: We believe the labor camp was near Cieszanów, Poland, in the fall of 1940. Source: Joe Rubinstein. (See Additional Research Notes for more information about the camp and SS Dolp.)

4. Author Note: August 1940, around 2,000 Jews were deported to work camps in the Lublin district to construct anti-tank ditches and fortifications between Germany and Soviet occupied Poland. Hundreds of Jews from Radom were sent to forced labor camps near the border with the Soviet Union, including Cieszanów. Source: Holocaust Education and Research Archive Team. "Radom." *Holocaust Research Project.* http://www.holocaustresearchproject.org/ghettos/radom.htm.

The Taking

5. Author Note: The events in this chapter are as Joe described. The physical descriptions of the soldiers have been enhanced. Source: Joe Rubinstein.

6. Author Note: In February, 1942 and April 28, 1942, raids were carried out in the Radom ghetto in an attempt to eliminate the individuals the Nazis feared would organize opposition to the imminent deportation of Radom's Jews to the extermination camps. SS men came to the ghetto with a list of names and took the feared agitators. Some of those on the list were murdered at the entrances of their homes; others were transported to a local prison and many were taken to Auschwitz. Source: Jewish Gen. Copyright ©1999-2014 by JewishGen, Inc. Updated 1 Aug 2009 by LA. "*Radom*," Encyclopedia of Jewish Communities in Poland, Volume VII (Poland), pp. 530-543. Translation of "*Radom*" by Pinkas Hakehillot Polin, Published by Yad Vashem, Jerusalem. http://www.jewishgen.org/yizkor/pinkas_poland/pol7_00530.html.

7. Author Note: It is unclear if Joe's name, or that of any of his older siblings who were not at the house, were on the Nazi lists. It is not known why Joe might have been targeted; he was not an activist. Joe believed it was because he was the oldest male in his home. Source: Joe Rubinstein.

Eye of the Storm

8. Author Note: The events in this chapter are as Joe described. Source: Joe Rubinstein.

The White Shroud

9. Author Note: The physical description of the Rabbi and minor details of the burial have been portrayed based on Jewish tradition, including Joe tossing dirt into the grave and the actions of his grandparents. The events of his father's last hours are as Joe described.

Joe's mother used to light kerosene lanterns on the graves of Joe's father and his brother Solomon. Source: Joe Rubinstein.

Strength Through Family and Faith

10. Author Note: The events in this chapter are as Joe described. Source: Joe Rubinstein.

From Generation to Generation

11. Author Note: The events in this chapter are as Joe described. Source: Joe Rubinstein.

Promises Kept

12. Author Note: The events in this chapter are as Joe described. Source: Joe Rubinstein.

The Girl in the Corner

13. Author Note: The events in this chapter are as Joe described. Minor details, including conversations, have been enhanced. Source: Joe Rubinstein.

Finding a Path

14. Author Note: The details of Joe working with Mr. Nagel are as Joe described. The neighbor calling them names as they played soccer was a representation of the growing anti-Semitism in Radom. Source: Joe Rubinstein.

Neighbor Turns on Neighbor

15. Author Note: Joe described Mr. Nagel as a politically astute and brilliant man. He openly shared his opinions with Joe while they worked. Specific details of their conversations have been supplemented based on Author's research.

Nowhere to Hide

16. Author Note: Joe huddled with his family under the kitchen table during the assault of Poland. Other details were supplemented based on Author's research.

The Dark Surge

17. Author Note: Details of where Joe was when the Germans invaded and the newspaper photo described were supplemented based on Author's research. Joe said the invasion happened so suddenly, the Nazis were everywhere in his town. Source: Joe Rubinstein.

Part Two:

18. Gitta Sereny, *Into That Darkness: An Examination of Conscience,* (New York: Vintage Books, 1983).

19. Source: United States Holocaust Memorial Museum, Washington, D.C. "Ohrdruf," *Holocaust Encyclopedia.* Last updated: June 20, 2014. Last accessed September 7, 2014. http://www.ushmm.org/wlc/en/article.php? ModuleId=10006131. * Selected excerpts were used and does not include the entire article.

The Truck

20. Author Note: Minor conversation details have been enhanced. Joe's words regarding the teenager's threats to get off the truck are as Joe described. Source: Joe Rubinstein.

21. Author Note: Joe said they spent the first day on the truck collecting more and more men. He believes the truck left Radom, because they eventually stopped outside unfamiliar buildings where they were left on the truck all night. Since the exact date Joe was taken remains unknown, there is confusion about how long it took for him to arrive at Auschwitz. Joe's best recollection is that he was on the truck for two days and one night, then at several smaller camps for a few months and finally he was taken to Auschwitz.

Joe said he was taken from his home about two weeks after the ghetto gates were closed, which occurred on April 7, 1941. Ten months later, two Nazi raids on the ghetto took place, in February 1942 and on April 28, 1942. We know by Joe's tattoo number that he arrived at Auschwitz with a group of about 606 other men from Radom on April 30, 1942, which I believe was likely the result of the April 28th raid. If Joe was taken shortly after the ghetto gates closed in 1941, it is unclear how he would have arrived with the others from Radom to Auschwitz on April 30, 1942. Had Joe been housed at smaller camps and eventually brought to Auschwitz the same day as the others from Radom?

My suspicion is that Joe may be confusing the time he says he went from "camp to camp" (which he believes happened before he went to Auschwitz) with the time several years later, after he left Auschwitz, when we know he was taken to many smaller camps by truck. But this is speculation on my part. Several times, throughout the course of researching this story, when I thought Joe must be confused, his accounts have later proved accurate in every instance.

The recorded temperature on April 28, 1942, in Poland was a low of 33 degrees F. (1.1 Celsius).

The Cold Unknown

22. Author Note: The events in this chapter are as Joe described. Source: Joe Rubinstein.

Toward the Dark

23. Author Note: Joe described the train as being so crowded that there was barely room to stand and that people cried out for their loved ones, cried out in prayer, and cried out in agony. The people surrounding Joe in line and those on the train are a compilation of Joe's broader description of his ordeal on the train to Auschwitz. They were never given any

food, and only once during their ordeal were they given any water. Minor details such as Joe hitting his head against the man next to him are representative of his experiences while on board.
Source: Joe Rubinstein.

The Arrival

24. Author Note: Joe said he had never heard of Auschwitz until the day he arrived there. He believes they arrived by train late in the afternoon. Inmates and soldiers are compilations of Joe's broader descriptions. Source Joe Rubinstein.

25. Source: Yad Vashem, "The Auschwitz Album," *The Holocaust Martyrs' and Heroes' Remembrance Authority.*
http://www.yadvashem.org/yv/en/exhibitions/album_auschwitz/ausch witz.asp.

Marked for Life

26. Author Note: Details of how Joe was shaved, sprayed with disinfectant, tattooed and given ill-fitting clothes are as Joe described. Individual inmates and guards are representative of his broader descriptions of those around him upon his arrival at Auschwitz. Source: Joe Rubinstein.

Source: Excerpts: "Tattoos and Numbers: The System of Identifying Prisoners at Auschwitz," *Holocaust Encyclopedia,* United States Holocaust Memorial Museum, Washington, D.C. Last accessed: September 5, 2014. http://www.ushmm.org/wlc/en/article.php? ModuleId=10007056.

28. Source: Danuta Czech, *Auschwitz Chronicle 1939-1945: From the Archives of the Auschwitz Memorial and the German Federal Archives,* p. 161. An Owl Book. (New York: Henry Holt and Company, 1989/1990).

29. Source: Danuta Czech, *Auschwitz Chronicle 1939-1945: From the Archives of the Auschwitz Memorial and the German Federal Archives,* p. 161. An Owl Book. (New York: Henry Holt and Company, 1989/1990).

Sustenance of the Starved

30. Author Note: Individual inmates and guards are representative of Joe's broader descriptions of those around him in his early days at Auschwitz. The one day here is representative of the many Joe spent at Auschwitz. Source: Joe Rubinstein.

31. Author Note: Joe was housed at Birkenau, one of the three camps of the Auschwitz complex. Source: Joe Rubinstein.

32. Source: Danuta Czech, *Auschwitz Chronicle 1939-1945: From the Archives of the Auschwitz Memorial and the German Federal Archives*, p. 161. An Owl Book. (New York: Henry Holt and Company, 1989/1990).

Day 2

33. Author Note: Individual inmates and guards are representative of Joe's broader descriptions of those around him at Auschwitz. The one day portrayed here is representative of his many days at Auschwitz. Source: Joe Rubinstein.

34. Source: Danuta Czech, *Auschwitz Chronicle 1939-1945: From the Archives of the Auschwitz Memorial and the German Federal Archives*, p. 162. An Owl Book. (New York: Henry Holt and Company, 1989/1990).

And Still They Come

35. Author Note: People surrounding Joe in line are representative of Joe's broader description of his ordeal at Auschwitz. Source: Joe Rubinstein.

36. Author Note: Children were often separated from the parents and that the outwardly religious Jewish men were the ones most despised by the SS and often the ones first to be brutalized and/or killed. Source: Joe Rubinstein.

A Day in the Life

37. Author Note: The one day portrayed here is representative of his many days at Auschwitz, as were the inmates eating with Joe. Joe said he saw people commit suicide by "touching the wire" nearly every day. Joe talked extensively about the vast number of different languages spoken by the inmates at Auschwitz. Source: Joe Rubinstein.

38. Source: Excerpt: Walter Laqueur, "Foreword," Danuta Czech, *Auschwitz Chronicle 1939-1945: From the Archives of the Auschwitz Memorial and the German Federal Archives*, p. xvi. An Owl Book. (New York: Henry Holt and Company, 1989/1990).

A Different Kind of Army

39. Author Note: The events in this chapter are as Joe described. Source: Joe Rubinstein.

Blisters

40. Author Note: The events in this chapter are as Joe described. Source: Joe Rubinstein.

The Icy Blanket

41. Author Note: Occasionally some of the inmates were given shovels to clear the Auschwitz grounds of snow. Those with shovels would scoop the snow into Joe's and other inmates' shirts to be transported. On the days they were not given shovels, inmates used their hands to scoop it into their shirts. Source: Joe Rubinstein.

Hallways of the Dead

42. Author Note: The events in this chapter are as Joe described. Source: Joe Rubinstein.

A Question Repeated

43. Author Note: Joe never found anyone he knew from Radom at Auschwitz. Source: Joe Rubinstein.

Swallowing Hell

44. Author Note: Descriptions of individual corpses and the insects around them have been enhanced. The one day here was representative of the many days Joe spent moving the bodies of the dead. Source: Joe Rubinstein.

45. After the poison gas had dissipated, prisoner work units, called sonderkommandos, were sent into the gas chambers, with pliers and scissors in hand and forced to scour the dead to remove their jewelry, yank out any gold teeth, and cut off long hair, all to be sent back to Germany. Sonnderkommandos were housed together away from the other inmates and were routinely killed after a few months on the job. Source: Shields, Jacqueline. "Concentration Camps, The Sonderkommando." *Jewish Virtual Library*. Last accessed: September 3, 2014. https://www.jewishvirtuallibrary.org/jsource/Holocaust/Sonderkommando.html.

46. Author Note: I believe Joe moved the bodies to pits outside one of the converted cottages (gas chambers). Joe recalls the corpses in the massive pits being sprayed with chemicals from large trucks, then covered with dirt by large bulldozers, but not burned. Thus, it is likely that Joe was no longer on the labor crews moving the bodies when the burning of the bodies in open pits began in late summer 1942. Joe said his job was confined to moving the bodies and did not involve removing victims' teeth and hair. He was housed with the general population.

47. Source: John C. Zimmerman, "How Reliable Are the Höss Memoirs?" *Holocaust, Holocaust Denial: Demographics, Testimonies and Ideologies.* http://www.holocaust-history.org/auschwitz/hoess-memoirs/.

The Green Grass of Radom

48. Author Note: Joe talked extensively about his love of watching his father's horses graze near their barn. Reports of inmates having eaten the grass was described by other inmates at Auschwitz, but never by Joe.

49. Irene Safran. Personal account (May 1978). United States Holocaust Memorial Museum. *At Auschwitz.* http://www.ushmm.org/remember/the-holocaust-survivors-and-victims-resource-center/benjamin-and-vladka-meed-registry-of-holocaust-survivors/behind-every-name-a-story/irene-safran/irene-safran-at-auschwitz, last accessed August 21, 2014.

Trains in the Night

50. Author Note: Joe took food to his neighbor who worked in the Radom rail yard. The details of Joe's thoughts of hearing trains in the night have been enhanced.

For a Crime I Didn't Commit

51. Author Note: The events in this chapter are as Joe described. The physical descriptions of inmates and guards have been enhanced. Source: Joe Rubinstein.

The Missing Half

52. Author Note: The individual capo is a compilation of Joe's broader description of supervising capos. The specific experiences represented in this chapter of Joe thinking about his twin are representative of his many thoughts about his brother and other siblings.

A Precious Gift of Warmth

53. Author Note: The events in this chapter are as Joe described. Source: Joe Rubinstein.

Shattered

54. Author Note: Joe believes the man from Radom bearing the terrible news of the fate of his family may have known his mother. The details of what the man witnessed during the raid on Radom has been enhanced. We do not know the exact date that Joe met the man, but believe it was sometime in the latter part of 1942.
Source: Joe Rubinstein.

Night

55. Author Note: Joe said that the nights at Auschwitz were the most difficult times for him, when he had time to think back on all the terrible things he had seen. Source: Joe Rubinstein.

An Experienced Prisoner

56. Author Note: The events in this chapter are as Joe described. Source: Joe Rubinstein.

For the Sport of It

57. Author Note: Joe described his utter despair and horror at having to witness, on several occasions, children being lined up and clubbed to death with clubs. Individual descriptions of the children, soldiers, and their actions have been enhanced. Source: Joe Rubinstein.

Stars of Hope

58. Author Note: The one night described here is a representation of the many nights Joe spent at Auschwitz with the details enhanced. Source: Joe Rubinstein.

One Stroke for Life

59. Author Note: The events in this chapter are as Joe described. Source: Joe Rubinstein.

Beyond the Gates

60. Author Note: The events in this chapter are as Joe described. Source: Joe Rubinstein.

61. "The idea of exterminating them by labor is the best." Joseph Goebbels, Berlin 1942. *Joseph Goebbels' Diaries: Excerpts, 1942-42. The Nizkor Project.* http://www.nizkor.org/hweb/people/g/goebbels-joseph/goebbels-1948-excerpts-01.html.

62. Author Note: After a few days of walking several miles to the coal mine and back in the wooden clogs, Joe asked for and received a pair of leather shoes. It is unclear if his designation as "Political Prisoner" had any influence in him being allowed to get different shoes. Source: Joe Rubinstein.

Crumbling Stone

63. Author Note: The events in this chapter are as Joe described. Source: Joe Rubinstein.

64. Author Note: Joe does not know the full name of his abuser, but believes his first name was Bill. Source: Joe Rubinstein.

65. Author Note: Joe lived at the Jawischowitz (Sub-Camp Auschwitz) while working at the Brzeszcze Coal Mine. Source: Joe Rubinstein.

A Good Shine

66. Author Note: The physical description of the German officer has been enhanced as were the details of how Joe first met the man. The officer's words were as Joe described. Source: Joe Rubinstein.

A Chance at Freedom

67. Author Note: The physical description of the miner has been enhanced. His offer of freedom was as Joe described. Source: Joe Rubinstein.

Pierre

68. Author Note: Joe said when they saw Allied planes, he would say to himself, "Drop the bombs! Drop the bombs." It is unclear if Pierre ever discussed seeing the Allied planes with Joe. Joe said once, when he had a bad headache, Pierre put a cold cloth over his head and that they did on occasion play checkers and cards with discarded materials. Joe woke one day, feeling fine, but everyone around him exclaimed that his skin was very yellow. He was sent to the camp hospital. Source: Joe Rubinstein.

Sickness and Salvation

69. Author Note: The events in this chapter of Joe's illness, the Polish doctor telling him that he would never have to go back to the mines and his staying on as the doctor's assistant are as Joe described. The man with the injured leg is a compilation of patients that the doctor would try to help despite the order not to do so. Source: Joe Rubinstein.

On the Move

70. Author Note: The description of the soldiers has been enhanced. The "taking" of Joe described in this chapter is representative of the many times after Joe left Auschwitz that he was taken by truck to various concentration camps and sub camps. Source: Joe Rubinstein.

Laja's Tears

71. Author Note: Joe said that when he thinks about his sister what he mostly remembers is her tears. His thoughts about seeing the tears of other children are representative of the many children Joe saw while at Auschwitz. Source: Joe Rubinstein.

An Inattentive Teacher

72. Author Note: The events in this chapter are as Joe described. Source: Joe Rubinstein.

Far from Home

73. Author Note: The description of the guards and the stopping of the truck is representative of the many times Joe traveled by truck. The details have been enhanced. The descriptions of the underground camp and his recollections of his father lifting him on his draft horse are as Joe described. Source: Joe Rubinstein.

74. Author Note: We are uncertain in which underground bunker complex Joe was held. It is possible it was Mittelbau-Dora, where a group from Buchenwald Concentration Camp were taken. We believe the timing fits, but we have no confirmation of the location, only that he worked at such a site. See Additional Research Notes.

And Then It Was Over

75. Author Note: The events in this chapter are as Joe described. After leaving the Theresienstadt Concentration Camp he walked with his two friends for "a while." They eventually crossed a bridge and entered a nearby town. The exact location is unknown. Source: Joe Rubinstein.

76. Author Note: While still at Theresienstadt, Joe was told that the camp's SS commandant, Karl Rahm, had been given the order to kill all the inmates as the war grew to an end, but that he ignored the order. In researching this story, the author could find no specific validation of that report. However, similar orders were reported to have been given to other concentration camp commandants, including Buchenwald's Hermann Pister.

From Ashes to Alive

77. Author Note: We believe the clothing shop was in Litoměřice, but it may have been another village near the Theresienstadt Concentration/Ghetto Camp. The events in this chapter are as Joe described. Source: Joe Rubinstein.

Part Three

Which Way?

78. Author Note: The events in this chapter are as Joe described. Source: Joe Rubinstein.

Picking Up the Pieces

79. Author Note: The events in this chapter are as Joe described. Source: Joe Rubinstein.

Beyond Words

80. Author Note: In his post-war search for his family, Joe was told repeatedly told by the authorities that his family was believed to have been killed at Treblinka following the liquidation of the Radom ghetto. Source: Joe Rubinstein.

81. Source: "Treblinka Death Camp History," Holocaust Education & Archive Research Team, *Holocaust Research Project.* http://www.holocaustresearchproject.org/ar/treblinka.html.

Dancing It Away

82. Author Note: The events in this chapter are as Joe described. Source: Joe Rubinstein.

A Night That Changed a Life

83. Author Note: The people and events in this chapter are as Joe described. His conversation with Irene's family, during their first dinner together, is a combination of many such meals. Source: Joe Rubinstein.

From Despair to Love

84. Author Note: The people and events in this chapter are as Joe described. His thoughts as he regarded his reflection in the mirror have been enhanced. Source: Joe Rubinstein.

85. **Author Note:** Before he wed, Joe was able to locate and visit his father's sister, Geitel, and her husband, Bernard Ackerman, who resided in Stuttgart, Germany, to secure their blessing for his marriage. It is unclear how his aunt and uncle survived the war. They had no remaining photos of Joe's family. After meeting Irene, Geitel and Bernard gave their blessing to the marriage.

Touché

86. **Author Note:** The events in this chapter are as Joe described. Joe believed the seller of the car was a former Nazi general. Author had no means to verify this information. Source: Joe Rubinstein.

Anywhere But Germany

87. The events of this chapter are as Joe described. Source: Joe Rubinstein.

Changing Tides

88. **Author Note:** Joe and Irene's wait at the camp for "displaced persons," their son spilling out of his crib with the motion of the ship, and Joe's reunion with the doctor from the hospital were as Joe described. Source: Joe Rubinstein.

89. **Author Note:** Documentation of the ship manifest show Joe, Irene, and their son departed Wentorf, Germany, on September 29, 1950, for the USA via "Grohn Embarkation Staging Centre." Joe and Irene thought that it was closer to November. The September date may have been when they were processed at Grohn. See Additional Research Notes.

Out of Darkness

90. Author Note: Their kissing the American soil and their walk to see Times Square the first day they arrived was as Joe and Irene described. Source: Joe Rubinstein.

For Just One Picture

91. Author Note: Joe does not have even one photo of his childhood family. Source: Joe Rubinstein.

Nightmares and Dreams

92. Author Note: The events in this chapter are as Joe described. Source: Joe Rubinstein.

The First Light of Dawn

93. Author Note: Joe has never been back to Radom since the day he was taken by the Nazis. He is torn between being eager to do so and unwilling to consider it. Source: Joe Rubinstein.

Epilogue – Threads of Gold

94. Author Note: The events in this chapter are as Joe described. Source: Joe Rubinstein.

95. Author Note: The details regarding Joe's employment experiences and history are as Joe described. Source: Joe Rubinstein.

Follow-Up Note from the Author

It has been one of the greatest honors and blessings of my life to write the story of this incredible man who somehow found the strength, time after time, to go on, not as merely a survivor, but as someone who thrived. Joe had a choice when he walked out of that concentration camp nearly seventy years ago—a choice to succumb to his sorrow or to move forward with joy. He chose joy and, thankfully, joy found him. He found the love of his life, and his desire to provide for his new family led him to become one of the most sought-after shoe designers in the world.

When Joe first shared his story with me, he said he wanted to get it all out, from "A to Z." He began with such clarity that I was reminded of the early scene in James Cameron's 1997 version of the *Titanic* when the elderly "Rose" could still describe the smell of the fresh paint. When Joe began to tell his story, in essence, this is how he began: "It was before dawn. I was sound asleep. There was a knock at the door. I went to open it wearing only a T-shirt and pajama bottoms. Two German soldiers were there, ordering me to come with them. Why? I hadn't done anything wrong. I wanted to change my clothes, but they told me I had everything I needed. Everything I need? I walked out in my bare feet. I didn't even get to say goodbye to my mother. They put me on a truck with several others. It was frigid. They drove us around, collecting more people. Some of the men died."

And then a shadow came over Joe and his next words were a quick summary: "And then I was taken to Auschwitz and I worked in a coal mine. Then after the war, I moved to New York." All the details were gone, and I knew I was witnessing how Joe had survived and why he was, and still is, known as "Smiling Joe." He had skipped the details in his mind. During the course of our many interviews, Joe would often say, "That's all there is," and every time he said it, I knew more was coming. I believe there is still much more that will forever remain unspoken.

Some memories may still be too painful for him to want to remember. Some of what Joe has told me, I do not have the ability to put into words, for much of what he experienced is simply beyond words.

When I began writing about Joe's life, I had A and Z, but very little in between. To get the rest caused Joe tremendous heartbreak and pain in reliving what he has spent a lifetime trying to forget.

This story, during the time he was held captive, is as I say often in the story ... the essence of what was taken—every last bit of Joe. And yet, somehow, when Joe was liberated, he made a choice to put it behind him enough to rebuild from the ashes of his life. What he did throughout his imprisonment, and the way he moved forward afterwards, was, and is, a testament to the human spirit, to Joe, and to his faith. Joe is, without question, one of the kindest and most joy-filled people I have ever known, which is even more remarkable given what he endured.

Throughout his ordeal during WWII, Joe never stopped believing that God was present with him. He believes it still.

Long before I ever met Joe, I visited the United States Holocaust Memorial Museum in Washington, D.C., and, like so many others, was profoundly affected by what I experienced there. I was especially shaken by the sight of thousands of shoes of the Holocaust victims, many of them the small shoes of infants and children, all piled high— like the bodies of those Joe helped throw into the pits at Auschwitz. While writing this book, I thought often of those shoes. Perhaps it was because I was repeatedly struck by the importance of shoes throughout Joe's life, including the wooden clogs of Holland and the fear Joe had that the blisters caused by them might cost him his life. As I wrote, I envisioned the people who once wore those museum shoes, of them slipping those shoes off, trusting that they would find them again after they had showered away the stench of the horrific train ride. It's hard to fathom that something as tangible as shoes could survive when the precious lives they held did not.

Under the direction of Mr. Nagel, Joe made many shoes and boots in the days before the war. I wonder now, could any of the shoes he so lovingly stitched together be in that pile? Could the bodies of the people he pushed in his cart have worn any of those same shoes? Could any of them be those of Joe's siblings or his mother? A mother who sacrificed so much to provide them for her children. I wonder. It is heartbreaking, such wonderings.

The first date I am certain of is April 30, 1942. On that date, it is recorded that 606 prisoners arrived from Radom, Poland, to Auschwitz and were given the numbers in the range corresponding to Joe's: 34207.

Other dates are less certain. There is even some confusion on the year in which Joe was born. He grew up believing it was 1922. His birth certificate, which Joe was able to secure after the war, shows 1920, a date that he now believes is accurate.

We believe that Joe was working under the direction of the Nazis, digging trenches in approximately August 1940. We have documents from the Buchenwald Concentration Camp showing that he arrived from Auschwitz and was assigned number 117.66. Another document shows that Joe was transported from Buchenwald on January 22, 1945, and arrived at the Ohrdruf Concentration Camp on January 24, 1945. Another undated document shows that later he was a survivor of the Theresienstadt Concentration/Ghetto Camp. All these documents validate Joe's recollections of the places he was held.

In between, there are missing pieces of the many smaller camps and sub-camps where Joe said he was imprisoned. I have done my best to reconstruct the puzzle of his time since the invasion of Poland in 1939, using the pieces that I have ... a puzzle that will never be complete, not since the day that a knock at his door changed everything. I have fought the urge to fill in every gap, every detail.

While we don't know the exact date he was taken from his family, what we do know is that he was taken.

Nancy Sprowell Geise—August 5, 2014

Timeline

February 24, 1910	**Ruwin and Reska**	Joe's parents marry in Radom, Poland. Ruwin Rubinsztejn (21), from Radom, son of Chaim Rubinsztejn and Chaja Fyrman, marries Reska Kierszenblat (18) from Tomaszow, daughter of Mendel Kierszenblat and Ruchla Wajcman. *
Date Unknown	**Solomon**	Joe's eldest brother, birthdate unknown, dies in childhood before Joe was born.
May 30, 1912	**Dawid Anszel**	Joe's brother, born in Radom.
September 16, 1920	**Chaim**	Joe's identical twin brother, born in Radom.
September 16, 1920	**Icek Jakub Rubinsztejn**	"Joe" born in Radom (During the war Joe's name was spelled "Juzek Rubinsztein," after the war "Jozef 'Joe' Rubinstein," in America: Joseph "Joe" Rubinstein). **
August 26, 1923	**Abram**	Joe's brother, born in Radom.
March 5, 1925	**Irene Gusenda**	Joe's future wife, born in Lallaing, France.
March 15, 1926	**Laja**	Joe's sister, born in Radom.
December 1926*	**Ruwin Rubinsztejn**	Joe's father passes away. (Joe believes his father died in December. The exact year is unknown.)

August 23, 1939	Molotov–Ribbentrop Pact is signed between Germany and the Soviet Union, allowing Germany to invade Poland without interference and agreeing to later divide and annex Poland between them.
September 1, 1939	Germany invades Poland.
September 3, 1939	Britain and France declare war on Germany.
September 8, 1939	Nazi march on Radom.
September 17, 1939	The Soviet Union invades eastern Poland.
September 27, 1939	Warsaw (Poland's capital) surrenders to the Germans.***
October 1939	Germany annexes former Polish territories. Poland is divided between the Germans and the Soviets.
September 1940	Joe and his brother Abram are sent to a forced labor camp to dig trenches in Cieszanów, Poland. Joe returns to Radom in the fall after getting ill.
April 7, 1941	Radom Ghetto gates are closed, imprisoning all area Jews.
December 7, 1941	Japan attacks Pearl Harbor.
December 8, 1941	United States declares war on Japan.
December 11, 1941	Germany and Italy declare war on the United States.
December 13, 1941	Hungary and Bulgaria declare war on the United States.
Date Unknown	Between April 7, 1941 – April 30, 1942, Joe is taken from his home by the Nazis. (See page 249.)
April 28, 1942	Nazis conduct a major raid on the Radom Ghetto where many men are taken from their homes and sent to Auschwitz.
April 30, 1942	Joe arrives at Auschwitz-Birkenau (Poland), is assigned #34207.

August 5, 1942 The small ghetto in Radom, the Glinice district, is "liquidated."

August 6–17, 1942 The larger ghetto in Radom in the Śródmieście district is "liquidated."

Date Unknown Joe is transferred to Jawischowitz sub-camp and the Brzeszcze Coal Mine (under Auschwitz authority) where he works as a coal miner. He later works as a doctor's assistant in a hospital treating coal miners.

October 10, 1944 Joe is treated at a hospital for a gastrointestinal illness.

June, 1944 Joe is transported from the Auschwitz controlled area to the Buchenwald concentration camp in Germany, is assigned #117.666, and works at a rock quarry there.

January 22, 1945 Joe leaves Buchenwald on "Transport S III."

January 24, 1945 Joe arrives at the Ohrdruf concentration camp, Germany (under Buchenwald authority).

Date Unknown Joe is sent to a heavily fortified, underground artillery, camp, possibly Dora-Mittelbau (Dora-Nordhausen or Nordhausen).

April 6-21, 1945 Joe arrives at Theresienstadt concentration/ghetto camp. in Czechoslovakia. (Estimated date.)

May 5 -6, 1945 SS Commandant Rahm and the rest of the SS abandon the Theresienstadt concentration/ghetto camp.

May 6, 1945 Joe walks out of the Theresienstadt concentration/ghetto camp to freedom. (Estimated date.)

May 9, 1945 Soviet troops take control of the Theresienstadt concentration/ghetto camp.

May 1945 Joe moves to Duisburg-Hamborn, Germany where he meets his future wife.

September 27, 1947 Joe and Irene marry in Duisburg-Hamborn.

May 27, 1949 Joe and Irene's son Chaim-Moni is born.

September 26, 1950 Joe, Irene, and their son leave Germany for America.

1965   **Seven Jews reside in Radom, Poland.** * * * *

* Joe believed his mother was from Radom. Her marriage certificate lists Tomaszow, Poland. It is unclear if that was her place of birth or where she was living at the time of her marriage. Her parents lived in Radom when Joe was growing up.

* * Throughout his life, Joe believed his birthday to be October 15, 1922. All documents from his time in the various concentration camps, including his Buchenwald information form, his resettlement processing center form in Wentforf for displaced persons, and the ship manifest, lists his birthdate as either October 15, 1922 or October 15, 1920. After the war, Joe obtained a copy of his birth certificate from Radom (one that had likely been re-copied by hand) stating that his birthday (and that of his twin Chaim) was actually two years earlier. It is uncertain which date is accurate. The September 16, 1920 birthdate is the one that Joe has since used. If Joe was born in 1922 instead of 1920, it would explain why he repeatedly talked about being a teenager when he was taken; i.e., he would have been 19 when he arrived at Auschwitz on April 30, 1942, rather than 21, the age he would have been if the September 1920 date was accurate. Family birth certificates sent from Radom show that Joe had another sibling, born May 3, 1917, named Szyja. Joe does not know anything about this sibling. Either the information on the re-copied birth certificate was inaccurate, or it is possible this was another of Joe's siblings that died before he was born (perhaps even shortly after birth). We do not have a birth certificate of the eldest son Solomon who passed away before Joe was born.

* * * The Polish resistance against the Nazis was one of the largest underground movements in Europe, with reportedly hundreds of thousands of Polish Gentiles aiding the Jews, notably during the time of the occupation of Warsaw. Despite their military defeat, the Polish government never surrendered, establishing a Polish government-in-exile based in London in 1940.

* * * * According to the Radom Regional Commission, 380,000 Jews from the entire Radom District lost their lives during the German occupation. A few hundred Jews settled in Radom for a short time after World War II, but soon left due to the hostility of the Polish population. By 1965, only seven Jews resided there. [1,2]

Timeline Information Sources:

1. Stefan Krakowski. *Encyclopaedia Judaica.* © 2008 The Gale Group. Last accessed: September 10, 2014.

2. Pinkas Halpern, index; A. Rutkowksi, in: BŻIH, 15–16 (1955), 75–182; 17–18 (1956), 106–8; Sefer Milḥamot ha-Getta'ot (19542), index; Sefer Radom (1961), a memorial book published in Hebrew and Yiddish.

Additional Research Notes

Below is more information related to Joe's story, including concentration camps, ships transporting displaced persons, camps for displaced persons, camp commandants/other Nazi officials and their fate, and famous shoe companies.

1. Concentration Camps

A. Auschwitz/Birkenau, Poland (Concentration Camp)

Author's Note: Joe arrived at Auschwitz on April 30, 1942 and was housed at its sister camp, Birkenau, or "Auschwitz II," where two days a week he was forced to move the bodies of the dead from the gas chamber to open pits. He was also required to do daily calisthenics and work in many other areas around the camp, including snow removal on the massive grounds. Joe was eventually assigned to a slave labor crew working in a nearby coal mine. For a short while, the inmate miners were forced to walk several miles each day to the coal mine and back. When Joe was finally moved from Birkenau to a camp near the coal mine, he left Auschwitz for the last time, but the mining camp remained under the authority of Auschwitz. Joe permanently lost the hearing in one ear from the repeated explosions of dynamite. Documents provided by the United States Holocaust Memorial Museum in Washington, D.C., show that in June 1944, Joe (Juzek Rubinsztein) was sent from the Auschwitz complex (we believe from the Jawischowitz Sub-camp/Brzeszcze Coal Mine) to Buchenwald, Germany. His official number while at Auschwitz was 34207. At Buchenwald, his number was 117.666. [1,2]

The **Auschwitz** Concentration Camp, located thirty-seven miles west of Krakow, near the Polish city of Oswiecim, was in an area annexed by Nazi Germany in 1939 after its invasion of Poland. Auschwitz was the largest of all the concentration camps and included three main camps, all of which used prisoners as forced labor: Auschwitz I opened in May 1940; Auschwitz II (also called Auschwitz-Birkenau) in early 1942; and Auschwitz III (also called Auschwitz-Monowitz) in October 1942.

The Auschwitz-Birkenau killing center was central to the Nazi plan of killing all the Jews of Europe. During the summer and autumn of 1941, Zyklon B gas was introduced as a mechanism for large-scale killing. In September of that year, the SS first tested Zyklon B at Auschwitz as an instrument of mass murder; eventually converting two farmhouses near Birkenau to use as gas chambers. The first "Provisional" gas chamber was operational in January 1942 and later dismantled. Provisional gas chamber II operated from June 1942 through the fall of 1944. Between March and June 1943, after the SS determined that larger facilities would be needed for the gassing of the masses, construction began on four large crematoriums, each containing a disrobing area, a large gas chamber, and crematorium ovens.

The SS staff at Auschwitz-Birkenau conducted "selections" of all new arrivals, choosing only those deemed fit for forced labor. Those deemed "unfit" were immediately sent to the gas chambers, which were disguised as shower installations to mislead the victims. The belongings of those sent to the gas chambers, including the gold fillings of victims and some of the women's hair, were confiscated for shipment back to Germany.

The Soviet Army liberated Auschwitz/Birkenau on January 27, 1945, rescuing 7,000 prisoners, most of whom were ill and dying. The Soviets found several hundred corpses believed to have been executed by the SS as the Soviet Army advanced. Soviet troops also discovered the ruins of the crematoriums; pits with the ashes of human beings; and some documents that were hidden by inmates who risked their lives during the last weeks before the liberation. It is estimated that a minimum of 1.3 million people were sent to the Auschwitz complex between 1940 and 1945. Of these, authorities estimated that 1.1 million were murdered. [3, 4]

Auschwitz/Birkenau Information Sources:

1. Danuta Czech. *Auschwitz Chronicle 1939-1945. From the Archives of the Auschwitz Memorial and the German Federal Archives.* New York: H. Holt (1990) p. 161. "606 prisoners sent by the Sipo and SD from Radom receive Nos. 33996-34601"

2. Joe Rubinstein. *Face-to-face interviews with Author Nancy Sprowell Geise*, November 2012 – August 2014

3. Documents for Juzek Rubinsztein: *Copy of Doc. No. 34646016#1 (/Image vorhanden/_R/R0747/00604@0.1 in conformity with the ITS Archives)*

4. United States Memorial Holocaust Museum. *Holocaust Encyclopedia. Auschwitz.*
http://www.ushmm.org/wlc/en/article.php?ModuleId=10005189, last accessed August 12, 2014

B. Buchenwald, Germany

Author's Note: Documents provided by The United States Holocaust Museum in Washington, D.C., show Joe arrived at Buchenwald from Auschwitz in June 1944 (classified as a "political prisoner") and assigned #117.666. He was transported out January 22, 1945, on "Transport S III," arriving at the Ohrdruf Concentration Camp on January 24, 1945. While at Buchenwald, Joe worked at a stone quarry. He said the dust laden air was worse to breathe than the air in the coal mine. [1, 2, 3, 4, 5]

Buchenwald was one of the largest concentration camps established within the "old" German borders (prior to 1937), about five miles northwest of Weimar, Germany. Buchenwald administered eighty-eight sub-camps across Germany, using the prisoners as forced labor in various construction projects, armaments factories, and stone quarries.

"On April 11, 1945, in expectation of liberation, starved and emaciated prisoners stormed the watchtowers, seizing control of the camp. Later that afternoon, U.S. forces entered Buchenwald. Soldiers from the 6th Armored Division, part of the Third Army, found more than 21,000 people in the camp. Exact mortality figures for the Buchenwald site can only be estimated, as camp authorities never registered a significant number of the prisoners. The SS murdered at least 56,000 male prisoners in the Buchenwald camp system." [6]

Buchenwald Information Sources:

1. Joe Rubinstein. *Face-to-face interviews with Author Nancy Sprowell Geise*, November 2012 – August 2014

2. Documents for Juzek Rubinsztein: *(I.T.S. FOTO NO. 007275)*

3. Documents for Juzek Rubinsztein: *File: GCC 2/222-IIC/17 Copy of Doc. No. 34646017#1 (/Image vorhanden/_R/R0747/00603@0.1) in conformity with the ITS Archives*

4. Documents for Juzek Rubinsztein: *Copy of Doc. No. 6973698#1 /RUBIN-RUDN/00209544/0001@1.1.5.3 in conformity with the ITS Archives*

5. Documents for Juzek Rubinsztein: *File: GCC2/181/IB/9 Copy of Doc. No. 34646015#1 (/Image vorhanden/_R/R0747/00605@0.1) in conformity with the ITS Archives*

6. Selected excerpts from: United States Memorial Holocaust Museum. *Holocaust Encyclopedia. Buchenwald.* http://www.ushmm.org/wlc/en/article.php?ModuleId=10005198, last accessed September 4, 2014

C. Cieszanów, Poland (Labor Camp)

Author's Note: Cieszanów, Poland, is the location where we believe Joe and his younger brother Abram worked digging trenches under the brutal commandant Herman Dolp. Joe eventually became very ill, vomiting blood, and was too sick to work. He was sent back to Radom, likely with a group of other ill and injured inmates, after a visit to the camp from Radom Jewish leaders. Abram returned to Radom a few weeks later. [1]

Cieszanów. After the invasion of Poland, German soldiers began indiscriminate and brutal treatment of the Jews, forcing them into labor. Food rations were meager. To negotiate a solution, the Judenrat (Jewish council) offered to supply the Germans with a mostly Jewish labor force, if they would agree to better treatment of the workers and to supply them with food.

In August 1940, around 2,000 Jews were deported to work camps in the Lublin district, engaged in the construction of a series of anti-tank ditches and fortifications between German and Soviet occupied Poland. Hundreds of teenagers and men from the Radom area were sent to forced labor camps near the border of the Soviet Union, including Cieszanów, where little preparations had been made regarding the workers' living conditions. Laborers were housed in wooden barracks with poor sanitation and little food. Food packages sent by relatives in Radom and other Jewish communities kept many of the workers from starvation.

An official delegation of the Radom Jewish community visited the camp and were horrified by the conditions. They were able to negotiate the release of many of the ill. Once back in Radom, the delegation was able to eventually help secure the release of all the other men by year's end. Many returned home gravely ill and/or with permanent injuries.

One thousand of the camp's laborers were sent to a similar camp in Stary Dzików. The Cieszanów camp was closed in November 1940, but re-opened in the spring of 1941.

At the labor camp in Cieszanów, Jewish laborers would sing bitterly in Yiddish:

Work, brothers, work fast. If you don't, they'll lash your hide. Not many of us will manage to last – Before long we'll all have died. [2, 3, 4, 5]

Cieszanów Information Sources:

1. Joe Rubinstein. *Face-to-face interviews with Author Nancy Sprowell Geise*, November 2012 – August 2014

2. Holocaust Education and Research Archive team. "Radom." *Holocaust Research Project* http://www.holocaustresearchproject.org/ghettos/radom.html

3. Lipson, Alfred. *The book of Radom; The story of a Jewish community in Poland destroyed by the Nazis*. Translation of Sefer Radom. Editors: Y. Perlow: Alfred Lipson, Tel Aviv. 1961

4. Virtual Shtetl. *History – Jewish Community before 1989-Cieszanów.*
http://www.sztetl.org.pl/en/article/cieszanow/5,history/

5. JewishGen, Inc. *Years of Disaster Under Nazi Rule. Translation of Sefer Radom (The book of Radom: The story of a Jewish community in Poland Destroyed by the Nazis).* Editors: Y. Perlow; [English section]: Alfred Lipson, Tel Aviv 1961. Original book can be found online at the NY Public Library site: Radom (1961a)
http://www.jewishgen.org/yizkor/radom/rade039.html

D. Dora-Mittleblau, Germany (Concentration Camp) and Other Possible Location Sites

Author's Note: I believe it is possible that Joe was among a group of inmates sent from Buchenwald to the underground complex at Dora-Mittelbau. At some point, Joe was housed in an underground bunker compound where large missiles were either stored or produced (he saw them being loaded onto trucks). The site was highly fortified. It is possible, however, that instead he was at a different site –possibly the underground factories that were code named Richard I and Richard II, which were begun in the spring of 1944 near Terezin.

Another possible location where Joe was housed was in the underground complexes near the Ohrdruf Concentration Camp. (The United States Holocaust Museum has documentation of Joe being at Ohrdruf.) Southeast of the nearby city of Gotha, these sites had code names such as Siegfried, Olga, Burg, and Jasmin. This site is possible, as the physical description of the complex matches very closely to what Joe reported, "It was a place of manmade bunkers, so fortified that I kept thinking that maybe Hitler was hiding there." Interestingly, there is speculation that the bunker complex near Ohrdruf was built as a backup location to Berlin for Hitler to hide. [1]

The Dora-Mittelbau (Dora-Nordhausen or Nordhausen) camp, in central Germany, was originally a sub-camp of Buchenwald, becoming its own independent concentration camp in 1944, consisting of many smaller sub-camps. With the onslaught of Allied bombing raids, the Nazis began using Buchenwald prisoners to dig massive tunnels into the mountains as part of a large underground industrial complex, including building the facilities used for the development of the production of V-2 missiles along with other experimental weapons, stored in the underground facilities and bombproof shafts. The Dora-Mittelbau (Dora-Nordhausen or Nordhausen) camp eventually became its own camp, with authority over several smaller sub-camps. Deprived of daylight and fresh air, and exposed to unstable tunnels, mortality rates were higher than many other concentration camps. Inmates who became ill or too weak to work were sent to Auschwitz-Birkenau or Mauthausen to be killed. In 1944, a compound to house forced laborers was built. An above ground-level compound to house the laborers was built in 1944 and eventually had an inmate population of at least 12,000.

In early April 1945, the Nazis began to evacuate the camp, with thousands of inmates killed in death marches. In April 1945, American troops liberated the camp, but only a few prisoners remained. (a) General Patton, accompanied by Colonel Robert Allen, reached Ohrdruf in April 1945. Allen wrote the following in his book *Lucky Forward: The History of Patton's 3rd US Army*, published by Vanguard Press, New York, 1947.

"The underground installations were amazing. They were literally subterranean towns. There were four in and around Ohrdruf: one near the horror camp, one under the Schloss, and two west of the town. Others were reported in near-by villages. None were natural caves or mines. All were man-made military installations. The horror camp had provided the labour. An interesting feature of the construction was the absence of any spoil. It had been carefully scattered in hills miles away. The only communication shelter, which is known, is a two floor deep shelter, with the code "AMT 10". [2, 3, 4]

Dora-Mittleblau and Other Possible Location Information Sources:

1. Joe Rubinstein. *Face-to-face interviews with Author Nancy Sprowell Geise*, November 2012 – August 2014

2. United States Holocaust Memorial Museum. *Holocaust Encyclopedia. Dora-Mittelbau.* http://www.ushmm.org/wlc/en/article.php?ModuleId=10005322, last accessed August 12, 2014

3. Terezin Memorial The Natural Cultural Monument. *The Litomerice forced labour camp.* http://www.pamatnik-terezin.cz/en/history-collection-research/historical-overview/the-litomerice-forced-labour-camp?lang=en

4. Missouri University of Science and Technology. *German Underground Structures in WWII*

E. Jawischowitz (Sub-Camp Auschwitz) and the Brzeszcze Coal Mine

Author's Note: We believe this was the Auschwitz sub-camp where Joe lived while working at the mine. The only documentation we have with Joe's name and HKB Jawischowitz is a medical form dated October 10, 1944, when he was seen for a gastrointestinal illness. Other documentation shows Joe having left the Auschwitz complex in June of 1944, so there is confusion as to the exact dates he was seen for this illness, where he was examined, and whether this medical visit was related to the illness that led to his working as an assistant to the coal mine camp doctor. [1]

Jawiszowice, an Auschwitz sub-camp, used to house inmates who worked in the Brzeszcze coal mine; a mine owned at the time by German, Herman Göring Werke. It was the first instance that the Germans put the prisoners from the concentration camps to work underground. In 1942, the number of inmates reached 2,000. The sub-camp's population consisted of Jews from all over Europe, including from Poland, Czechoslovakia, Russia, Yugoslavia, France, Germany and Austria. The prisoners worked in very difficult conditions and, because so many had little or no mining experience, there were frequent accidents. Inmates were subjected to beatings by supervising prisoners and the SS guards, often resulting in death. Attempted suicides by prisoners were common. It is estimated that from October 1942 to December 1944, at least 1,800 of the inmates were deemed unfit for work and sent to the gas chambers of Birkenau.

Some of the civilian workers in the mine, along with the people of Brzeszcze and Jawiszowice, regardless of their own personal risk, helped the inmates, bringing them food, assisting them with their work, and even helping them to escape. (Something Joe experienced firsthand.)

On January 19, 1945, the camp was evacuated, with the SS leading 1,900 inmates on a more than 50 kilometer march to Wodzisław Śląski, executing many of the ill and exhausted along the way. Dozens of those ill inmates were left behind at the camp and cared for by the area citizens. [2,3,4]

Jawischowitz and the Brzeszcze Coal Mine Information Sources:

1. Joe Rubinstein. *Face-to-face interviews with Author Nancy Sprowell Geise*, November 2012 – August 2014

2. Documents for Juzek Rubinsztein: *Copy of Doc. No. 559402#1 (/0124-0323/0321/0210@1.1.2.1) in conformity with the ITS Archives*

3. Documents for Juzek Rubinsztein: *Copy of Doc. No. 839129#1 (/AU000503/163@1.1.2.5) in conformity with the ITS Archives. October 20, 1944*

4. Urząd Gminy W. Brzeszcach. *Route of Remberance. Jawischowitz sub-camp. (2009 – 2014)* http://www.trasapamieci.brzeszcze.pl/home/memorials-and-plaque/jawischowitz-sub-camp/

F. Ohrdruf, Germany (Sub-camp of Buchenwald)

Author's Note: The United States Holocaust Memorial Museum provided documentation of Joe arriving in Ohrdruf on January 24, 1945, after leaving Buchenwald on January 22, 1945. (1) (2)

The Ohrdruf camp, a sub-camp of Buchenwald, was created in 1944 near the town of Gotha, Germany. It served as a forced labor camp to work on a railway leading to a proposed communication center, but that was never completed because of the American troop advance. In early April, the SS forced the majority of camp inmates on a death march to Buchenwald, killing many of those too ill to walk. Ohrdruf was the first Nazi camp liberated by the Fourth Armored Division of the U.S. troops. The atrocities they discovered are well documented, including piles of dead bodies, many covered with lime, others left partially incinerated on pyres.

On April 12, the supreme commander of the Allied Forces in Europe, General Dwight D. Eisenhower, visited the camp with General George S. Patton and General Omar Bradley.

Below are excerpts from United States Holocaust Memorial Museum, Washington, D.C., *Holocaust Encyclopedia. "Ohrdruf."*

"After his visit, Eisenhower cabled General George C. Marshall, the head of the Joint Chiefs of Staff in Washington, describing his trip to Ohrdruf:

"... the most interesting—although horrible—sight that I encountered during the trip was a visit to a German internment camp near Gotha. The things I saw beggar description. While I was touring the camp I encountered three men who had been inmates and by one ruse or another had made their escape. I interviewed them through an interpreter. The visual evidence and the verbal testimony of starvation, cruelty and bestiality were so overpowering as to leave me a bit sick. In one room, where they were piled up twenty or thirty naked men, killed by starvation, George Patton would not even enter. He said that he would get sick if he did so. I made the visit deliberately, in order to be in a position to give first-hand evidence of these things if ever, in the future, there develops a tendency to charge these allegations merely to "propaganda."

"Eisenhower and he wanted the world to know what happened in the concentration camps. On April 19, 1945, he again cabled Marshall with a request to bring members of Congress and journalists to the newly liberated camps so that they could bring the horrible truth about Nazi atrocities to the American public. He wrote:

"We continue to uncover German concentration camps for political prisoners in which conditions of indescribable horror prevail. I have visited one of these myself and I assure you that whatever has been printed on them to date has

been understatement. If you could see any advantage in asking about a dozen leaders of Congress and a dozen prominent editors to make a short visit to this theater in a couple of C-54's, I will arrange to have them conducted to one of these places where the evidence of bestiality and cruelty is so overpowering as to leave no doubt in their minds about the normal practices of the Germans in these camps. I am hopeful that some British individuals in similar categories will visit the northern area to witness similar evidence of atrocity.

"That same day, Marshall received permission from the Secretary of War, Henry Lewis Stimson, and President Harry S. Truman for these delegations to visit the liberated camps."

"Ohrdruf made a powerful impression on General George S. Patton as well. He described it as *"one of the most appalling sights that I have ever seen."* He recounted in his diary that:

"In a shed ... was a pile of about 40 completely naked human bodies in the last stages of emaciation. These bodies were lightly sprinkled with lime, not for the purposes of destroying them, but for the purpose of removing the stench.

When the shed was full—I presume its capacity to be about 200, the bodies were taken to a pit a mile from the camp where they were buried. The inmates claimed that 3,000 men, who had been either shot in the head or who had died of starvation, had been so buried since the 1st of January.

"*When we began to approach with our troops, the Germans thought it expedient to remove the evidence of their crime. Therefore, they had some of the slaves exhume the bodies and place them on a mammoth griddle composed of 60-centimeter railway tracks laid on brick foundations. They poured pitch on the bodies and then built a fire of pinewood and coal under them. They were not very successful in their operations because there was a pile of human bones, skulls, charred torsos on or under the griddle which must have accounted for many hundreds.*"

The 4th Armored Division's discovery of the Ohrdruf camp opened the eyes of many U.S. soldiers to the horrors perpetrated by the Nazis during the Holocaust." [3]

Below are excerpts from The Jewish Virtual Library titled: U.S. Army & the Holocaust.

"Generals George Patton, Omar Bradley, and Dwight Eisenhower arrived in Ohrdruf on April 12, the day of President Franklin D. Roosevelt's death. They found 3,200 naked, emaciated bodies in shallow graves. Eisenhower found a shed piled to the ceiling with bodies, various torture devices, and a butcher's block for smashing gold fillings from the mouths of the dead. Patton became physically ill. Eisenhower turned white at the scene inside the gates, but insisted on seeing the entire camp. *"We are told that the American soldier does not know what he was fighting for,"* he said. *"Now, at least he will know what he is fighting against."*

Within days, Congressional delegations came to visit the concentration camps, accompanied by journalists and photographers. General Patton was reportedly so angry at what he found at Buchenwald that he ordered 1,000 civilians to see what their leaders had done, to witness what some human beings could do to others. The MPs were so outraged they brought back 2,000. Some turned away. Some fainted. Even veteran, battle-scarred correspondents were struck dumb. In a legendary broadcast on April 15, Edward R. Murrow gave the American radio audience a stunning matter-of-fact description of Buchenwald, of the piles of dead bodies so emaciated that those shot through the head had barely bled, and of those children who still lived, tattooed with numbers, whose ribs showed through their thin shirts. "I pray you to believe what I have said about Buchenwald," Murrow asked listeners. *"I have reported what I saw and heard, but only part of it; for most of it I have no words."* He added, *"If I have offended you by this rather mild account of Buchenwald, I am not in the least sorry."*

It was these reports, the newsreel pictures that were shot and played in theaters, and the visits of important delegations that proved to be influential in the public consciousness of the still unnamed German atrocities and the perception that something awful had been done to the Jews." [4]

Ohrdruf Information Sources:

1. Documents for Juzek Rubinsztein: *Copy of Doc. NO34646019#1 (/Image vorhanden/_R/R07/0060@0.1) in conformity with the ITS Archives*

2. Documents for Juzek Rubinsztein: *File Gcc2/222-IIC/17. Copy of Doc. No.34646017#(/Image Vorhanden/ R/R0747/00603@0.1) in conformity with the ITS Archives*

3. Selected excerpts from the United States Holocaust Memorial Museum, Washington, DC. *Holocaust Encyclopedia. Ohrdruf.* http://www.ushmm.org/wlc/en/article.php? ModuleId=10006131. Last accessed September 7, 2014

4. Selected excerpts from: Mitchell G Bard. *U.S. Policy During WWII: U.S. Army & the Holocaust. 1998.* Jewish Virtual Library. *Article above references: U.S. Army & the Holocaust. 1998.* Jewish Virtual Library, lists it source: Encyclopedia Judaica. © 2008 The Gale Group. All Rights Reserved. I. Gutman (ed.), *Macmillan Encyclopedia of the Holocaust* (1990); A. Grobman, *Battling for Souls, The Vaad Hatzalah Rescue Committee in Post-War Europe* (2004). http://www.jewishvirtualli-brary.org/jsource/Holocaust/usarmy holo.html

G. Theresienstadt, Czechoslovakia (Camp-ghetto)

Author's Note: Theresienstadt was the last camp where Joe was held captive. He walked out of the camp after the SS abandoned it. The United States Holocaust Memorial Museum in Washington, D.C., provided arrival documentation of Joe at Theresienstadt, but no date is listed. It is likely that Joe arrived in Theresienstadt during the time period described below (April 6-21, 1945). Joe was there only briefly before the camp was abandoned by the SS. Joe and two of his inmate friends witnessed several of the Nazi guards putting civilian clothes over their uniforms. Joe asked one of his friends, "What are they doing?" His friend replied, "It's over. They are going to try and hide." Later, once the camp gates were open, Joe and his friends simply walked out of the camp and made their way to a nearby town. They found a clothing store. The shopkeeper looked at the three men in their striped clothing and said, "We know who you are. Take whatever you want. We owe you more than that." Joe selected a suit, put it on, and left his inmate clothing on the floor. The store owner then tried to give Joe money, which he refused. [1,2]

The **Theresienstadt** "camp-ghetto" existed from November 24, 1941 to May 9, 1945, and had a highly developed cultural life. The camp-ghetto served as an ongoing propaganda and deception strategy for the Nazis, telling the public that the Jews from Germany were being resettled in the east to perform forced labor for the war, and that the elderly Jews were sent to the Theresienstadt ghetto to "retire" in the "spa town." In reality, the ghetto served as a center for deportations to other Nazi ghettos and killing centers. Succumbing to pressure following the deportation of Danish Jews to Theresienstadt, the Germans permitted the International Red Cross to visit in June 1944, following the deportation of Jews from Denmark to Theresienstadt.

With ample preparation, the Nazis created an elaborate hoax, having intensified deportations from the ghetto shortly before the visit, and then having the ghetto "beautified." Gardens were planted, houses painted, and barracks were renovated. The Nazis staged social and cultural events for the visiting dignitaries. Once the visit was over, the deportations from Theresienstadt resumed, ending in October 1944.

Between April 20 and May 2, 1945, approximately 13,500 and 15,000 prisoners were brought to the camp-ghetto, primarily from Buchenwald and Gross-Rosen sub-camps.

After visiting the camp again on April 6 and April 21, 1945, the International Red Cross took over its administration on May 2, 1945, when SS Commandant Rahm and the rest of the SS fled on May 5 and 6. On May 8, the area around the camp became a battlefront of the remaining German and SS units fighting the Soviet Red Army. On May 9, Soviet troops took control of the camp.

Of the approximately 140,000 Jews transferred to Theresienstadt during its operation, nearly 90,000 were deported to other concentration camps and killing centers. Roughly 33,000 died in Theresienstadt itself. [3, 4, 5]

Theresienstadt Information Sources:

1. Joe Rubinstein. *Face-to-face interviews with Author Nancy Sprowell Geise*, November 2012 – August 2014

2. Documents for Juzek Rubinsztein: *Copy of Doc. No. 34646020#1 (/Image vorhanden/_R/R0747/00600@0.1 (in conformity with the ITS Archives)*

3. Selected excerpts from the United Holocaust Memorial Museum. *Holocaust Encyclopedia. Theresienstadt.* http://www.ushmm.org/wlc/en/article.php? ModuleId=10005424, last accessed September 5, 2014

4. Selected excerpts from the United States Holocaust Memorial Museum. *Holocaust Encyclopedia. Theresienstadt: Final Weeks, Liberation, and Postwar Trials.* http://www.ushmm.org/wlc/en/article.php? ModuleId=10007505, last accessed September 25, 2014

5. Selected excerpts from the United States *Holocaust Memorial Museum. Holocaust Encyclopedia. Theresienstadt: SS and Police Structure.* http://www.ushmm.org/wlc/en/article.php?ModuleId=10007462, last accessed August 12, 2014

H. Treblinka, Poland (Extermination Camp)

Author's Note: The site where Joe's beloved family is believed to have perished. [1]

The **Treblinka** Extermination Camp, in the secluded woods of northeastern Poland, fifty miles from Warsaw, was established in 1941 as a forced labor camp; becoming one of only six extermination centers carrying out the Nazi's goal of exterminating the Jewish people. The ghettos of Warsaw and

Radom districts became the main source of deportations to Treblinka. The numbers of victims murdered at Treblinka were estimated at 900,000 between July 1942 and August 1943; the exact number may never be known because the Nazis destroyed most of the documentation. Within a four-month period in 1942, approximately 346,000 Jews were deported to Treblinka II alone from the Radom District. In July of 1944, Soviet troops overran Treblinka, but not before the Germans killed an estimated 300-700 of the remaining Jewish prisoners. [2, 3, 4]

While much of the physical evidence of the camp was destroyed by the retreating Germans, later, several Nazi SS soldiers testified as to what they witnessed while stationed there. The quotes below are partial excerpts from their testimonies:

Kurt Franz: *"I cannot say how many Jews in total were gassed in Treblinka. On average each day a large train arrived. Sometimes there were even two."* *(i)*Only selected excerpts were used.*

Willi Mentz: *"When I came to Treblinka the camp commandant was a doctor named Dr. Eberl. He was very ambitious. It was said that he ordered more transports than could be "processed" in the camp. That meant that trains had to wait outside the camp because the occupants of the previous transport had not yet all been killed. At the time it was very hot and as a result of the long wait inside the transport trains in the intense heat many people died. At the time whole mountains of bodies lay on the platform. Following arrival of a transport, six to eight cars would be shunted into the camp, coming to a halt at the platform there. The commandant, his deputy Franz, Kuettner and Stadie or Maetzi would be here waiting as the transport came in."*

"When the Jews had got off, Stadie or Maetzig would have a short word with them. They were told something to the effect that they were a resettle-ment transport, that they would be given a bath and that they would receive new clothes. They were also instructed to maintain quiet and discipline. Then the transports were taken off to the so-called 'transfer' area. The women

*had to undress in huts and the men out in the open. The women were than led through a passageway, known as the "tube," to the gas chambers." **(ii)*Only selected excerpts were used.***

SS Oberscharfuehrer Heinrich Matthes: *"All together, six gas chambers were active." **(iii)*Only selected excerpts were used.***

Treblinka Information Sources:

1. Joe Rubinstein. *Face-to-face interviews with Author Nancy Sprowell Geise,* November 2012– August 2014

2. Shamash. Jewish Virtual Library. *Treblinka. Testimonies of SS at Treblinka.* http://www.jewishvirtuallibrary.org/jsource/Holocaust/treblinkatest.html

3. United States Holocaust Memorial Museum. *Holocaust Encyclopedia. Treblinka.*
http://www.ushmm.org/wlc/en/article.php?ModuleId–10005193, last accessed September 4, 2014

4. Holocaust Education & Archive Research Team. *Treblinka Death Camp History.*
http://www.holocaustresearchproject.org/ar/treblinka.html, last accessed September 6, 2014. And Holocaust Education & Archive Research Team. Radom. http://www.holocaustresearchproject.org/ghettos/radom.html

i. Kurt Franz. Quoted in: *The Good Old Days* – E. Klee, W. Dressen, V. Riess, The Free Press, NY, 1988, p. 247-249

ii. Willi Mentz. Quoted in: *The Good Old Days* – E. Klee, W. Dressen, V. Riess, The Free Press, NY, 1988, p. 245-247

iii. Heinrich Matthes. Quoted in: *Belzec, Sobibor, Treblinka–the Operation Reinhard Death Camps.* Indiana University Press – Yitzhak Arad, 1987, p. 121

2. Ship Transporting Displaced Persons

USS General R. M. Blatchford

Author's Note: The United States Holocaust Memorial Museum in Washington, D.C., provided documentation of a ship manifest listing twenty-six persons (including the names of Joe, Irene, and their son) leaving Wentorf for the USA via Grohn Embarkation Staging Center on September 29, 1950. However, the ship manifest does not include the name of the ship. The document (502 IRO Documentation Office Wentorf BAOR 3), lists: Jozef Rubinstein (along with his wife and son), passenger No. 151818 433272 occupation "Coal Miner" destined for 15 Park Row, New York, N.Y.

Joe and Irene said their ship was a military transport called "Blackfort." All further research, including the opinion of a resource coordinator from the United States Holocaust Museum in Washington, D.C., indicate that likely the ship's name was actually the *USS General Blatchford*, which was used for the transportation of displaced persons leaving ports in Germany for the United States and Australia. Joe told me that they were initially told they would be relocated to Australia, but that they successfully were able to change the location to New York. Irene stated that they did not go through Ellis Island. Research indicates that since the individuals were processed in Germany by U.S. officials, the *USS General Blatchford* did not process through Ellis Island. (1)

USS General R. M. Blatchford **(AP-153)** was named in honor of U.S. Army general Richard M. Blatchford. She was a Squire-Class transport ship for the U.S. Navy in World War II, launched August 27, 1944, with a capacity of 3,823 troops.

After WWII (1946), she was transferred to the U.S. Army as *USAT General R. M. Blatchford* and was later transferred to the Military Sea Transportation Service as *USNS General R. M. Blatchford*. In October of 1949 and February 1950, she carried at total of nearly 2,500 displaced persons from Europe to Sydney, Australia, and was one of nearly 150 voyages made by forty ships bringing WW II refugees to that country.

The *USNS R.M. Blatchford* made at least two trips from Bremerhaven, Germany, across the Atlantic Ocean with refugees from Germany, Poland, Russia, Czechoslovakia and other countries and arrived at the Port of New York.

General R. M. Blatchford received two battle stars for service during the Korean War. She continued operating in the Atlantic until she was transferred to the Pacific in 1965 to carry troops to Vietnam.

She was sold to commercial operations under the names *SS Stonewall Jackson* and *Alex Stephens*, before being acquired by the Department of Commerce in 1979 and scrapped in 1980. [1,2,3,4,5,6,7]

USS General R. M. Blatchford Information Sources:

1. Joe and Irene Rubinstein. *Face-to-face interviews with Author Nancy Sprowell Geise,* November 2012 – August 2014

2. 502 IRO Documentation Office Wentorf BAOR 3. September 26, 1950. *Ship manifest.* "Twenty-six persons who departed from Wentorf for the USA via Grohn Embarkation Staging Centre on September 29, 1950." Included on the list: "Jozef Rubinstein, coal miner; Irene Rubinstein, housewife; Chaim-Moni, minor."

3. Naval History and Heritage Command. *Dictionary of American Naval Fighting Ships.* http://www.history.navy.mil/danfs/g3/general_r_m_blatchford.htm

4. Gary Priolo. NavSource Online. *NavSource Naval History.* AP-153 / USAT / T-AP-153 *General R. M. Blatchford.* http://www.navsource.org/archives/09/22/22153.htm

5. Immigrant Ships, Transcribers Guild, *General Blatchford.* Created & Maintained by the ISTG™Immigrant Ships Transcribers Guild. http://immigrantships.net/v5/1900v5/generalblatchford19491111.html

6. FifthFleet.net, *Ships of the Fifth Fleet*

7. National Archives Microfilm Publication T715. New York Passenger Arrival Records, 1820 – 1957. National Archives and Records Administration. *General R. M. Blatchford*

3. Camp for Displaced Persons: Wentorf bei Hamburg, Germany

Author's Note: Joe and Irene, along with their son, stayed at the Wentorf camp for several months prior to boarding the ship that would bring them to America. During their time there, they were housed in cramped quarters, sharing a small apartment with another couple, hanging a sheet between two areas of the apartment for privacy. [1]

Wentorf bei Hamburg. After liberation, the Allies began preparations to repatriate Jewish displaced persons to their homes. Some refused to go, many were fearful of doing so, and others had nowhere for which to return.

Allied authorities and the United Nations Relief and Rehabilitation Administration (UNRRA) began housing displaced Jewish persons in camps and urban centers in Germany, Austria, and Italy. From 1945 to 1952, more than 250,000 Jewish displaced persons (DPs) lived in camps and urban centers. Some were housed in former concentration camps and German army camps.

UNRRA established the Central Tracing Bureau to help survivors locate relatives. Public radio broadcasts and newspapers contained lists of survivors and their whereabouts. In the camps for displaced persons, schools (with teachers from Israel and the United States) were established. Athletic clubs were formed along with many musical and theatrical troupes. Religious holidays were celebrated and more than 170 publications came to life.

On May 14, 1948, the United States and the Soviet Union recognized the state of Israel and passed the Displaced Persons Act in 1948, authorizing 200,000 displaced persons to enter the United States. By 1952, most of the DP camps were closed, with 80,000 Jewish displaced persons living in the United States, 136,000 in Israel, and another 20,000 in other nations, including Canada, South Africa, and Australia.

One of these camps was **Wentorf bei Hamburg**, a municipality in the district of Lauenburg, in Schleswig-Holstein, Germany. Located on the river Bille, near Geesthacht and Hamburg, Germany, it was a site for a large DP camp for primarily Eastern European refugees. [2, 3]

Wentorf bei Hamburg Information Sources:

1. Joe and Irene Rubinstein. *Face-to-face interviews with Author Nancy Sprowell Geise*, November 2012 – August 2014

2. United States Holocaust Memorial Museum. *Holocaust Encylopedia. Displaced Persons.* http://www.ushmm.org/wlc/en/article.php? ModuleId=10005462, last accessed September 13, 2014

3. Bogdan Karasek. *Wentorf Displaced Persons Camp.* http://www.dpcamps.org/wentorf.html

4. Camp Commandants and Other Nazi Officials Related to Joe's Experiences

A. Herman Dolp* (1889-1947**)

Author's Note: Herman Dolp was commandant of several forced labor camps in the Belzec area including Cieszanów, where 3,000 Jews from Warsaw, Radom, and Czestochowa were put to work from August 20, 1940. Cieszanów is where we believe Joe encountered Dolp, the man Joe and his fellow forced-laborers referred to as "The Swinehund." Joe said that Dolp was often drunk. Joe witnessed Dolp ride his horse to where men were digging trenches, take out his gun, and shoot several of the men who lifted their heads. Dolp then turned his horse and rode away. (1)

SS Herman Dolp, a professional locksmith by trade, was married with four children when he was promoted to Standartenführer (colonel) in 1931. In November of 1939, while intoxicated, Dolp tried to rape a young Polish woman who was friend of a German official. Dolp was court-martialed on February 4, 1940, and demoted two ranks to Sturm-bannführer (major). Less than a week later, he was reassigned to Lublin to the Selbstschutz (armed ethnic German collaborators), where he gained a reputation as the most brutal and vicious of all the SS man on Odilo Globocnik's staff.

Author's Note: Globocnik was the Austrian-born SS leader responsible for ordering the raid on the Radom Ghetto and sending its residents to Treblinka to be murdered, including, it is believed, Joe's family. (See information page on Odilo Globocnik.)

During his command of the forced labor march of Jewish POWS from Lublin, hundreds were murdered. In the spring of 1940, Dolp supervised the digging of defensive trenches along the border with the Soviet Union, primarily a stretch of border between the Bug and Sans Rivers, and was assigned authority over several forced labor camps in Belzec, housing the forced labor. Dolp reportedly only allowed the Jews to go to the toilets at certain times. Many, suffering from severe dysentery, were killed if they were caught using the toilets outside allotted times. Dolp was promoted to Obersturmbannfihrer in April 1944, for his "good work." Conflicting reports show Dolp missing; others report he died after being injured in a battle in Romania late in 1944. [2, 3, 4, 5]

* Variations of the spelling of Dolp's first name exist in research: Herman or Hermann.
** The year Dolp died is in question.

Herman Dolp Information Sources:

1. Joe Rubinstein. *Face-to-face interviews with Author Nancy Sprowell Geise*, November 2012 – August 2014

2. David Silberklang. *Willful Murder in the Lublin District of Poland in*: Chapter 15 in Michael L. Morgan and Benjamin Pollock book: *The Philosopher as Witness: Fackenheim and Responses to the Holocaust*. Albany: State University of New York Press, 2008.

http://books.google.com/books?id=6jWgi9ky2OUC&pg=PA185&lpg=
PA185&dq=Silberklang,+David.+Willful+Murder+in+the+Lublin+Dist
rict+of+Poland

3. Holocaust Education and Research Archive team. *Radom. Holocaust
Research Project*
http://www.holocaustresearchproject.org/ghettos/radom

4. Dixon, Ian. January 1991. *Research. Herman Dolp.* http://www.red-
cap70.net/A%20History%20of%20the%20SS%20Organisation%201924
-1945.html/D/DOLP,%20Hermann.html

5. Aktion Reinhard Camps. *Belzec Labour Camps.* 2005.
http://www.deathcamps.org/belzec/labourcamps.html

B. Odilo Globocnik (1904 – 1945)

Author's Note: Globocnik was the SS leader who ordered the raid on the
Radom Ghetto, sending thousands of residents to Treblinka to be
murdered, including, it is believed, Joe's family. Herman Dolp, the man
Joe witnessed shoot several of those around him when he was digging
trenches, worked on Globocnik's staff (after his time as commandant of
the forced-labor camp in Cieszanów) and was considered the most vicious
and ruthless of all those on Globocnik's staff. (See Herman Dolp notes.)

Austrian-born **Odilo Globocnik** volunteered for the Waffen-SS and
served during the German invasion of Poland in 1939. Reichsführer SS
Heinrich Himmler appointed Globocnik police leader in the Lublin
district of the General Government. In 1941, Globocnik, on orders from
Heinrich Himmler, oversaw construction work on the extermination
camp Belzec, followed by Sobibor and Treblinka in 1942.

In the summer of 1942, Odilo Globocnik sent SS Wilhelm Blum to
Radom with orders to begin the "liquidation" of the ghetto. August 5,
1942, Jews in the smaller of the two Radom ghettos were forced to assemble
at a site near the railway line. Then, between August 16 and 18, 1942, the
larger ghetto was liquidated. Some were selected for forced labor, some

of the women and children were shot and buried in mass graves. Most of the people were deported to Treblinka and killed within hours of arriving. Those who tried to hide in the ghetto during the raids were executed on the spot.

Under his organization and supervision of Operation Reinhard, more than 1.5 million Polish, Slovak, Czech, Dutch, French, Russian, German, and Austrian Jews were killed, and the properties and valuables of murdered Jews were seized. The Operation Reinhard headquarters was responsible for coordinating the timing of the transports to the camps.

With the advance of Allied troops near the end of the war, Globocnik retreated with some of his staff into Austria, hiding high in the mountains in an alpine hut near Weissensee. On May 31, 1945, Globocnik was captured by a British armored cavalry unit, the Fourth Queen's Own Hussars, at the Möslacher Alm. He was taken to Paternion for interrogation, where he committed suicide by biting on a cyanide capsule. Later, rumors began about Globocnik having survived; later shown to be a hoax. [1, 2, 3, 4, 5]

Odilo Globocnik Information Sources:

1. *Holocaust Research Project. Radom.* http://www.holocaustresearch-project.org/ghettos/radom.html

2. Mark Mazower. *Hitler's Empire: How the Nazis Ruled Europe.* Penguin Books: Reprint edition (August 25, 2009)

3. Joseph Poprzeczny. *Odilo Globocnik, Hitler's Man in the East.* Jefferson and London. McFarland & Company (2004)

4. William L. Shirer: *The Rise and Fall of the Third Reich.* Secker & Warburg; London; 1960

5. Susan Zuccotti. *Under His Very Windows: The Vatican and the Holocaust in Italy.* Yale University Press, 2002

C. Adolf Hitler (1889- 1945)

Author Note: Hitler was the mastermind of the events that resulted in the murder of Joe's family and his captivity in the concentration camps.

Adolf Hitler was born on April 20, 1889, in Braunau am Inn, Austria. His father, Alois Hitler (1837–1903), was born out of wedlock to Maria Anna Schickelgruber in 1837. In 1876, Alois Schickelgruber changed his name to Hitler. Alois Hitler's illegitimacy would cause speculation as early as the 1920s that Hitler's grandfather was Jewish. Reliable evidence to support Hitler's possible Jewish ancestry has never been found.

Adolf Hitler desired a career in the visual arts and had a tumultuous relationship with his father who believed he should instead enter the civil service. After the death of his father and later his mother in 1907 from cancer, Hitler took the entrance exam to the Vienna Academy of the Arts but was denied. Despite being left a significant inheritance by his parents, Hitler squandered it away until he became impoverished, living in homeless shelters. During his time in Vienna, he had personal and business interactions with Jews and was occasionally dependent on them for his living. Following WWI, Hitler appears to have adopted an anti-Semitic ideology that was influenced by German racist nationalism promoted by politician Georg von Schönerer and the Mayor of Vienna, Karl Lueger. Both men reinforced anti-Jewish stereotypes and deemed the Jews as enemies of the German middle and lower classes.

In 1932, Hitler became a predominant figure in Germany in part by the German population's frustration over their poor economy, their continued humiliation over their defeat in WWI, and their discontent over the peace terms of the Treaty of Versailles. Hitter's charismatic speeches fueled his broad support, creating the path to him being named leader of the National Socialist German Workers Party (Nazi Party), as the chancellor of Germany in 1933.

Nazi dictator Adolf Hitler committed suicide in Berlin, April 30, 1945. [1,2,3]

Adolf Hitler Information Sources:

1. United States Holocaust Memorial Museum. *Holocaust Encyclopedia. Theresienstadt Timeline.* http://www.ushmm.org/wlc/en/article.php?ModuleId=10007460, last accessed September 5, 2014

2. United States Holocaust Memorial Museum. *Adolf Hitler: Early Years, 1889–1913.* http://www.ushmm.org/wlc/en/article.php?ModuleId=10007430, last accessed November 3, 2014

3. History. *In This Day in History. January 30th, 1933: Adolf Hitter is named Chancellor of Germany.* http://www.history.com/this-day-in-history/adolf-hitler-is-named-chancellor-of-germany

D. Dr. Rudolf Höss (1900 – 1947)

Author's Note: Höss was the commandant of Auschwitz during most of Joe's incarceration.

Rudolf Franz Ferdinand Höss, born in Baden-Baden in southwest Germany, was in training for the priesthood before his father's death and WWI. He joined the German army in 1916, was wounded and twice awarded the Iron Cross. In 1922, he renounced his affiliation with the Catholic Church and joined the Nazi Party, joining the SS in 1933. In 1940, he was assigned commandant of the newly built Auschwitz Concentration Camp.

SS commander Heinrich Himmler told Höss in May 1941 of Hitler orders for the final solution of the Jewish question. Himmler told Höss, "I have chosen the Auschwitz camp for this purpose." Höss converted Auschwitz into an extermination camp, where later its gas chambers were capable of killing 2,000 people an hour. Höss lived with his family on the camp-grounds and wrote poetry about the "beauty" of Auschwitz.

In 1945, with the approaching Red Army, Höss fled Auschwitz. He was eventually tracked down by a German Jew, Hanns Alexander. Höss was arrested by the Allied military police in 1946, who handed him over to the Polish authorities.

In his autobiography and despite his pivotal role in the Final Solution, Höss said, "May the general public simply go on seeing me as a blood-thirsty beast, the cruel sadist, the murderer of millions, because the broad masses cannot conceive the Kommandant of Auschwitz in any other way. They would never be able to understand that he also had a heart and that he was not evil."

Only steps from his former villa near Crematorium I of the main camp of Auschwitz, Rudolf Höss was hanged on the morning of April 16, 1947. [1, 2]

Rudolf Höss Information Sources:

1. Mitchell G. Bard. *U.S. Policy During WWII: U.S. Army & the Holocaust. 1998. Jewish Virtual Library.* https://www.jewishvirtuallibrary.org/jsource/biography/Hoess.html

2. United States Holocaust Memorial Museum. *The Frankfurt Trial.* http://www.ushmm.org/information/exhibitions/online-features/collections-highlights/auschwitz-ssalbum/frankfurt-triall, last accessed November 8, 2014

E. Karl Rahm (1907 – 1947)

Author's Note: Rahm was the commandant of Theresienstadt during Joe's brief incarceration there. Joe said that shortly before the SS abandoned the camp, Rahm was given the order to kill all the inmates (which is consistent with orders given to other camp commandants, but has not been independently verified). Joe said Rahm ignored the order. [1]

SS First Lieutenant Karl Rahm served as commandant of Theresienstadt. During his time as commandant, Rahm was ordered to commission an elaborate and hoax-ridden film called *The Fuhrer Gives the Jews a Town*. The film depicts prisoners receiving fake packages and swimming, and Rahm welcoming young children off arriving trains. When the cameras were gone, the same children were sent to the gas chambers of Auschwitz. The film was not believed to have been shown during the war.

Rahm abandoned the camp on May 5, 1945 as the Soviet moved in. Rahm, along with several other members of the SS, was sentenced to death and executed in Litomerice. [2, 3, 4]

Karl Rahm Information Sources:

1. Joe Rubinstein. *Face-to-face interviews with Author Nancy Sprowell Geise*, November 2012 – August 201

2. United States Holocaust Memorial Museum. *Holocaust Encyclopedia. Theresienstadt: SS and Police Structure.* http://www.ushmm.org/wlc/en/article.php?ModuleId=10007462, last accessed September 26, 2014

3. United States Holocaust Memorial Museum. *Holocaust Encyclopedia Theresienstadt: Final Weeks, Liberation and Postwar Trials.* http://www.ushmm.org/search/results/?q=Theresienstadt+Final+Weeks %2C+Liberation%2C+and+Postwar+Trials, last accessed September 25, 2015

4. Holocaust Education & Archive Research Team. *Terezin/Theresienstadt.* http://www.holocaustresearchproject.org/othercamps/terezin.html

F. Franz Paul Stangl (1908 – 1971)

Author Note: Stangl was the commandant of Treblinka, the believed site of the murder of Joe's beloved family.

Austrian-born Stangl was the commandant of the Sobibór and Treblinka extermination camps. He was arrested in Brazil in 1967, tried and found guilty of mass murder of more than 900,000 people, and was sentenced to life in prison. He died of heart failure in 1971. He admitted to his crimes, saying, *"My conscience is clear. I was simply doing my duty."* [1]

In 1970, Stangl was interviewed by author Gitta Sereny, used later in his book: *Into That Darkness: An Examination of Conscience* (1983). When asked if he ever got used to liquidations, Stangl answered, "One did become used to it." Below are excerpts from that interview:

"It was months before I could look one of them in the eye. I repressed it all by trying to create a special place: gardens, new barracks, new kitchens, new everything; barbers, tailors, shoemakers, carpenters. There were hundreds of ways to take one's mind off it; I used them all."

"In the end, the only way to deal with it was to drink. I took a large glass of brandy to bed with me each night and I drank."

"'When I was on a trip once, years later in Brazil,' he said, his face deeply concentrated, and obviously reliving the experience, 'my train stopped next to a slaughterhouse. The cattle in the pens, hearing the noise of the train, trotted up to the fence and stared at the train. They were very close to my window, one crowding the other, looking at me through that fence. I thought then, "Look at this, this reminds me of Poland; that's just how the people looked, trustingly...," adding later, 'Those big eyes which looked at me not knowing that in no time at all they'd all be dead.'"

"I remember Wirth standing there, next to the pits full of blue-black corpses. It had nothing to do with humanity, it couldn't have; it was a mass—a mass of rotting flesh. Wirth said, 'What shall we do with this garbage?' I think unconsciously that started me thinking of them as cargo."

"...I rarely saw them as individuals. It was always a huge mass. I sometimes stood on the wall and saw them in the tube. But how can I explain it—they were naked, packed together, running, being driven with whips like..."

"When asked if he could have stopped such abuse, he said, 'No, no, no. This was the system. Wirth had invented it. It worked and because it worked, it was irreversible.'" [2]

Franz Paul Stangl Information Sources:

1. Jewish Virtual Library. *Franz Strangl.* http://www.jewishvirtualli-brary.org/jsource/biography/Stangl.html

2. Gitta Sereny. *Into That Darkness: An Examination of Conscience.* Vintage (1983). Only selected excerpts were used. http://www.ama-zon.com/Into-That-Darkness-Examination-Conscience/dp/0394710355

5. Shoe Companies Where Joe Worked

A. Herbert Levine

In 1949, **Herbert Levine, Inc.** began production of shoes in a factory on 31 West 31st Street in New York, where it produced 400 pairs a week. By 1954, that number was 5,000, with more than 200 employees. For over thirty years, The Herbert Levine Company designed creative and innovate shoes. Herbert ran the business end while Beth was head designer. Beth would later be referred to as "America's First Lady of Shoe Design." The company brought back into fashion boots called mules in the mid-1960s. The company would become world-renowned for its craftsmanship, creative, and fun styles.

Herbert Levine shoes were worn by such stars as Julie Andrews, Marilyn Monroe, Rita Hayworth, Natalie Wood, Dinah Shore, Lauren Bacall, Peggy Lee, Joan Collins, Cher, Linda Evans, Rosemary Clooney, Betty Grable, Gladys Knight, Debbie Reynolds, Arlene Francis, Phyllis Diller, Helen Hayes, Barbra Streisand, Carol Channing, Ali MacGraw, Barbara Walters, Angela Lansbury, and others.

In 1955, Marilyn wore a pair of Herbert Levine's Spring-o-Lators, captured in many pictures, including the series taken by photojournalist Eve Arnold. Marilyn's red stilettos from Herbert Levine are now part of the Bata Shoe Museum collection in Toronto. The Herbert Levine Company made many custom pairs of the so-called "Gigi Stocking Shoes" for Marlene Dietrich. Nancy Sinatra wore Herbert Levine boots for *These Boots Are Made for Walkin'* on stage and for promotion.

Herbert Levine shoes were worn by many First Ladies of the United States, including Jackie Kennedy, Mamie Eisenhower, Lady Bird Johnson, and Patricia Nixon. Herbert Levine shoes are collected by more than twenty museums around the world, including the Costume Institute at the Metropolitan Museum of Art. The company closed in 1975. Herbert passed away in 1991, followed by Beth in 2006 at the age of 92. [1, 2, 3, 4]

Herbert Levine Information Sources:

1. Joe Rubinstein. *Face-to-face interviews with Author Nancy Sprowell Geise*, November 2012 – August 2014

2. *Beth Levine Shoes historical website.* http://www.bethlevineshoes.com

3. Helene Verin. *"Beth Levine Shoes."* April 1, 2009. http://www.amazon.com/Beth-Levine-Shoes-Helene-Verin/dp/1584797592

4. kickshawproductions. *Vintage Fashion Guild.* http://vintagefashionguild.org/label-resource/levine-herbert/

B. Nina Shoes

Nina Shoes was founded in 1953 by brothers Mike and Stanley Silverstein, who were Cuban immigrants. The company was named after Stanley's firstborn daughter. They began in New York with a small boutique on Prince Street in Manhattan's SoHo, making famous a fashion clog with a stiletto heel, designed after the clogs their father had made in Cuba. "By the end of the 1950s, Nina's fashion clogs were on the feet of stylish women everywhere, including the Miss Universe contestants."

In 2012, Nina Footwear celebrated its sixtieth anniversary with a collection based on its archives beginning in 1953 called "Nina Originals." [1, 2]

Nina Shoes Information Sources:

1. Official Website: *Nina Shoes.* About Us. http://ninashoes.com, last accessed September 20, 2014

2. Lauren Parker. L Accessories Magazine. November 13, 2012. *Nina Celebrates 60th with Retro Collection.* http://www.accessoriesmagazine.com/58187/nina-celebrates-60th-with-retro-collection#.VBhCGlZH2FI

C. Sbicca of California Footwear

Sbicca Footwear, a ninety-two-year-old company based in Southern California, was originally founded in 1920 by the Sbicca family in their home in Philadelphia. The business was moved to California after World War II. "In the 1970s Sbicca revolutionized the shoe business when it began producing its 'Molded Unit Bottoms' out of polyurethane. This gave Sbicca the competitive advantage of producing footwear on a lightweight, flexible bottom that is fashionable as well as comfortable.

In 2010, the Sbicca of California brand was purchased by another family-owned business, Palos Verdes Footwear. This company is owned by the Lovely family and is the parent company of the Volatile, Very Volatile, Volatile Kids, Volatile Handbags, Grazie, and Encanto Footwear brands." [1]

Sbicca of California Footwear Information Source:

1. Official Website: *Sbicca of California.* Our Story. http://www.sbiccafootwear.com/content.php?pgID=9

Glossary of Terms Related to Joe's Story

A

anti-Semitism Term used to refer to the hatred of Jews and Judaism.

Auschwitz/Birkenau See Additional Research Notes/Concentration Camps.

B

bar mitzvah A celebration of a Jewish boy's thirteenth birthday, marking his obligation to observe religious commandments and teachings.

Birkenau See Additional Research Notes/Auschwitz/Birkenau.

blitzkrieg 1) A term that means "lightning war"; 2) Hitler's invasion strategy of attacking a nation suddenly and with overwhelming force, used in the invasions of Poland, France, and the Soviet Union.

borscht Soup made with beetroot popular in many Eastern and Central European countries.

British Mandated Palestine 1922, Great Britain was called upon by the League of Nations to facilitate the establishment of a Jewish national home (Land of Israel) in Palestine-Eretz Israel (Land of Israel). November 29, 1947, the UN General Assembly adopted the resolution to partition Palestine. Britain announced the termination of its Mandate over Palestine to take effect on May 15, 1948. On May 14, 1948, the state of Israel was proclaimed.

Buchenwald See Additional Research Notes/Concentration Camps.

Brzeszcze See Additional Research Notes/ Concentration Camps/ Jawischowitz.

C

capo (kapo) A Nazi concentration camp prisoner given privileges in return for supervising prisoner work gangs. Many of those with criminal background and violent personalities were selected, often brutalizing other fellow inmates.

challah A sweet, yellow bread (often braided), served on Shabbat and other Jewish holidays, named for the commandment to set aside a portion of the dough from any bread.

Chamberlain, Neville (1869-1940) Britain's prime minister from 1937 to 1940, remembered for his advocacy of a policy of appeasement toward Nazi Germany and its 1938 annexation of Austria and the Sudetenland, mistakenly believing the agreement would bring "peace in our time."

Cieszanów See Additional Research Notes/Labor Camp.

camp for displaced persons See Additional Research Notes/Wentorf bei Hamburg.

D

displaced person People who are unable or unwilling to return to their home country.

Dolp, Herman See Additional Research Notes/Camp Commandants.

Dora-Mittelbau (Dora-Nordhausen or Nordhausen) See Additional Research Notes/Concentration Camp.

E

Eisenhower, Dwight (1890 -1969) U.S. Army general who held the position of Supreme Allied Commander in Europe, known for his work in planning the Allied invasion of Europe. In 1953, he became president of the United States and was elected to two terms. (See Additional Research Notes on Ohrdruf Concentration Camp.)

F

final solution The Nazis' term for their plan to exterminate the Jews of Germany and other German-controlled territories during World War II. (The term was used by the Nazis at the Wannsee Conference of January 1942.)

G

gas chambers Large chambers built and used by the Nazi in the death camps to execute people with poison gas.

Gestapo The brutal Nazi secret police force, headed by the infamous Hermann Göring. The Gestapo was responsible for sending many Jews throughout Europe to Nazi concentration camps during the war.

ghetto A part of a city, especially a slum area, occupied by a minority group or groups. During WWII it was the areas where Jews were forced to live.

Globocnik, Odilo See Additional Research Notes/Camp Commandants.

Great War Term often used to refer to WWI. July 28, 1914 – November 11, 1918.

H

Hebrew 1) A member of or descendant from one of a group of northern Semitic peoples including the Israelites; 2) The Semitic language of the ancient Hebrews.

Herbert Levine, Inc. See Additional Research Notes/Famous Shoe Companies.

High Holidays The holidays of Rosh Hashanah, the Days of Awe, and Yom Kippur are commonly referred to as the High Holidays or the High Holy Days.

Hitler, Adolf See Additional Research Notes/Camp Commandants and Other Nazi Officials.

Holocaust 1) The killing of millions of Jews and other people by the Nazis during World War II; 2) Situation in which many people are killed and many things are destroyed especially by fire; 3) Originally a term meaning a sacrifice burned entirely on an altar.

Höss, Rudolf See Additional Research Notes/Camp Commandants.

I

Instytut Pamieci Narodowej—**Institute of National Remembrance** The Institute, established in 1998 by the Polish Parliament is headquartered in Warsaw, Poland. Its purpose is for the research, prosecution and legislation to investigate Nazi and Communist crimes committed in Poland between 1939 and 1989, and to document and report its findings to the public.

Israel 1) A country on the Mediterranean: formed as a Jewish state May 1948. Capital: Jerusalem. 2) The people described as descended from Jacob; the Hebrew or Jewish people. 3) An alternate name for Jacob. 4) The northern kingdom of the Hebrews. 5) A group considered by its members or by others as God's chosen people. 6) A male given name.

J
Jawischowitz See Additional Research Note/Concentration Camps.

Jew A person whose mother was a Jew or who has converted to Judaism. According to the Reform movement, a person whose father is a Jew is also a Jew.

Jewish Religion The religion of the Children of Israel, that is, the Jewish people.

Jewish Star Magen David, the Shield of David, or the Star of David. The six-pointed star emblem associated with Judaism.

Judaism The religion of the Jewish people.

Judenrat (Judenraete) Jewish councils (municipal administrations) established during World War II by the Germans to ensure that Nazi orders and regulations were implemented. Jewish council members also sought to provide basic community services for Jews forced into ghettos.

K

kapo (capo) See Capo.

Kanada (Canada) Considered a country of great wealth, the term "Kanada" became the slang used by the guards and inmates at Auschwitz to describe the vast warehouses of the personal property taken from the thousands of victims heading for the gas chambers.

kosher a Jewish sanctioned law; ritual for selling and serving food.

L

labor camp Camp where Jews and others were pressed into forced labor for military or government purposes.

Lebensraum A term meaning "living space." Adolf Hitler used it to justify territorial conquests in the 1930s. Hitler used the idea of Lebensraum to claim that the German people's "natural" territory extended beyond the current borders of Germany and Germany's need to acquire more.

Luftwaffe The German air force.

liquidation The term used to refer to the act of moving people out of the ghettos by force, through execution, transportation to concentration, extermination, or forced labor camps, or by setting fire to the ghetto and burning any people in hiding alive.

M

Magen David (shield of David, Star of David) The six-pointed star emblem associated with Judaism.

Matzah Unleavened bread traditionally served during Jewish celebration of Passover.

menorah 1) A nine-branched candelabrum the Jewish use to hold

Chanukkah candles. 2) A seven-branched candelabrum used in the Jewish Temple.

muselmann Slang term used to describe inmates in the concentration camps that were near death by means of starvation, exhaustion, and despair.

N
Nagel The Englishman who taught Joe the trade of making boots and shoes in Radom, Poland, shortly before the war. His influence on Joe had far-reaching implications when Joe began designing some of the most sought-after shoes in the world.

The Nazi (National Socialist German Workers') Party Founded in Germany, January 5, 1919, based on a centralist and authoritarian structure, with national, militaristic, racial, and anti-Semitic policies.

Nina Shoes See Additional Research Notes/Shoe Companies.

O
Operation Reinhard The Nazi code name for the planned deportations and extermination of Jews as part of the "Final Solution" including: construction of extermination camps; deportation coordination of Jews from the different government districts to the extermination camps; the killing of the Jews in the camps; and the confiscation of Jewish belongings and valuables. The three extermination camps established under Operation Reinhard were Belzec, Sobibór, and Treblinka.

Ohrdruf See Additional Research Notes/Concentration Camps.

Orthodox A major movement of Judaism, with strict observance of Jewish law and teachings.

P
Passover A Jewish holiday commemorating the Exodus from Egypt; also marks the beginning of the harvest season.

prayer Observant Jews pray three times daily and say blessings over many day-to-day activities.

prayer shawl See tallit.

R

rabbi Jewish term for master/teacher; trained and ordained to professional religious leadership.

Radom Ghetto In March of 1941, an order was issued to establish a ghetto in Radom. A "large ghetto" was set up at Walowa Street in the Śródmieście District as well as the "small ghetto" at the Glinice District; together housing approximately 33,000 local Polish Jews were forced to live in the two ghettos. The Germans began to liquidate the Radom Ghetto in Operation Reinhard. The deported Jews were sent to extermination camps, primarily Treblinka and Auschwitz.

Radom, Poland A city in central Poland located south of Poland's capital, Warsaw.

Rahm, Karl See Additional Research Notes/Camp Commandants.

Roosevelt, Franklin Delano (1882–1945) President of the United States throughout most of WWII until his death in 1945; worked with Allied leaders in the fight against Nazi Germany, Italy, and Japan.

S

Sabbath The seventh day of the week beginning Friday evening to Saturday evening as a day of worship and rest.

Sbicca of California Footwear See Additional Research Notes/Shoe Companies.

Shabbat The Jewish Sabbath.

shalom A Jewish greeting and parting: hello or goodbye.

Shoah The biblical word Shoah (meaning "destruction") became the standard Hebrew term for the murder of European Jews in other languages besides Hebrew.

skull caps See yarmulkes.

Sonderkommando Male prisoners of the Nazi concentration camps, forced to dispose of the corpses.

SS (*Schutzstaffel*) The German term for Hitler's personal bodyguards. Used by the Nazis throughout the war, including operations of the concentration camps and the extermination of Jews and others.

Stangl, Franz Paul See Additional Research Notes/Camp Commandants.

Star of David The emblem, a six-pointed star, commonly associated with Judaism. During the Holocaust, Jews were required to wear Stars of David on their sleeves, shirts and/or jackets.

Sudetenland The term used by the Adolf Hitler in referring to the area of Czechoslovakia's northern and western border regions, known collectively as the Sudetenland, for Nazi annexation.

synagogue Jewish house of worship.

T
Tachrichuim Traditional Jewish clothing for burying the dead made up of simple white shrouds.

Tallit (prayer shawl) A Jewish garment worn during morning services, with tzitzit (fringes) attached to the corners.

Tallit Katan A Jewish four-cornered garment resembling a poncho worn under a shirt.

Tefillin Phylacteries (small leather box) worn by the Jews, consisting of leather pouches containing scrolls with passages of scripture.

The Jewish People (Children of Israel) A reference to the Jews as a nation of people with a shared history and shared group identity. Not used as a reference to a territorial or political entity.

Torah 1) The body of wisdom and law contained in Jewish Scripture, sacred literature, and other oral traditions. 2) The five books of the Bible (sometimes called Five Books of Moses, constituting the Pentateuch: Genesis, Exodus, Leviticus. 3) A leather or parchment scroll of the Pentateuch used in a synagogue for liturgical purposes.

Torah readings Weekly portions of the Torah and the Prophets read in Jewish synagogues.

Torah scroll Parchment on scrolls on which the Torah is read in Jewish synagogues.

Theresienstadt See Additional Research Notes/Concentration Camps.

Treblinka See Additional Research Notes/Concentration Camps.

Truman, Harry S. President of the United States who succeeded Franklin D. Roosevelt in April 1945, following Roosevelt's death. Truman led the country through the final months of WWII, including use of two atomic bombs against Japan, resulting in Japan's surrender.

Tzittzit Fringes or tassels at the corner of garments worn by Jewish males as a reminder of the commandments.

U

United States Holocaust Memorial Museum, Washington D.C. According to its website: "A *living* memorial to the Holocaust, the United States Holocaust Memorial Museum inspires citizens and leaders worldwide to confront hatred, prevent genocide, and promote human dignity.

"Today we face an alarming rise in Holocaust denial and anti-Semitism—even in the very lands where the Holocaust happened—as well as genocide and threats of genocide in other parts of the world. This is occurring just as we approach a time when Holocaust survivors and other eyewitnesses will no longer be alive.

"Since its dedication in 1993, the Museum has welcomed more than 36 million visitors. On September 27, 1979, President Carter's Commission on the Holocaust submitted its recommendation for Holocaust remembrance and education in the United States. On October 5, 1988, President Ronald Reagan said in the laying of the Cornerstone for the museum on the National Mall: *'We must make sure that {...} all humankind stares this evil in the face.'* On April 7, 1990, two workers at the site buried two milk cans containing the pledges of remembrance signed by Holocaust survivors. On April 22, 1993, President Clinton dedicated the Museum, stating, *"This museum will touch the life of everyone who enters and leave everyone forever changed."*

United Nations Relief and Rehabilitation Administration (UNRRA)
A relief organization that was created at a forty-four-nation conference at the White House on November 9, 1943. Its mission was to provide economic assistance to European nations after WWII and to assist and repatriate refugees. The U.S. government funded close to half of UNRRA's budget.

USS General Blatchford See Additional Research Note/Ship Transporting Displaced Persons.

V

Yad Vashem, Jerusalem, Israel. World Center for Holocaust Research. Established in 1953. According to its website: "As the Jewish people's living memorial to the Holocaust, Yad Vashem safeguards the memory of the past and imparts its meaning for future generations. Established in 1953, as the world center for documentation, research, education and commemoration of the Holocaust, Yad Vashem is today a dynamic and vital place of intergenerational and international encounter. For over half a century, Yad Vashem has been committed to four pillars of remembrance: Commemoration: Documentation: Research; Education" www.yad-vashem.org/, last accessed September 5, 2014.

W

Wehrmacht German armed forces from 1935-1945.

Wentorf bei Hamburg See Additional Research Notes/Displaced Persons Camp.

Y

Yarmulkes (skull caps) A head covering worn by some Orthodox and Conservative Jewish males. Some wear yarmulkes only during Jewish services, and others wear them only at home, and some wear them at all times.

Yiddish Language spoken by Jews in primarily Eastern Europe or other areas where European Jews have migrated, a combination of elements of German and Hebrew.

Z

Zermirot Jewish hymns sung around the table during Shabbat and Jewish holidays.

złoty Polish form of money.

Sources for Glossary Terms:

1) *A Teacher's Guide to the Holocaust.* Produced by the Florida Center for Instructional Technology, College of Education, University of South Florida © 2005.

2) *Jewish Virtual Library.* http://www.jewishvirtuallibrary.org/.

3) *Judaism 101 Glossary of Jewish Terminology.* http://www.jewfaq.org/glossary.htm.

4) "Judaism: Definition and More," *The Free Merriam Webster Dictionary.* http://www.merriam-webster.com/dictionary/judaism.

5) *Answers.com.*

6) "World War II (1939-1945) Key People and Terms." *SparkNotes.* http://www.sparknotes.com/history/european/ww2/terms.html.

7) *FreeTranslation.com.*

8) United States Memorial Holocaust Museum, Washington D.C. Excerpts from "About the Museum." http://www.ushmm.org/information/about-the-museum. Last accessed September 17, 2014.

9) *Webster's New Collegiate Dictionary,* 1979 Edition.

10) Vad Yashem. "The Holocaust: Definition and Preliminary Discussion." *The Holocaust Resource Center.* Last accessed September 17, 2014. http://www.yadvashem.org/yv/en/holocaust/resource_center/the_holocaust.asp.

Discussion Questions

1. In reading Joe's story, what was/were the hardest part(s) for you? Why?

2. In what ways do you feel that Joe's early years helped him survive the horrors that were to come and to find the strength to go on living?

3. Joe has never returned to Poland since the day he was taken from his home in 1942. If you were Joe, would you have returned to your country? If so, what would you be looking to gain? If not, why? What do you think has kept Joe from returning?

4. President Eisenhower said, after seeing firsthand the horrors at the Ohrdruf Concentration Camp (where Joe was held for a while) and upon its liberation, that they now knew what they had been fighting against. What do you think he meant by this?

5. Were you surprised Joe went to Germany immediately after the war? Would you have done so? Why or why not?

6. What do you think would have been the hardest part for Joe while living among the German people?

7. Joe and Irene were an unlikely pair. A Catholic girl raised in Germany during the war, marrying a young Jewish man who spent the war in captivity. What do you think has been the key to their long and happy life together? Have you ever formed a strong alliance, friendship, or marriage with an unlikely person? If so, in what ways did your differences affect your relationship? Can incompatibility actually be a strength?

8. Many events happened to keep Joe alive, including being taken in the first place, as everyone in his family who was left behind was killed. Do

you believe these were miracles or random occurrences? Have you ever experienced a miracle?

9. Why do you think Joe survived when so many others perished?

10. How do you think Joe was able to continue living with joy, when everyone he knew and loved was dead?

11. How do you think you would have reacted, if you had been Joe and the gates to the concentration camp were opened and suddenly you were free, but at the same time you realized that you had no money, no home, no possessions, no country, and no one in your family living? What would you have done? Where would you have gone and why?

12. When asked about his survival, Joe says that for some reason God kept him alive. Did you see God or a great power at work in Joe's story? If so, in what ways?

13. In many of the Holocaust photos, German soldiers are laughing amidst the atrocities they were committing. How is this possible? Were they evil people? How did they justify such evil, even to themselves? How honest do you think they were with their families about what they were doing?

14. Have you ever been ashamed of your actions against others and wished you could go back in time and redo them? How have you coped with your guilt?

15. Could anything have been done to stop the Holocaust? If so, what? Why was it allowed to happen? Was it a total breakdown in morality in a country known for great cultural contributions to the humanities?

16. Many countries, weary of WWI, did little or nothing to heed the warnings of the massive Nazi buildup. In what ways did such inaction allow the Nazis to build up their war machine? Could they have been

stopped sooner? What actions could have prevented Germany's early aggressive successes? Were other world leaders negligent in any way?

17. Hitler committed a great deal of manpower and other resources in fighting two wars—the one against the Allies and the other against the Jews. How did these two "wars" affect each other?

18. When he learned the fate of his family, Joe said, "I will never forgive them for what they did to my family." If you were Joe, how would you relate to his feelings? How would you have coped with such feelings? Have you ever been able to forgive someone for something that you never felt you could? How vital is forgiveness in moving forward? Are some things unforgivable?

19. How much of the Holocaust can be blamed on the German people's complacency until it was too late to fight or stop? Are we just as complacent today? Are similar things happening in the world today that we are ignoring?

20. Joe was determined not to give in to despair. Have there been times in your life when you were overwhelmed by despair? How did you get beyond it?

21. Joe said that even before he heard the news, he "knew" that his family was dead. Why do you think he felt this way? Have you ever experienced anything similar?

22. Joe witnessed a man being beaten when the Nazis kept asking him, "Who are you?" And his response was, "German." The beating did not stop until he finally said, "Jewish." If you had been that man, what do you think would have been your response and why?

23. In what ways have you been like Joe, able to find hope in the darkest of moments?

24. When Joe went to receive a second tattoo mark under his number, the man doing the tattooing said to him, "You don't look Jewish to me. I'm not giving you that mark." Have you ever experienced having to hide some part of you that you did not want revealed to others? Is it possible to look Jewish when Jewishness is not related to race, only religion?

25. When Joe was given the tattoo on his arm by the Nazis, he was marked for life. If you were Joe, how would such a mark affect you, initially and later, if like Joe, it remained even seventy years later? Would you have had it removed? Why or why not? Is being reduced to a number a dehumanization process you would never want to forget?

26. In what ways do you see the evil at work in Joe's time happening again today?

27. If evil is a breakdown of morality, is there a solution to overcoming it?

28. What common traits do you see of those in the so-called, "Greatest Generation," of Joe's era that gave them the ability to overcome so much? Is such a thing a myth or a reality? Do you see such traits in the younger people of today?

29. What was the most uplifting part of Joe's story for you? Why?

30. There is spiritual power in an authentic life such as Joe's because his story is not a solution but more a soul condition. How would you explain the spiritual power that comes from yielding to meaning like Joe does? Despite everything, Joe saw another vision of life possible and lived it, owing much to an infusion of hope for humanity. How is this possible?

If you could share any of your kind thoughts with Joe, what would they be?

You can!
Please send us your feedback and/or notes to Joe:

Via my website: *www.nancygeise.com*
or email me directly at: nancy@nancygeise.com.

Acknowledgments from Nancy Sprowell Geise

To God and Jesus Christ, for my life and the love woven throughout all of it.

I am deeply indebted to so many wonderful people who have helped in bringing this story to life. I owe my deepest gratitude to Joe for trusting me to write his remarkable life story and for showing me what it means to live a joy-filled life and to never give up hope, no matter the challenges.

To Irene, for her loving encouragement of Joe in the telling of his often painful and difficult experiences and to her for sharing the tragic details of losing her beloved brother. I will forever remember Irene easing our long and emotional conversations with her delicious teas and goodies.

To Joe's son, Dan, and his wife, Julie, I thank you for helping to coordinate interviews, photos, and research material. To Joe and to everyone in his family, I thank you for your patience in the long wait for this book's completion.

I'm forever grateful –

To my husband, Doran—my greatest of life editors. Without his love and support, I could never have begun, nor finished, this book. I am so thankful for his wisdom, insight, and tender concern throughout this long process, not only for me, but also of Joe, and for his ability to bring me back to the light each day, after hours of being immersed in the dark places of the Nazi concentration camps.

To my three daughters, Crystal, Hallie, and Natalie, who are the light of my life.

To my parents, Bob and Lucretia Sprowell, for their never-ending support and unconditional love.

To my many, many family and friends who never stopped encouraging me in another writing journey.

To my incredible, retired high school English teacher, John Forssman, for his continual prodding, insight, and encouragement. Without him, this book would not have been written.

To draft readers: John and Sharon Forssman; Sara Hunt; Charlotte Bates; Sybil Wiegman; Jenny Bergstrom; Sheryl McCarthy; Leisa Doran; Sue Fackler; Jane Goble; Jamie Meyer; Carole Fraley; Clare Sprowell; Lucretia Sprowell; Cheryl Davis; Cindy Frost; Connie and Bruce Berman; and Doran, Dale, Crystal, Hallie, and Natalie Geise. A special thanks to Dan Wilson, Julie Wilson, and Mark Wilson for their insight and helpful corrections and additions.

To the many staff associated with the United States Holocaust Memorial Museum in Washington, D.C., for their dedication to helping us all never forget; including Peter Black, Geoffrey P. Megargee, and especially, many, many thanks to Michlean Amir, Resource Coordinator, whose help and insight was invaluable.

To Dr. David Silberklang: Yad Vashem – Senior Historian, International Institute for Holocaust Research and author: *Gates of Tears: The Holocaust in the Lublin District,* and to Dr. Michael Berenbaum of The Sigi Ziering Institute and Professor of Jewish Studies, American Jewish University, for their help in answering numerous research questions.

To photographer Crystal Geise (*crystalisphoto.com*), for her wonderful photos of Joe and Irene, and for her technical help in so many areas including website development.

To my extraordinary content and copy editor, Donna Mazzitelli, (writingwithdonna.com). Without Donna's tremendous services, this book would not have gone to print.

To publisher Merry Dissonance Press (*merrydissonancepress.com*).

To copy editor Melanie Zimmerman.

To Polly Letofsky of MyWord!Publishing.

I had the privilege of attending the "Extravaganza of Author U" in Denver, Colorado, earlier this year and had the opportunity to participate in their version of "The Shark Tank." After hearing a little of Joe's story, an amazing array of professionals offered their services to help bring this story to light.

I am forever indebted to the following incredible and very generous professionals:

Georgia McCabe, Social Media Sensei (*Georgia@georgiammcabe.com*), for whom I am so grateful for her extraordinary drive, passion, insight, and willingness to help in all phases of the marketing of this book.

Nick Zelinger, NZ Graphics (*nzgraphics.com*) for his book cover and interior layout designs. Nick is amazing!

Susie Scott and her team at i25 productions (*i25productions.com*), including her very talented photographer and videographer, Nicholas DeSciose, DeSciose Productions (*desciose.com*), for the development of a promotional video and the powerful cover photo.

Judith Briles (Author U) *AuthorU.org*

Mark Coker (Smashwords) *Smashwords.com*

Amy Collins (Newshelves) *newshelves.com*

Kathi Dunn (Dunn + Associates Design) *dunn-design.com*

Daniel Hall (Daniel Hall Combined Enterprises) *greatproductsupport.com*

John Kremer (Open Horizons; Book Market) *bookmarketingbestsellers.com*

Penny Sansevieri (Author Marketing Experts, Inc.) *amarketingexpert.com*

Justine Schofield (Pubslush) *pubslush.com*

Joan Stewart (The Publicity Hound) *http://PublicityHound.com*

Lynn Hellerstein *DRH@LynnHellerstein.com*

... and many others who offered to help

A thanks beyond my ability to put into words to the men and women of the Armed Forces, whose immense sacrifices throughout WWII helped bring freedom to Joe and so many others.

A special note of gratitude to our beloved Golden Retriever, "Prairie Dog," for staying by my side through every word written and every tear wept during this often difficult journey. Prairie Dog died at age fourteen the day after I completed the manuscript. I think some part of her knew she had to wait until we finished this together. I could not have gone through this without her.

And finally, in writing this book, I grew to love a family that I wish I could have known, a family that should never have been taken from us. I'm so grateful for the lives of Irene's brother, Walter Gusenda, and for Joe's family—his mother Reszka "Rachel" and his siblings: Dawid "Anszel," Chaim, Abram, and Laja Rubinsztejn, who remind us all of the precious lives behind the dry-number statistics of those lost during the war and the millions of Holocaust victims.

They were all so much more.

About the Author ...
Nancy Sprowell Geise

Seven years ago Holocaust survivor Joe Rubinstein told author Nancy Sprowell Geise that he would never publicly share his experiences at Auschwitz and several other of the most notorious Nazi concentration camps. Two years ago he changed his mind.

When Nancy began writing Joe's story, she had no idea the impact it would have on her life as she immersed herself in Joe's world and his remarkable journey of survival and triumph.

Author Nancy Sprowell Geise's debut novel, *The Eighth Sea*, became an Amazon bestseller, ranked on Amazon Best Seller List #1 in Historical Fiction and #1 Historical Romance (free Kindle downloads). #1 Historical Genre Literature & Fiction; #1 Religion and Spirituality Fiction (Kindle). *The Eighth Sea* was a Quarter Finalist of the *2012 Amazon Breakthrough Awards*.

Nancy Sprowell Geise was raised in Ames, Iowa, and is a graduate of Iowa State University. She and her husband, Doran, have lived in Austin, Texas; Fort Collins, Colorado; and Topeka, Kansas. They have three grown daughters.

Nancy divides her time between writing and speaking engagements. Her hilarious and moving life experiences provide great fodder for her writing and storytelling endeavors.

Final Note from the Author

Can You Help Joe Find a Photo of His Family?

I am convinced that somewhere out there a photo of Joe's family from Poland exists. On the Timeline you will find the names and birthdates of some of his family.

If you have any information about such a photo, please contact me.

Let's Stay Connected

To stay connected, please be sure to find me online by visiting my website at www.nancygeise.com. You can also connect with me on Facebook, LinkedIn, Twitter, and Goodreads.

Joe and I would love to hear from you. Please send us your feedback and notes via my website, or email me directly at nancy@nancygeise.com.

And one last favor …

If you have enjoyed this book, please be sure to visit Amazon and Goodreads to leave a review.

Thank you!

About the Press

Merry Dissonance Press is a book producer/indie publisher of works of transformation, inspiration, exploration, and illumination. MDP takes a holistic approach to bringing books into the world that make a little noise and create dissonance within the whole in order that ALL can be resolved to produce beautiful harmonies.

Merry Dissonance Press works with its authors every step of the way to craft the finest books and help promote them. Dedicated to publishing award-winning books, we strive to support talented writers and assist them to discover, claim, and refine their own distinct voice. **Merry Dissonance Press** is the place where collaboration and facilitation of our shared human experiences join together to make a difference in our world.

For more information, visit http://merrydissonancepress.com/.

More Praise for
Auschwitz #34207 ...

"Debut biographer Geise (*The Eighth Sea*, 2012) tells the remarkable story of Joe Rubinstein, a survivor of the Holocaust.

The author writes that Rubinstein was born Icek Jakub Rubinsztejn, in Radom, Poland, in the 1920s, 'when the world paused from its madness—between the great and terrible war and the one yet to come.' Along with three brothers, he was raised in a devoutly Jewish home. His family was poor, and barely scraped by after the early death of Rubinstein's father. At the age of 12, Rubinstein was hired at a lumberyard, where he worked to supplement the family income. Later, he learned shoemaking, and in that job, he first became aware of the Nazi movement and growing anti-Semitism.

Then, in September 1939, his world changed, as the Germans invaded Poland. Joe and his brother Abe are forced to dig trenches around the city for fortification, and he experienced the cruelty of Nazi commanders who randomly shot and killed people in the work camp. When the Nazis sequestered the Jews of Radom, Rubinstein was taken prisoner—barefoot and in the middle of the night—and shipped to a prison camp at Auschwitz, where he was stripped, shaved and tattooed with the number 34207. He remembered thinking, 'You mark me like an item to be sold! Who are you to do this to me?'

The harrowing details of his next several years are mind-numbing and nauseating; indeed, Geise's account of the horrid prison conditions, beatings and mental abuse almost defies human understanding. The disturbing black-and-white archive photographs accompanying the text will nearly overwhelm readers, who may need to take frequent breaks from the material. Fortunately, in the final section, Geise recounts Rubinstein's inspiring climb out of darkness, as he finds true love, starts a new life in America and, in an ironic twist, becomes one of New York's most renowned shoe designers.

With its thorough chapter endnotes, helpful timeline, extensive research citations and suggested discussion questions, this biography may serve as an ideal teaching tool for students of the Holocaust.

A riveting, well-documented account of survival that's harrowing, inspiring and unforgettable." —*Kirkus Review*

Made in the USA
Monee, IL
16 March 2022